EDDIE SCOTT

MISARANA

Carnival

INTRODUCTION

My sea-faring career, which began while I was a teenager, took me all over the world and I have been lucky enough to have experienced many wonderful cultures. I owe much to my sea-faring past, but food and cooking has always been my passion. Whenever I went away to sea, I would take a big bag of spices with me. Captain Don Campbell of the fine ship *Lesley PG* (a small oil tanker that I worked on in the Caribbean) discovered my talents as a chef. He would cover my afternoon watch every Thursday to allow me to show the ship's cook how to make a proper curry. In May 2022, life changed in a flash. There I was, on national TV, crowned as *MasterChefUK* Champion! I never dreamt in a million years that this would happen! I believe that this was only possible thanks to the fact that in my life I've always been driven by my passion.

Since winning *MasterChefUK*, I have spent time honing my skills in my favourite restaurant – Pipe and Glass in South Dalton, just a few minutes from where I live in East Yorkshire. If you haven't visited (you should get it on your list), they do the best Sunday roast in the country! I was also lucky enough to have the opportunity of cooking at world-renowned Restaurant Gordon Ramsay on Royal Hospital Road. And now, I proudly present my debut cookbook *Misarana*. I have to say, writing this book has been fun and I hope it will bring you pleasure in your kitchen.

Misarana translates to 'fusion' in Punjabi. This cookbook is full of Indian twists on classic European dishes with real, fusion flavour. I have brought together all my favourite food memories – cooking home-made food with my Punjabi grandparents, eating in bustling French bistros, or on vibrant street food stalls in India – and created some mouth watering recipes. In this book, I aim to reinvigorate cooking at home and bring vibrancy and freshness to the kitchen. My greatest dining experiences have been in wonderful, inexpensive, communal places – with the electric buzz of people scoffing overloaded plates: steak frites in France or the intoxicating aroma of sizzling lamb kebabs on a smoking, white-hot charcoal grill, in India. I have brought these amazing experiences to life on the pages that follow. This book is full of recipes which reflect my love of simple food with emphasis on flavour. From midweek meals to slow Sundays, these are twists on familiar dishes for all kinds of schedules, brought to life with vibrancy and spice.

Many of my childhood memories are from time spent in the kitchen. At the age of around five, my mum stood me on a stool and carefully instructed me how to stir the scrambled eggs – a job which is still mine whenever I'm at home. I grew up around a love of cooking; at the end of summer, we would pick apples, pears, crab apples and damsons from the garden and slowly cook them into compotes, jellies and jams. As a teenager, I started teaching myself the classic French techniques, replicating elaborate recipes from the great masters: Raymond Blanc and Michel Roux. Cooking is something that I've always done and I have always pushed myself to achieve perfection.

It's not just cooking though – I love everything that goes with it. I remember my first experience of a French supermarket and the stunning variety and quality of produce that was available. Live lobsters and crabs in a supermarket is unheard of in the UK. I get inspiration from cooking with the best produce, and I also have an obsession with cookware. As a child, the family regularly visited the town of Villedieu-les-Poêles in France, home to the wonderful Mauviel factory, which makes the finest pans in the world. I have always appreciated cooking with the best cookware.

My family and I would spend long summer holidays camping in France. However, when I talk about France and French food, I'm not describing *haute cuisine*; I'm talking about hearty and simple fare. I love to show people honest, lesser-known regional dishes, which I have known and loved my whole life. My recipes are built on this philosophy.

My parents, both teachers, had the luxury of having time to do this each year. As a family, we preferred to go off the beaten track and do our own thing. We could forget about our normal lives and live new and exciting ones each year. I loved the adventure of it all; the route would change, depending on where we felt like visiting. Biarritz for surfing and *confit de canard*, Haute-Savoie for the Alps and mountain cheeses! These holidays were always kept to a strict budget – but who said you had to spend money to have a great time anyway? Most days we would cook at the campsite. We had a well-equipped, professional set-up: a large gas stove, a barbecue, a gas camping fridge, pots and pans; everything you needed to cook a gourmet meal. Food was always at the centre of these holidays. My parents both loved to cook and discover new French specialities and the days would be spent deciding what to eat using local, seasonal produce: fresh sardines, grilled simply with lemon juice, with courgettes and a dressed tomato salad was a favourite – bursting with energy and freshness. Wherever we found ourselves, we would cook the classic dishes of each region; cassoulet in the

South West, mussels in Normandy. We used to visit the salt pans of Guérande, where some of the world's most famous salt is sourced. These experiences shaped the way I think about food today.

We would also eat out, but only in places where you'd never find a tourist, or a menu written in English; all recommended to us very carefully, of course, by locals. We were never the sort of family who would turn up to a restaurant without research, or on a whim. I'm talking about little bistros frequented by workers at lunch; people who knew where the real food was served. I loved the buzz of these places and how informal they were. Unfussy interiors, nothing flash, busy and bustling with lots of chatter and crashing of cutlery and crockery, with an amazing smell wafting through the dining room; communal plates of cheese and wine in the centre of the table. Menus would be short and classic: home-made pâté for starter, or prawns with mayonnaise. A main course of rabbit in mustard with tagliatelle (or chips) was a classic, with *fromage blanc* and berries for dessert. All with cheese and coffee for about a tenner. You had to be quick at lunch; if you arrived too late, everything would have inevitably run out. The food was always simple, but made with so much care. Simply delicious.

My favourite type of restaurant was the supermarket cafeteria, a French institution. Families and workers visit these self-service restaurants, usually at lunchtime to get a quick, tasty, no-frills meal. The best cafeterias were always on the outskirts of large cities, where there was a busy lunch trade. They were exciting places: the food would be simple, cheap and have daily changing specials of local delicacies. My favourite cafeteria meal was steak haché, a minced steak formed into a thin burger then grilled to pink perfection, served with chips and stewed green beans; a meal fit for a king. Banana split for dessert was legendary! These were magical places where the chefs put a lot of care into the food and knew how to make the most out of affordable ingredients. Looking back, these meals shaped the way I want to eat. Simple food, with big flavour, cooked with care.

I am half-Indian and my Punjabi heritage is the other part of my background that has inspired me. My Indian grandparents were both brilliant cooks. They would rarely go out for dinner and would religiously cook at home, creating amazing meals from whatever was cheap that day at Leicester market. I spent a lot of time with my grandparents growing up, watching my grandmother make dal, or an array of vegetable curries, frying crisp pakora over

her giant wok full of smoking oil. Their house was always full of the beautiful smells of Indian spices, and the frying of onions, garlic and ginger. The eye-tingling aroma of fresh ground garam masala straight from the coffee grinder, filling the house with a cloud of intoxicating spice. Buying packets of ready-ground spice powders was never an option. They only wanted to cook with authentic ingredients, to create food with the best flavour.

I didn't have to learn how to cook Indian food; I absorbed the knowledge without even realising. My grandparents taught me the art of cooking with spice and the expertise required to perfectly balance a dish. My grandmother would give me different spices to smell and taste, explaining very carefully which would go into each dish, and which ingredients paired with each spice. It is so easy to throw in a bunch of spices in a haphazard fashion and more often than not, you are left with something which is not quite as harmonious as you would like. It is all too easy to overpower and lose the delicate flavours of the ingredients you are trying to emphasise and upset the balance. I remember watching my grandmother burn aubergines for her special aubergine sabzi. It is beautifully creamy and smoky with an amazing depth of flavour and layering of spice. Her yellow dal was so fresh, singing of green chillies, coriander and ginger.

My fusion recipes show you how to use spice effectively, to introduce a new complexity and flavour into your everyday cooking. It may seem like each of these dishes requires a large number of ingredients, but there is actually a core arsenal of spices that all my recipes depend on, and will be used time and time again while cooking from this book. This book simplifies the process of Indian spicing and aims to make this more accessible and achievable. These flavours unlock a different world to the soulless jars of korma sauce you can buy in the supermarket, which bear scant resemblance to the famous Old Delhi Mutton Quorma you would find in Karim's restaurant in the back streets of the ancient city.

Indian cuisine has contributed so much to Britain's modern-day food culture: mulligatawny soup, black pepper, kedgeree, chicken tikka masala, coronation chicken... the list goes on. Despite this, it is all too easy for people to throw Indian food into a category which isn't taken very seriously. For many, it's seen as poppadoms with a sickly sweet, gloopy mango chutney, followed by a heavy bowl of rice and curry with homogenous flavour, made from a base sauce of 'spices'. When you take into account the huge diversity of regional cuisines across India, you start to realise that Indian food has to be one of the most misunderstood, under-appreciated cuisines in the world. The food in India is a world apart from what most British people believe it to be – because this is the Indian food that we have all been exposed to for generations. Cooks from India would open restaurants and have to make do with ingredients they had access to in the UK, as well as deciding whether to make their food more palatable to the British taste. But now things are changing, and this cookbook reflects that change, showing the enhancement that real, authentic Indian flavours can add to classic European dishes. We now have the luxury of being able to buy the sweetest mango in our local supermarket during the Indian mango season. Let's use them!

I want to change people's mindset when it comes to Indian food and fusion cooking and give people an insight into the fascinating and varied regional cuisines of India. I hope to enthuse my readers – perhaps to even travel to Mumbai and eat the perfect *vada pav* one day – but for now, to transport you to my culinary world. This book is full of flavourful, no-nonsense, everyday recipes that marry my love of classic European food with my love of India. It's based on traditional and regional recipes – recipes that everyone will be able to relate to and get excited about eating. Inspired by my favourite places to eat, these are wholesome dishes, which are both light and vibrant or rich and indulgent. I want to stimulate your senses and introduce Indian flavours as a vital foundation of home cooking. We're not talking about poppadoms and chutney; think Goan vindaloo pulled-pork buns with apple fennel slaw, roasted duck legs with a Punjabi-spiced bean cassoulet, coriander and fennel smoked salmon waffles with ginger and lime crème fraîche.

The wonderful thing about my life-changing journey of food, is that it's only just the beginning. The world of food is one that never stops changing and one where, as a cook, you never stop learning. For me, the greatest pleasure of cooking is being able to share my love of food and the dishes which mean the most to me. I hope you will find pleasure in sharing these recipes and ideas with your loved ones. Because, let's face it, the best memories are always spent sharing food with friends and family.

BREAKFAST & BRUNCH

Late breakfasts in our relentlessly busy lives bring to mind the idea of slowing down and taking the time to enjoy a leisurely start to the day. There's nothing like the satisfaction of ignoring the clock and feeling unusually refreshed. Wouldn't life be better if we could wake up mid-morning every day? The intoxicating aroma of fresh coffee and the whirring of the juicer signals the weekend. Only the most vibrant fresh juice will do – none of that UHT cartoned stuff, thank you. You sink into your armchair and flick through the pages of your brand-new cookbook, *Misarana*, which was delivered just a day ago but you haven't had the time to read. It has that wonderful new book smell ... almost as alluring as the coffee. I think it's time for something to eat!

For me, India offers some of the greatest breakfast dishes. When we go to visit family in Punjab, each morning we are treated to the famous paranthe, accompanied with cups of fragrant masala chai. Paranthe are perfectly stuffed flatbreads, made from wholewheat flour, fried in ghee until flaky and crisp on the outside. The usual stuffings are paneer, green chilli and cauliflower or potato and they are served in American pancake-style stack formation – piled up high in the centre of the table, laden with slowly melting butter. They are eaten with unsweetened home-made yoghurt and a selection of home-made fiery pickles. It's all about contrast: the rich buttery fried paranthe against creamy, but tangy yoghurt. The whole experience is elevated with the punch of pickle – a wonderful combination. When we were kids, my brother and I could eat paranthe non-stop. On a good day, we could get through at least five of them each. 'You cook 'em, Nani and we'll eat 'em', was the motto we lived by.

But breakfast in India isn't just paranthe – we're only scratching the surface. Eggs are a breakfast staple in India, from masala omelettes to scrambled eggs spiced with tomato, green chillies, red onion and coriander. In South India, dosa is the king of breakfast. Dosa is a thin and crisp, fermented-rice pancake, which is served with a creamy coconut chutney. Chole bhature is another Punjabi classic – a dark and spicy chickpea curry, accompanied with puffy fried bhatura bread.

Everywhere you look you'll see chai being made and sold in tiny tall glasses, paper cups or clay pots. Poured from a height from gigantic aluminium teapots to give a bit of cappuccino-like froth – it's what espresso is to Italians, served in small cups to allow many cups to be consumed over the course of the day.

Watching the chai wallahs expertly brewing their chai is pure theatre. The spices are crushed on a stone and thrown into a huge pot of concentrated tea and heavily reduced milk, so thick that it's covered in a thin blanket of fatty skin. Some sugar is added to balance the spices and the pot is furiously boiled to further concentrate the flavours and reduce the milk to an even silkier, creamy consistency. It's not a case of boiling a kettle and adding water; chai making is art and a way of life. People stand and have a chat at their local tea stall over a steaming hot cup of chai – it's the best way to start the day.

There is so much variation and vibrancy to discover in India, and in this chapter I will show you some of the breakfast and brunch dishes that I love to cook at home. The recipes are inspired by my love of traditional Indian breakfast staples and some familiar ideas closer to home. Here's to an exciting start to the day, like you've never tasted before!

DELHI STREET BREAD OMELETTE

MAKES 2 LARGE
OMELETTES
(SERVES 4)

6 medium eggs
½ red onion, finely diced
½ fresh tomato, diced
3 green finger chillies,
    finely chopped
A small handful (8g/¼oz)
    of fresh coriander
    (cilantro), chopped
1 tsp garam masala
1 tsp Kashmiri chilli
    powder
Scant ½ tsp ground
    turmeric
60g (2oz/4 tbsp) butter
A splash of vegetable or
    sunflower oil, for frying
2 thick slices of white
    bread, halved
40g (1½oz) mature
    Cheddar cheese, grated
Salt and pepper

In Delhi, the day starts with a hot cup of fragrant chai and, of course, that staple of any Indian breakfast – eggs. You'll find street stalls offering all manner of eggs and omelettes, prepared in a variety of ways. Highly skilled chefs stand at their turbo gas stoves, behind barricades of egg boxes, with pans of foaming butter and perform a lightning-fast sequence of chopping, beating and tossing without the slightest hesitation. Nothing is more pleasurable than a spicy omelette to start the day – and none better than the one from the famed Khan Omelette Corner of Old Delhi. It is made by adding slices of bread to the eggs as they are cooking – the bread soaks up the runny egg and forms part of the structure of the omelette – almost like a savoury eggy bread. A very special way to start the day … Dilli- (Delhi) style!

In a large bowl, whisk the eggs with the red onion, tomato, green chillies, fresh coriander, garam masala, chilli powder and turmeric. Season with 2 pinches of salt and some ground black pepper. Whisk again.

Heat a 24cm (9½in) non-stick frying pan over a high heat. When the pan is hot, add half of the butter with a tiny splash of oil. The butter will sizzle and begin to melt immediately. Swirl the butter around the pan and, when melted, pour in half of the egg mixture.

Immediately add two halves of the bread on top of the runny eggs, (side by side, in the centre of the omelette) and flip the bread slices over so that they are coated in egg (like eggy bread). Cook the omelette over a very high heat for 2 minutes to build up a nice crust on the underside, shaking the pan to make sure that the omelette has not stuck.

Using a spatula, flip the omelette over and sprinkle half of the grated cheese over the top. Cook for a further 1 minute, to toast the bread, before folding in half to make a sandwich with the cheese in the centre. The omelette should be perfectly cooked, with a very slightly moist centre and dark golden exterior. Remove from the pan and keep warm on a serving plate whilst you repeat to make the second omelette with the remaining eggs.

Enjoy with lashings of ketchup and chilli sauce!

STREET MASALA CHAI

MAKES 2 MEDIUM
OR 4 SMALL CUPS
OF CHAI

6 green cardamom pods
4 cloves
2cm (¾in) cinnamon stick
5 black peppercorns
15g (½oz) fresh ginger
3 Assam or English
    Breakfast tea bags
    or 3 tsp loose-leaf
    Assam tea
1 heaped tbsp
    granulated sugar
250ml (9fl oz/1 cup)
    whole milk

There's nothing like starting the day with a cup of fragrant masala chai and it's so simple to make – just a few spices, some tea bags, milk and sugar are all that's required.

In a pestle and mortar, crush the spices for a couple of minutes, until you have a powder (don't worry about the cardamom husks – they won't break down). Add the ginger and crush well.

Add the ginger and spices to a heavy-based saucepan with 250ml (9fl oz/1 cup) cold water and the teabags. Bring to a boil over a high heat and simmer for 3 minutes.

Add the sugar and milk and bring back to the boil. Boil hard over a high heat for another 3 minutes, stirring if the pan looks like it might boil over. This fast boiling helps reduce and intensify the milk in the chai, giving it a creamy texture. Remove the tea bags and strain the chai through a tea strainer into glasses.

CARDAMOM BISCUITS FOR YOUR CUPPA!

MAKES ABOUT
15 BISCUITS

250g (9oz/1¾ cups
    plus 2 tbsp) plain
    (all-purpose) flour
50g (1¾ cups) pistachio
    nuts, roughly chopped
150g (5½oz/¾ cup) caster
    (superfine) sugar
A pinch of salt
1 tsp green cardamom
    powder, or the seeds of
    10 cardamom pods ground
    to a fine powder in a mortar
    and pestle
200g (7oz/scant 1 cup)
    unsalted butter, melted

These biscuits are deliciously crumbly and have a gentle cardamom flavour, and are perfect to dunk into a cup of chai or tea.

In a mixing bowl, mix together the dry ingredients. Add the melted butter and bring together to form a dough. Don't over-mix, as this will make the biscuits less short and crumbly.

Unroll a double thickness rectangle of cling film (plastic wrap). Place the dough in the middle and roll into a thick sausage, around 14cm (5½in) long. Wrap tightly and place in the fridge for 2 hours.

Preheat your oven to 170°C fan/375°F/Gas 5. Line a baking tray with baking parchment. Remove the dough from the fridge and remove the cling film. Cut the log into slices on an angle, each around 5–7mm (¼–⅜in) thick, and place on the baking tray.

Bake in the oven for 12–15 minutes, until lightly golden. Allow to cool on a wire rack before enjoying. The biscuits will keep for 2 days in an airtight container.

SHAHI SHEERMAL BUNS

SERVES 6

150ml (5fl oz/scant ⅔ cup)
    whole milk
75g (2½oz/5 tbsp)
    unsalted butter, melted,
    plus extra for greasing
2 generous pinches of
    saffron
300g (10½oz/2¼ cups)
    strong white bread flour,
    plus extra for dusting
30g (1oz/2½ tbsp) caster
    (superfine) sugar
7g (¼oz) sachet of
    instant dried yeast
1 tsp salt
1 egg, at room temperature
1 egg yolk mixed with 1 tbsp
    whole milk, to glaze

Filling:
75g (2½oz/5 tbsp)
    unsalted butter, softened
150g (5½oz/¾ cup)
    muscovado sugar
1 tsp green cardamom
    powder, or the seeds of
    10 green cardamom pods
    ground to a fine powder
20g (⅔oz) cashew nuts,
    finely chopped
20g (⅔oz) pistachio nuts,
    finely chopped
20g (⅔oz) blanched
    almonds, finely chopped

Syrup:
100g (3½oz/½ cup) caster
    (superfine) sugar
1 tsp green cardamom
    powder
2 tsp rosewater
A pinch of saffron

Sheermal is a bread, similar to naan, but enriched with ghee and spiked with saffron. In Old Delhi and the district of Hazrat Nizamuddin, you might come across the shahi sheermal. Shahi *means 'royal' and this version is turbocharged: sweet, fluffy, indulgent, topped with nuts and dipped in a warm cardamom syrup. It's the perfect accompaniment for dunking into a cup of tea.*

For the dough: warm the milk and butter for 30 seconds in a microwave or in a small pan. Add the saffron and allow to infuse for an hour. Meanwhile, grease a roasting tin measuring roughly 35 x 25cm (14 x 10in) with a small amount of softened butter.

Add the dry ingredients to the bowl of a stand mixer fitted with a dough hook and mix until combined. Beat the egg into the saffron milk and pour into the bowl. Knead the dough on medium speed for around 10 minutes, until you are left with a smooth dough. (Alternatively, if you don't have a stand mixer, this can be done by hand.) Form the dough into a ball and place back in the bowl. Cover with cling film (plastic wrap) and leave in a warm place for 45 minutes–1 hour until doubled in size.

Whilst the dough is proving, make the filling. In a bowl, beat together the butter, sugar and cardamom until smooth. Set aside.

When doubled in size, roll out the dough on a floured work surface to a rectangle around 4mm (⅛in) thick. Spread the filling over the dough and scatter with the nuts. Roll the dough up, along the length, into a tight sausage shape. With a sharp knife, cut the log into eight equal rounds, around 4cm (1½in) thick. Arrange the buns, evenly spaced out, in the greased baking tray. Cover with cling film and prove again for around 45 minutes–1 hour, until they have doubled in size and have filled the tray with no gaps. Preheat your oven to 180°C fan/400°F/Gas 6. When the buns have risen, brush them with the egg and milk glaze, and place into the top of the oven. Bake for around 25–30 minutes, until golden.

While the buns are baking, place all the ingredients for the syrup into a saucepan with 100ml (3½fl oz/scant ½ cup) water and bring to the boil over a high heat. Allow to reduce for 4 minutes before turning the heat off and allowing the syrup to cool a little. As soon as the buns come out of the oven, brush with a generous amount of the warm syrup. Enjoy when cool enough to handle.

WAFFLES WITH SMOKED SALMON, CORIANDER, LIME & GINGER CRÈME FRAÎCHE

SERVES 4

Crème fraîche:
200g (7oz, generous
  ¾ cup) full-fat crème
  fraîche (Isigny is best)
15g (½oz) fresh coriander
  (cilantro), finely chopped
2 green finger chillies,
  finely chopped
2cm (¾in) piece of
  ginger, finely grated
2 tsp coriander seeds
  and 1 tsp fennel seeds,
  coarsely crushed in
  a mortar and pestle
Zest of 1 lemon
A pinch of black pepper

Waffles:
100g (3½oz/scant ½ cup)
  unsalted butter,
  plus extra, melted,
  for greasing
200g (7oz/¾ cup)
  self-raising flour
½ tsp salt
1 medium egg
200ml (7fl oz/generous
  ¾ cup) buttermilk

Pickled cucumber:
½ cucumber
100ml (3½fl oz/scant
  ½ cup) white wine
  vinegar
60g (2oz/5 tbsp) caster
  (superfine) sugar

To serve:
200g (7oz) good-quality
  smoked salmon
50g (1¾oz) salmon
  caviar (optional)
Lemon wedges

A restaurant in Copenhagen inspired this recipe – Restaurant Barr, a former shipping warehouse overlooking the waterfront. They serve a fluffy, crisp waffle with an unmistakable nutty brown butter flavour, topped with herby soured cream and salty salmon roe – what a mouthful! It was flawlessly executed, and yet, so simple. I've taken this marvellous idea, but added flavours of ginger, lime and coriander, which really lift the smoked salmon. Don't worry if you don't have a waffle-maker; the batter can also be cooked as pancakes, so no specialist equipment is required. And if you don't feel like making waffle batter, you can spread the crème fraîche onto toasted bagels for a simplified version.

For the crème fraîche: stir all the ingredients together, then refrigerate for an hour to set.

In a small saucepan, heat the butter for the waffles over a medium-low heat for 10–15 minutes, or until it is hazelnut-brown in colour and smells nutty. Allow to cool slightly.

Put the flour and salt in a large bowl. Add the egg, buttermilk and cooled butter. Whisk to make a thick batter, then leave in the fridge for 30 minutes to rest.

Thinly slice the cucumber and put it in a bowl with a generous pinch of salt. Warm the vinegar, sugar and 100ml (3½fl oz/scant ½ cup) water together in a small pan until dissolved. Pour the hot liquid over the cucumber. Leave to steep for at least 30 minutes.

To cook the waffles, preheat your waffle-maker. Brush the irons with some melted butter and spoon a generous dollop of batter into the machine. Cook for 5–6 minutes until golden. Repeat with the rest of the batter.

To serve, spread some crème fraîche onto a waffle. Top with two slices of smoked salmon and salmon roe, if using. Enjoy with the pickled cucumber and a spritz of lemon juice.

GREEN CHILLI PARANTHE

MAKES APPROXIMATELY
8 PARANTHE

Dough:
400g (14oz/3 cups) medium
    chapatti flour (if you
    can't find chapatti flour,
    wholemeal flour will
    be just fine), plus extra
    for dusting
1 tsp salt
250ml (9fl oz/1 cup)
    lukewarm water
1 tbsp oil
Vegetable or sunflower oil,
    for frying

Filling:
3 tbsp vegetable or
    sunflower oil oil
2 tsp cumin seeds
¼ tsp asafoetida
2 onions, finely diced
2cm (¾in) piece of ginger,
    finely grated
2 garlic cloves, finely grated
15 green finger chillies,
    finely chopped
A large bunch of fresh
    coriander (cilantro),
    finely chopped
½ tsp dried mango
    powder (amchoor)
Salt

Tamarind banana (optional):
100ml (3½fl oz/scant
    ½ cup) maple syrup
1 tsp tamarind paste
½ banana, sliced

To serve:
60g (2oz/4 tbsp) butter
100g (3½oz/scant ½ cup)
    natural yoghurt (optional)

*Paranthe really are the most famous North Indian breakfast and,
when done properly, I can eat hundreds of these stuffed flatbreads.
Fifteen green chillies are not as hot as they sound once cooked!*

For the filling, heat the oil in a large frying pan over medium heat.
When hot, add the cumin seeds and allow them to sizzle in the hot
oil, to release their aromas. Add the asafoetida and onions, along
with a pinch of salt. Cook for 8–10 minutes until softened and
lightly golden. Add the ginger, garlic and green chillies and fry for
3 minutes until lightly golden. Remove from the heat and add the
coriander and dried mango powder. Set aside in a bowl to cool.

To make the dough, mix together the flour and salt in a bowl.
Make a well in the centre, pour in the warm water and oil and
bring it all together with your hands. Remove the dough from the
bowl and knead for 10 minutes, until it is smooth. Cover in a bowl
with cling film (plastic wrap) and allow to rest for 20 minutes.

If serving with the banana, combine the tamarind paste and maple
syrup in a bowl. Add the banana and set aside until ready to serve.

Divide the dough into eight equal portions. Split the first portion
in half, dust with flour and roll out both halves so that you have two
10cm (4in) circles. Place a dollop of the filling into the centre of
the dough. Brush the edge with a little water and place the other
circle of dough on top. Seal well around the edges with your fingers.
Dust with a little more flour, then roll the paranthe to a circle about
16cm (6¼in) in diameter and around 3–4mm (⅛in) thick – as
thin as you can without the filling piercing the dough. Repeat until
you have used up all of the dough, placing the paranthe between
sheets of baking parchment as you go so that they don't stick
together. Keep covered with cling film, so that they don't dry out.

To fry, heat a heavy frying pan over a medium heat. When hot, place
a paranthe carefully in the pan and cook for 1 minute on each side.
Brush the top with oil, flip over and cook for a further 2 minutes.
By this time, the paranthe should puff up, which indicates that it
is ready. Remove from the pan and repeat with the other breads.
Keep wrapped in a tea towel, to keep warm.

Place a knob of butter on each paranthe and serve with the
tamarind banana or just with a dollop of yoghurt.

ALOO JEERA ROSTI

MAKES 1 LARGE ROSTI SERVES 4

400g (14oz) waxy potatoes (Charlotte or Ratte work well)
Vegetable or sunflower oil, for drizzling
2 tsp cumin seeds
1 tsp chilli flakes
3 garlic cloves, finely grated
200g (7oz) paneer cheese
1 tsp ground cumin
1 tsp ground coriander
½ tsp ground turmeric
½ red onion, finely diced
1 green finger chilli, finely chopped
A small handful of fresh coriander (cilantro), finely chopped
70g (2½oz/⅓ cup) unsalted butter
8 rashers of bacon
2 tbsp white wine vinegar
4 very fresh eggs
1 avocado, peeled and pitted
Juice of ½ lime
Salt and pepper

Betty's tearoom is a Yorkshire institution; the first time I visited, I fell in love with the place. The cake trolley is of course legendary. But, the special thing for me is the rösti – buttery on the inside, crisp and golden on the outside, oozing with cheese – irresistible! Potatoes are a staple of India and form the base of so many exciting dishes. Jeera (cumin) potatoes are a simple but superb dish of North India, and buttery rösti, layered with the warmth and flavour of spice, really takes this dish to the next level.

Boil the potatoes whole in a pan of salted water for 8 minutes, so they are still al dente. Drain and allow to cool.

Warm a frying pan over a high heat. When hot, drizzle with oil and add the cumin seeds, chilli flakes and garlic. Allow to sizzle for 2 minutes, or until golden.

Coarsely grate the boiled potatoes and paneer into a large bowl. Add the toasted spices, ground spices, red onion, green chilli, fresh coriander and a generous pinch of salt and pepper. Mix well.

Heat a 24cm (9½in) frying pan over a low heat. Melt half of the butter with a splash of oil (this stops the butter burning). Add the rösti mix, lightly press down and fry for 10–12 minutes, until nicely golden. Flip the rösti out onto a plate. Add the remaining butter to the pan, then return the rösti to the pan, other side down. Cook for around 10–12 minutes, until golden. Remove from the pan and keep warm.

In the same pan, add a splash of oil and fry the bacon until crisp.

To poach the eggs, fill a deep pan with water and bring to a gentle simmer. Season the water with salt and the vinegar. Crack each egg into a ramekin. When the water is simmering, take a spoon and swirl the water to make a vortex. One by one, drop the eggs into the water, close to the surface. Poach for 3½ minutes, then remove the eggs onto kitchen paper using a slotted spoon.

To serve, slice the avocado and dress it with the lime juice and a pinch of salt. Cut the rösti into four. Top each slice with a couple of slices of avocado, two rashers of bacon and a poached egg.

BLOODY MEERA

Rasam seasoning:
½ tsp cumin seeds
½ tsp fenugreek seeds
½ tsp black peppercorns

Rasam:
1 tbsp vegetable or
    sunflower oil
1 tsp black mustard seeds
1 tsp cumin seeds
¼ tsp asafoetida
Leaves from 1 sprig
    of fresh curry leaves
2 garlic cloves, finely grated
1½ tsp Kashmiri chilli
    powder
2 green finger chillies,
    finely chopped
500ml (17fl oz/2 cups)
    tomato juice
1 tsp brown sugar
Juice of 1 lime
A small handful of chopped
    fresh coriander (cilantro)
Salt

To serve:
Ice cubes
200ml (7fl oz/¾ cup
    plus 2 tbsp) vodka
4 celery sticks

How do you cure the intolerable hangover? I suggest hair of the dog! A spicy, tangy, invigorating tomato-based cocktail, spiked with a hit of vodka, I hear you say...Well, in that case, the Bloody Meera is just what you're after. It is, of course, an exciting twist on a classic Bloody Mary. The base of my brunch cocktail is from a traditional South-Indian tomato broth – rasam. It is a light, fragrant and tangy tomato soup, made by gently infusing tomatoes with curry leaves, green chilli, lime and a whole host of revitalising spices. In South India, it is customary to end a meal with a warming cup of rasam, like a digestif. I think this cocktail is a brilliant, exciting way to start the weekend; a drink that will definitely lift and wake up the senses. The rasam can be made well in advance and stored in the fridge.

For the rasam seasoning, add the cumin, fenugreek and black pepper corns to a spice grinder or mortar and pestle and crush to a fine powder.

In a medium saucepan, heat the oil over a medium heat. Add the black mustard and cumin seeds and fry for 1 minute to release their oils. Add the asafoetida, curry leaves and garlic to the pan and fry for 2 minutes. Add the chilli powder, green chillies, tomato juice, sugar, lime juice and rasam seasoning to the pan, along with 100ml (3½fl oz/scant ½ cup) water. Turn the heat up to high and bring to the boil. Simmer for 3 minutes, then turn the heat off. Season with salt and add the fresh coriander. Allow to cool, then put in the fridge to chill before making the cocktail.

To serve, pour the rasam into a large jug filled with ice. Add the vodka and give everything a good stir. Pour into four glasses and garnish each with a stick of celery.

MASALA BEANS & BLACK PUDDING ON TOAST

SERVES 4

4 thick slices bread
(sourdough is ideal)
Butter, for spreading
Vegetable or sunflower oil,
for frying
4 black pudding slices
(about 240g/8½oz)
100g (3½oz) mature
Cheddar cheese, grated
Salt and pepper

Masala beans:
20g (²/₃oz/1½ tbsp)
unsalted butter
1 tsp cumin seeds
3 garlic cloves, finely
grated to a paste
2cm (¾in) piece of ginger,
finely grated to a paste
1 tsp chilli flakes
2 x 400g (14oz) tins
baked beans
1 tsp ground coriander
1 tsp ground cumin
1 tsp garam masala

Now, this may sound mad, but you couldn't really buy baked beans in France in the 1990s and it's something us Brits can't live without so we always packed a couple of emergency tins. One thing you *could* get in France, however, was black pudding or *boudin noir* as it's called – another of our much-loved breakfast essentials! The breakfast I always remember eating was this very combination of beans piled high onto a hefty hunk of buttered French baguette, crowned with wonderful boudin noir. Black pudding can really stand up to spice, so I'm recreating this memory, but with some fire in the beans. I much prefer to use tinned baked beans than attempting to make my own – what's the point in pretending; the tinned ones are FAR superior.

For the beans, melt the butter in a saucepan over a medium heat. Add the cumin seeds and allow them to sizzle in the butter for 30 seconds, to release their aroma. Add the garlic and ginger pastes and chilli flakes and fry for 2–3 minutes. Add both tins of beans, along with 50ml (1¾fl oz/3½ tbsp) of water and the ground coriander and cumin. Cover with a lid and gently simmer for 5 minutes, stirring occasionally. Add the garam masala and simmer gently for a further 5 minutes.

Toast the bread until golden and spread with some butter.

Set a frying pan over a medium heat and, when hot, add a splash of oil. Fry the black pudding slices for 2–3 minutes on each side until nicely caramelised. Remove from the heat.

Preheat your grill (broiler) to 250°C (480°F).

To serve, place the slices of toast on a baking tray. Top each slice with a generous ladle of beans. Sprinkle each with a pinch of salt and a grind of black pepper. Crumble the black pudding over the beans, followed by the cheese. Place under the hot grill for around a minute and a half, until the cheese has melted. Serve and enjoy.

TANDOORI BODEGA SANDWICH

MAKES 6 SANDWICHES

Sausage patties:
½ piece of mace
1 tbsp dried fenugreek leaves
 (kasoori methi)
½ tsp fennel seeds
½ tsp chilli flakes
½ tsp garam masala
½ tsp ground cumin
½ tsp ground coriander
1 tsp Kashmiri chilli powder
1 tsp garlic granules
1 tsp salt
1 tsp ground black pepper
2 tbsp Greek yoghurt
450g (1lb) minced
 (ground) pork
Vegetable or sunflower
 oil, for frying

Eggs:
30g (1oz/2 tbsp) butter
½ red onion, finely diced
1 fresh tomato, diced
A small bunch of coriander
 (cilantro), finely chopped
3 green finger chillies,
 finely chopped
1 tsp Kashmiri chilli powder
½ tsp ground turmeric
6 eggs
Salt and pepper

To serve:
6 slices of burger cheese
Butter, for spreading
6 English muffins or brioche
 burger buns, halved
Ketchup

Let's face it, McDonalds do a pretty amazing breakfast. It's something that we shouldn't love, but we all do! It's a classic American breakfast offering … but the best breakfast sandwiches I've had were from your quintessential New York 'bodega'. The bodega is essentially a corner shop, owned by Latin American immigrants. They sell the usual confectionery, cigarettes, the American equivalent of Frosty Jack's turbo cider, Echo Falls wine and toilet paper. But somewhere, hidden from view, you can hear the sizzling of bacon, sausage and eggs and a frenzy of punters waving $5 notes at a stern-looking bloke sitting behind the cash register. These places usually grill the best sandwiches with any combination of egg, ketchup, cheese, sausage and bacon – sandwiched between a thick grease-toasted bun. Heaven!

To make the sausage patties, grind the mace, fenugreek leaves, fennel seeds and chilli flakes in a spice or coffee grinder (or you can do this by hand in a mortar and pestle). Add this and all the remaining patty ingredients aside from the oil to the pork and mix thoroughly with your hands. Divide the mixture into six equal portions and roll into balls, then flatten into thin burger patties around 5mm (¼in) thick. (These can be made well in advance and kept in the fridge, but make sure to remove them 30 minutes before frying.)

Heat a splash of oil in a large frying pan over a medium–high heat. When hot, season the patties with salt and add them to the pan. Fry for 2–3 minutes on each side until golden and caramelised. After the first flip, top each patty with a slice of cheese. Remove from the pan and keep warm in a low oven.

For the eggs, melt the butter in the same pan, over a medium heat. Add all the ingredients, except the eggs and fry for 2 minutes to soften. Crack in the eggs and season with a generous pinch of salt and pepper. Gently turn the eggs in the pan with a spatula to make a chunky scrambled egg. Once cooked, remove from the pan.

To serve, butter the muffins and toast lightly in the frying pan or under a hot grill (broiler). Add a generous dollop of ketchup to the bottom half of each muffin. Add some egg, followed by the sausage patty. Top with the other half of the muffin and tuck in!

PISTACHIO, ROSE & RASPBERRY CROISSANT

**MAKES 4
CROISSANTS**

70g (2½oz) pistachios
70g (2½oz) unsalted
  butter, at room
  temperature
70g (2½oz/⅓ cup) caster
  (superfine) sugar
1 large egg, plus 1 egg yolk
¾ tsp rosewater (Nielsen-
  Massey brand is best)
4 good-quality all-butter
  croissants
16 fresh raspberries
1 tbsp whole milk
30g (1oz) flaked (sliced)
  almonds
Icing (confectioners')
  sugar, for dusting

I have an obsession with proper almond croissants. You'll find them in bakeries in France, breathing new life into yesterday's leftover unsold croissants. These croissants are sliced open and stuffed with almond frangipane. As they bake, the frangipane starts to ooze out, leaving unctuous lava flows of buttery frangipane. They are liberally dusted with icing sugar and thrown into the shop window. The ones I've tried in the UK are never usually any good. So, here's an easy recipe – so that you don't have to resort to mediocre supermarket ones – with a gentle Indian twist: frangipane made from pistachios and the wonderful fragrance of rose.

Preheat your oven to 170°C fan/375°F/Gas 5.

In a food processor, grind the pistachios to a fine powder. You don't want to overdo this, as you'll release the oils and end up with a paste. Set aside.

In a bowl, cream together the butter and sugar until light and creamy. Add the whole egg and thoroughly whisk in. Stir through the ground pistachios and rosewater.

Slice a cavity in the centre of the croissants so that you have pockets to fill with frangipane. Spoon or pipe a generous amount of frangipane into each croissant, and insert four raspberries. Press the croissants shut and place onto a baking sheet.

Combine the egg yolk with the milk to make an egg wash, then brush the croissants with the egg and sprinkle with flaked almonds. Bake in the centre of the oven for 30–35 minutes – they should be golden in colour. Allow to cool before dusting with icing sugar through a fine sieve or tea strainer.

FRUIT CHAAT SALAD

SERVES 4

*Any of the following
    fruit combinations:*
1 ripe mango (you can tell
    they are ripe when they
    feel very soft to the touch
    and smell sweet)
½ pineapple
½ ripe papaya
Or
1 apple
2 ripe pears
1 banana
1 orange
Or
A handful of strawberries
2 peaches or nectarines
½ cantaloupe melon

Dressing:
1 tbsp honey
1 tbsp chopped mint
1cm (½in) piece of
    ginger, grated
Zest and juice of 1 lime
1 tbsp extra virgin olive oil
1 green chilli, finely sliced
A pinch of salt
1 tsp chaat masala

When you're on holiday, the fruit always seems to taste of sunshine, that much sweeter, that much riper. I gather that it's probably a psychological effect of, firstly, not having to cut the fruit yourself and, secondly, having it expertly presented to you on a platter. It may also be to do with the fact that there is a little extra secret seasoning on the fruit, to bring out a subtly different flavour. Many of the years I spent working on ships in the Merchant Navy were in the sunny Caribbean. The crew I worked with were from Guyana and would always enjoy pineapple with a sprinkling of salt. To my amazement, it turned the pineapple into an entirely different fruit – intensifying the sweetness and, equally, adding a faint mouth-puckering salinity. In many countries around the world there is a tradition of this: in Mexico, you might add chilli, lime and coriander to the salt and in India you'll find street vendors making fruit chaats. They cut ripe tropical fruit with long sabres, then dust it with a tangy seasoning of salt, chaat masala and red chilli powder, which cleverly cuts the sweetness of the fruit and has a tantalising effect on the tastebuds. Give this a go; you'll never look at a fruit salad in the same way again – ever! You can use any seasonal fruit in this salad so buy whatever you love to eat. Enjoy this fruit salad, imagining that you're sitting on a bustling street corner in India.

....

Prepare the fruit you have selected, peeling, stoning and chopping where necessary. Arrange it on a beautiful platter.

For the dressing, whisk together all of the ingredients except the chaat masala in a bowl. Spoon the dressing over the fruit and dust with the chaat masala.

CHOLE MASALA WITH CAVOLO NERO & CRISPY EGG

SERVES 4

3 tbsp vegetable oil,
    plus 1 tbsp for the eggs
2cm (¾in) cinnamon stick
1 tsp cumin seeds
4 cloves
2 black cardamom pods,
    lightly crushed
1 large onion, finely diced
2cm (¾in) piece of ginger,
    finely grated
3 garlic cloves, finely grated
2 fresh plum tomatoes,
    grated
1 green finger chilli,
    roughly chopped
½ tsp ground cumin
½ tsp ground coriander
¼ tsp ground turmeric
1 tsp garam masala
½ tsp amchoor powder
    (dried mango)
1 tsp salt
1 x 400g (14oz) tin
    good-quality chickpeas
1 tea bag
1 tbsp pomegranate
    molasses
8 stalks cavolo nero, woody
    stalks removed and leaves
    roughly chopped
4 medium eggs
4 pinches of chilli flakes
Salt and pepper

To serve:
4 slices thick crusty bread
Butter, for spreading

Chole masala is a very famous dish from the Holy City of Amritsar and one that my grandparents would often cook for special occasions. It is a chickpea curry, simmered in a fragrant, mildly acidic sauce made with fresh tomato, ginger and garlic, usually served with a crisp, inflated puri bread. This is my adapted version of the classic chole masala. I'm serving mine with crispy fried eggs, which make a fantastic leisurely brunch dish, to be enjoyed with crusty and generously buttered sourdough bread.

Warm the oil in a large deep sauté pan with a lid over a medium heat. When hot, add the whole spices. Allow to sizzle for 1 minute, then add the onion and fry until deep golden brown – at least 10–15 minutes. Add the ginger and garlic and stir for a further 2 minutes. Add the tomatoes and green chilli and cook for a further minute, before adding the ground spices and salt. Stir to coat everything in the wonderful spices, then add 100ml (3½fl oz/scant ½ cup) of water. Simmer for 10 minutes with the lid on, stirring from time to time. The result should be a beautifully dark and rich masala sauce. Add a splash more water if it becomes too dry.

Add the chickpeas, tea bag and pomegranate molasses, along with 200ml (7fl oz/generous ¾ cup) water and bring to a simmer. Once simmering, reduce the heat and cook uncovered for 10 minutes. Add the cavolo nero to the pan for the last 5 minutes. By this time, the curry will be beautifully thick and the chickpeas tender. If it is too liquid, then turn up the heat and allow to reduce further until thickened. Remove the tea bag and, with the back of a spoon, gently crush some of the chickpeas. Keep warm whilst you fry the eggs.

Heat a large frying pan which can hold four eggs comfortably over the highest heat, until the pan is smoking hot. Or use a smaller pan and fry the eggs two at a time. Add 1 tbsp of oil and immediately crack the eggs into the pan. Sprinkle each egg with a pinch of salt, pepper and chilli flakes and cook until the eggs are cooked on top and crispy underneath. This should take around 2 minutes over a high heat.

To serve, toast the bread. Butter each slice generously and top with a nice amount of chickpea curry and a crispy fried egg.

PORRIDGE WITH DATE COMPOTE & GINGER YOGHURT

SERVES 2

100g (3½oz/1 cup)
    rolled porridge oats
500ml (17fl oz/2 cups)
    whole milk
3 green cardamom
    pods, bruised
1 tsp garam masala
A pinch of salt
4 tbsp Greek-style ginger
    yoghurt, or 4 tbsp
    Greek yoghurt mixed
    with 2 pieces of finely
    chopped stem ginger
    in syrup

Compote:
125g (4½oz) dates
1 tbsp granulated sugar
4 cloves
3cm (1¼in) cinnamon
    stick
1 star anise

The key to perfect porridge is a loose, velvet consistency. After the oats have cooked, you want the mixture to be very runny, because, as it cools, it will start to set – and you want your porridge to ooze with creaminess. Coupled with a spiced date compote and ginger flavoured yoghurt – a combo that marries beautifully – I think this is just about the best porridge going! The compote can be kept in a sterilised jar in the fridge for up to four days.

For the compote, put the dates, sugar and spices in a medium saucepan with 175ml (6fl oz/¾ cup) water. Bring to a simmer, then turn the heat down to low and put a lid on the pan. Simmer gently for 10 minutes until the dates are soft. Remove the whole spices and blend the dates to a smooth purée.

For the porridge, set a medium saucepan over a moderate heat. Add the oats, 200ml (7fl oz/generous ¾ cup) water and 400ml (14fl oz/1¾ cups) of the milk, along with the spices and salt. Once simmering, turn down the heat to low. Continue to cook, stirring from time to time, for around 5–6 minutes, until the oats are tender.

Stir in the remaining milk, then serve in wide bowls. Swirl in a couple of spoonfuls of date compote and as much ginger yoghurt as you like.

TOMATO & GINGER CHUTNEY BACON SANDWICH

MAKES 1 SANDWICH

3 rashers smoked back
 bacon (Denhay smoked
 bacon is my favourite)
2 thick slices white bread
Plenty of softened salted
 butter, for spreading
2 tsp Tomato and Ginger
 Chutney (see page 233)

Chutneys play a crucial role in every South-Indian meal. They add excitement to the table – a meal just isn't the same without a good chutney to dip into! A breakfast dosa will always be served with a deliciously rich coconut chutney. For a simple evening meal, you might add some ghee and chutney to plain boiled rice. It takes seconds to make, but is one of my all-time favourite meals; each grain of rice soaks up the bright flavours of the chutney. My wife, Nami, who is from Hyderabad in South India, makes sure that we are never without at least two types of South-Indian chutney. She introduced me to an ultimate snack: ginger chutney spread onto buttered toast with a pinch of salt – this is absolutely next-level toast! I'm taking this idea one step further by adding bacon to the mix, to make what I think is an unbeatable bacon sarnie.

Preheat the grill (broiler) function of your oven to 250°C (480°F).

Place the rashers of bacon onto a baking tray and put into the centre of the oven for 3–4 minutes – you want to cook the bacon slowly so that it crisps up and renders the fat. Remove the rashers from the oven and pour off any liquid. Turn the rashers over, then return them to the grill for a further 2–3 minutes, until nicely golden. You can also fry the bacon in a pan, if you like.

Toast the bread lightly and, while still warm, spread generously with butter. Add a good smear of chutney to both sides before adding the bacon rashers and sandwiching together.

TAJ PALACE PERFECT FRENCH TOAST

SERVES 4

4 large eggs
4 heaped tbsp caster
  (superfine) sugar
100ml (3½fl oz/scant
  ½ cup) whole milk
1 tsp vanilla bean paste
  or vanilla extract
4 slices 5cm (2in) thick
  white bread
50g (1¾oz/3½ tbsp)
  unsalted butter

To serve:
2 tbsp caster (superfine)
  sugar (or use icing/
  confectioners' sugar)
Maple syrup

I have a sound knowledge of both the eating and cooking of French toast. I've made this dish for as long as I can remember, based on the French toast my mum used to make us every Saturday morning. It is also a very popular dish in India – perhaps that's why my mum used to cook it? In India, it sometimes goes by the name 'Bombay toast' and, funnily enough, I discovered on my last trip to India that the perfect French toast can be found on the breakfast menu of the Taj Mahal Palace Hotel in Mumbai. Many people tell me that brioche makes the best French toast, but I tend not to agree. In my opinion, I find the texture too dense and overwhelmingly rich in taste. The perfect French toast is simply made from an unsliced soft white sandwich loaf. Slice it yourself, about two inches thick – just like they do at the Taj.

Find yourself a roasting pan that's big enough to fit the bread slices without overlapping. In a bowl, whisk together the eggs, sugar, whole milk and vanilla. Pour the mixture into the pan and add the bread slices to soak up the mixture. After 5 minutes, turn the bread over and leave until all the egg mixture has been absorbed.

Heat a large frying pan over a medium-low heat and melt half of the butter. Add as many pieces of bread as you can comfortably fit in the pan – you'll probably have to do this in two batches, or in two pans. Be careful as the bread will be very delicate.

Keep the heat on medium-low and cook for 5–6 minutes on each side, until lightly golden. After turning, dot the pan with an extra few knobs of butter.

Sprinkle the slices of French toast with caster sugar and if you have a chef's blowtorch, caramelise the sugar to make a crunchy brûlée topping. If you don't have a blowtorch, simply swap out the caster sugar and dust with icing sugar through a fine sieve or tea strainer instead. Serve with plenty of maple syrup and if you like, some skinless sausages – just as my mum used to.

A SPOT
OF LUNCH

My ideal lunch would be an extravagant, sprawling alfresco spread laid out on a crisp white tablecloth, accompanied by a few glasses of wine or a jar of beer, followed by an afternoon siesta on a deckchair somewhere breezy and shady. I've got to admit that this isn't an everyday reality, but it's how I would live each day if I had the opportunity. In fact, I've found that midday is the best time of day for an indulgent banquet. I have always seized any opportunity to sit around a table ready to enjoy a great meal. The point is that lunch is easily overlooked and, amid the pressures of modern life, is easily relegated to a brief and expedient pause. Lunch for most people is a grab-and-go sandwich or a soggy meal deal. I've always admired how the French lunch: every shop or office will close its doors at 12 on the dot for the daily two-hour closure. There are no sandwiches being scoffed over tapping keyboards or kettles being boiled to fill instant noodle pots. In France, work stops and you'll spend the well-earned break having a very civilised meal in a simple café or restaurant, where time has been taken to create something traditional, home-made and delicious – washed down with a glass of wine ... *Bien sûr!* Why not?

In this chapter I've been inspired by some of the amazing lunches we enjoyed as a family growing up. Take Le Welsh Complet on page 57, for example. Le Welsh may sound like a curious thing, but it is the French version of Welsh rarebit! Complet refers to the beautifully fried egg which is placed on top of the melted cheese and ham, completing this hearty meal. As a family, we have enjoyed this dish for the past 25 years – even today, every trip to the Flandres area of France starts with a Welsh! We eat it in the same supermarket cafeteria in Boulogne-Sur-Mer each time. When I was very young, around 10, we would go on an exciting day trip to France for my birthday. Not because my parents wanted to go on a booze cruise – it was purely my choice. I loved the adventure of going on the ferry and then heading to our cafeteria for a Welsh and a banana split; a very special birthday treat indeed.

With Keralan Mussels on pages 50–51, I wanted to create a recipe which unites my love of family holidays in Normandy and travelling to the fishing port of Kochi in Kerala – two worlds, which feel so close in spirit I've even taken inspiration from the similarities between Indian cuisine and my home town. I can't think of a more legendary city for fish and chips than Hull. Maybe I'm biased, as it's now my home, but with its fishing heritage it's a city where fish and chips is deeply engrained in its beating heart. You simply can't come to this part of the world without trying the famous 'Hull pattie'. This sage and onion-flavoured potato cake is battered and deep-fried in beef dripping and it's a wonderful thing when served with chips and, of course, the local chip spice, which you'll find on the counter of every fish and chip shop in town. It plays a huge part in the identity and culture of this city.

It's funny how similar ideas are, because if you were to put a pattie into a breadcake (a bap, bun, cob or roll to most people) and make a 'pattie butty', you wouldn't be far off another famous Mumbai snack – the people of Mumbai have the vada pav. This is similar to the pattie – it's a potato cake which is mixed with spices and green chillies, deep-fried in a batter of chickpea flour then sandwiched in a pav (bread roll). In fact, as I've written this book I've noticed more shared flavours and techniques in French and Indian dishes than you might expect. It has allowed me to explore these commonalities and come up with some my own takes on classic dishes infused with less traditional flavours and which should, hopefully, liven up your lunches.

THE HULL PATTIE PAV

MAKES 4 SANDWICHES

Dripping or vegetable oil,
    for frying
12 fresh sage leaves
4 green finger chillies, slit
4 brioche burger buns
Green Chutney (see page 233)

Potato filling:
400g (14oz) peeled potatoes
    (Maris Pipers work well)
½ red onion, finely diced
2 green finger chillies,
    finely chopped
Zest of ½ lemon
1 heaped tsp dried sage
1 tbsp finely chopped fresh
    coriander (cilantro)
½ tsp ground turmeric
1 tsp salt

Batter:
80g (2¾oz/¾ cup) gram
    flour (if you can't find
    chickpea flour, then use
    plain/all-purpose flour)
20g (²/₃oz/3 tbsp) cornflour
    (cornstarch)
½ tsp baking powder
1 tsp salt
225ml (8fl oz/scant 1 cup)
    cold sparkling water

Masala:
1 tbsp vegetable oil or ghee
1 tbsp desiccated (dried
    shredded) coconut
½ tsp chilli flakes
1 tsp garlic granules
½ tsp garam masala
1 tsp Kashmiri chilli powder

This recipe pays homage to both the Hull pattie and vada pav and I'm sure that I've created something quite unique in doing so.

To make the filling, cut the potatoes into 3–5cm (1¼–2in) chunks and place in a medium pan. Cover with water and a generous amount of salt and bring to the boil. Simmer for 15 minutes then drain and mash with either a potato ricer or masher. Allow to cool.

When the potatoes have cooled, add the other ingredients to the mash and mix well. Divide into four equal balls and shape into round burger-shaped patties.

To make the batter, put the dry ingredients in a large bowl. Slowly whisk in the cold water until you have a batter similar in consistency to double (heavy) cream. Set aside in the fridge.

To make the masala, set a non-stick frying pan over a medium heat. When hot, add the oil, desiccated coconut and chilli flakes. Toast for 2–3 minutes until the coconut is lightly golden then transfer to a plate lined with kitchen paper then grind in a spice grinder until fine. Put in a bowl and stir through the remaining masala ingredients. Set aside.

Warm a deep, heavy-based saucepan. Fill with oil to a depth of approximately 6–7cm (2½–2¾in), making sure that it comes no more than halfway up the sides of the pan. You can also use a deep fryer, set to 180°C (350°F). If using a pan, I recommend that you use a temperature probe to monitor the temperature and never leave the hot oil unattended. When the oil is hot (at approximately 180°C/350°F), dip each pattie into the batter. Allow the excess batter to run off, so that it is coated in a thin, even layer. Lower the pattie into the hot oil. Agitate the pattie immediately as this stops it from sticking to the bottom of the pan. Fry in batches for 4–5 minutes until crisp and golden brown. Remove the patties from the oil and allow to drain on a plate lined with kitchen paper.

Deep-fry the sage leaves for 30–45 seconds until crisp and fry the whole green chillies for 2 minutes, until softened. Place the sage and chillies onto a piece of kitchen paper to absorb the oil.

Slice the burger buns in half and spread each side with a spoonful of the green chutney. Sprinkle the base with some masala and place a pattie inside each one. Top with a green chilli and a couple of fried sage leaves. Place the lids on the buns and serve.

BOMBAY BAGNAT

SERVES 4

3–4 new potatoes (Jersey
Royals, La Ratte or
Charlotte work well)
1 large crusty round loaf
of bread
Softened salted butter,
for spreading
Green Chutney
(see page 233)
2 balls mozzarella
(buffalo is best), sliced
into 3mm ($1/8$in) slices
$1/2$ cucumber, sliced
120g ($41/4$oz) store-bought
cooked beetroot (chilli
beetroot, if you can
find it), sliced
$3/4$ tsp chaat masala
$1/4$ red onion, very
finely sliced
2 tomatoes
$1/4$ jar flame-roasted
red peppers (about
6 pieces), drained
Salt and pepper

The Bombay sandwich is probably the ultimate street food snack in Mumbai. Although the filling is the same as the classic, I'm serving my Bombay sandwich un-toasted and in the style of the pan bagnat. This is a famous sandwich from Nice, which involves hollowing out a whole loaf of bread and filling it with gorgeous Mediterranean salad ingredients.

Put the whole potatoes in a pan and cover with water and a generous pinch of salt. Bring to the boil and cook for 25 minutes, until tender. Drain and allow to cool, then finely slice them.

Slice the top 3cm ($11/4$in) off the bread loaf so that it comes off in one piece; this will be the lid of the sandwich. Tear out the soft bread from the inside of the loaf, leaving 1cm ($1/2$in) around the bottom and sides before hitting the crust (keep the excess bread for breadcrumbs).

Take the empty loaf of bread and spread the inside with a layer of softened butter. Next, spread the inside of the loaf with a good layer of the green chutney (3–4 tablespoons). Add an even layer of mozzarella to the bottom of the loaf, followed by cucumber then beetroot. Season with salt, pepper and a light sprinkle of chaat masala. Add the potato slices, sprinkling them lightly with chaat masala and a couple of spoonfuls of green chutney. Add the sliced onion, followed by the tomatoes, red peppers and another layer of mozzarella, seasoning with salt and pepper and chaat masala every other layer. By this time, you should have used up most of your ingredients and you should have filled the loaf. Add another layer of green chutney and place the lid on top. Wrap the loaf tightly in cling film (plastic wrap) and leave in the fridge for at least 2 hours to allow the bread to soak up the flavours.

KERALAN MUSSELS

SERVES 4
AS A STARTER,
2 FOR MAIN

1kg (2lb 4oz) mussels
(Scottish farmed
mussels are widely
available)
1 tbsp coconut oil
2 green cardamom pods,
lightly crushed
2 banana shallots,
thinly sliced
2cm (¾in) piece of
ginger, finely grated.
3 garlic cloves, finely grated
2 sprigs fresh curry leaves
3 green finger chillies,
sliced
1 x 410g (14oz) tin
coconut milk
1 tsp ground turmeric
½ tsp chilli powder
1 tbsp tamarind paste
1 large tomato,
roughly diced
Juice of 2 limes
2cm (¾in) piece of ginger,
cut into fine matchsticks
Salt and black pepper

Mango salsa (optional):
½ very ripe mango
A small bunch of fresh
coriander (cilantro)
2 green finger chillies,
sliced
1 tbsp tamarind paste
Juice of ½ lime

When I remember the idyllic summers that I spent with my family by the coast in Normandy, the first thing that I think of is moules–frites. Mussels are to the French what fish and chips are to the British. It's a simple, convivial and generous dish – best enjoyed sitting outside with a glass of crisp white wine in your hand, enjoying the fresh Atlantic breeze. We used to visit the small fishing town of Granville, and I always remember the sensational mussels. We would walk up the quayside, trying to decide which of the busy brasseries looked like they served up the best seafood. You can enjoy mussels with the usual marinière sauce of white wine, cream, garlic and parsley but, in Normandy things are done a little differently. The mussels are cooked in local cider, parsley, chervil and thick Norman crème fraîche – which, to me, is far superior. The French buy mussels by the tonne during the summer months. I love watching the busy markets; fishmongers dressed in oilskins, shovelling great piles of the shiny molluscs into bags for never-ending queues of customers. I love the sweet, saline smell which fills the air.

Kerala, on the south-west coast of India, is famous for its fishing heritage and its wide-ranging repertoire of spicy fish and seafood dishes. The area around the city of Kochi is built on a network of serene palm tree-lined backwaters and lakes where you'll see little wooden fishing boats hauling their catch. Dinner in the busy Hotel Seagull in Fort Kochi, with its sublime fresh seafood and packed terrace with views over the water, made me feel like I was in Granville all over again. We enjoyed a brilliantly vibrant fish curry, made with curry leaf, coconut, lime, green chilli and ginger washed down – of course – with a cold Kingfisher beer. I wanted to create a recipe which unites my love of these two worlds, which feel so close in spirit. This is a wonderful way of eating mussels and they marry so well with the spicy coconut broth.

You'll find mussels in good supermarkets. I like to buy the farmed Scottish ones, as they are always very clean and you'll hardly find any broken ones. Clean them under a running tap, remove any beards and discard any broken ones. When cooked, discard any mussels which haven't opened.

Check and clean the mussels under running water. Remove any stringy beards or barnacles and discard any that are broken. Keep in a bowl in the fridge.

To make the mango salsa, slice off one cheek from the mango, cutting around the stone. With a spoon, scoop out the flesh, leaving behind the skin. Dice the mango into 5mm (¼in) cubes and place in a small bowl. Remove the leaves from the coriander stalks and set the leaves aside for the mussels. Finely chop a few of the stalks and add them to the salsa with the other salsa ingredients and a pinch of salt and mix to combine.

Heat a large, deep pan with a lid over a medium heat. When hot, add the coconut oil and the cardamom pods. Allow the spices to sizzle in the oil for 1 minute to release their aroma. Add the shallots, ginger and garlic and fry for 3–4 minutes, until lightly golden. Add the curry leaves, taking care, as they may splutter in the hot oil and cook for a further minute.

Add the green chillies, coconut milk, turmeric, chilli powder, tamarind paste, tomato, the juice of 1 of the limes and a generous few grinds of black pepper. Increase the heat to high and bring to the boil. Allow the sauce to reduce on a high heat for 3 minutes.

Add the mussels to the pan and stir well. Cover with a lid and allow to steam on a high heat. Check after 3 minutes: if the mussels have all opened, remove from the heat; if not, allow to cook for a further minute, when they should have opened. Don't overcook, as this will make the mussels quite rubbery.

To serve, spoon some of the mango salsa into the bottom of some wide bowls, and top with a hearty portion of mussels. Spoon over plenty of broth and season with more lime juice. Scatter over the ginger juliennes and the reserved coriander leaves.

CRISPY CHICKEN TIKKA BUTTERMILK SANDWICH

**MAKES 4
SANDWICHES**

8 skinless chicken
   thigh fillets
130g (4½oz/1 cup) plain
   (all-purpose) flour
Vegetable or sunflower
   oil, for frying

Marinade:
200ml (7fl oz/generous
   ¾ cup) buttermilk
3 garlic cloves, finely grated
2cm (¾in) piece of ginger,
   finely grated
Juice of ½ lemon
1 tsp salt
1 tbsp Kashmiri chilli
   powder
1 tsp garam masala
1 tsp dried fenugreek leaves
   (kasoori methi)

To build:
8 thick slices bread (or
   4 brioche burger buns)
Mayonnaise
1 Little Gem (Baby Bibb)
   lettuce, finely shredded
¼ red onion, shredded
2 tomatoes, sliced
½ cucumber, finely sliced
   (or pickled gherkins)
Mint and Coriander
   Chutney (see page 232)

This is a proper sandwich: chicken marinated in tandoori spices with buttermilk – which adds tang and tenderness – fried to crisp golden perfection in hot oil and sandwiched between thick slices of bread. It's an irresistible snack; I'm sure you'll all agree. You can add slices of cheese, if you like; in fact, the fun is in customising this treat to your taste – so if you want to add hot sauce or kimchi, be my guest.

....

To make the marinade, mix together all the marinade ingredients in a large bowl. Add the chicken, stir to coat, cover and leave to marinate in the fridge for anywhere between 1–24 hours; the buttermilk will help to tenderise the chicken. Remove from the fridge 30 minutes before cooking.

To fry the chicken, put the flour on to a tray and dredge the thighs in an even coating of flour.

Heat the oil to 170°C (325°F) in a deep-fat fryer or in a deep saucepan no more than halfway full. Be very careful never to leave the stove unattended. You can monitor the temperature with a digital probe.

When the oil is hot, add the chicken thighs to the pan in batches and fry for 5–6 minutes, or until golden and cooked through. Remove with a slotted spoon and transfer to a plate lined with kitchen paper, to absorb any excess oil.

To build the sandwich, spread your slices of bread (or buns, if you prefer) with plenty of mayo. Add some shredded lettuce, red onion and tomato and cucumber to four of the slices of bread. Top each with two chicken thighs and a good tablespoon of mint and coriander chutney, then sandwich with a second piece of bread. Cut in half and enjoy.

MASALA CHIPS

SERVES 4, AS A SIDE

1kg (2lb 4oz) Maris Piper
    or King Edward potatoes
1 litre (35fl oz/4¼ cups)
    sunflower oil
Or
1 bag of shop-bought
    chips (French fries)
½ packet of chives,
    finely chopped

Sauce:
4 tbsp sweet chilli sauce
4 tbsp hot chilli sauce
    (e.g. Maggi or Sriracha)
4 tbsp ketchup
½ tsp ground turmeric
1 tsp garam masala
2cm (¾in) piece of
    ginger, finely grated
2 garlic cloves,
    finely grated

Yoghurt dip (optional):
1 shallot, finely chopped
A small bunch of
    fresh coriander
    (cilantro), chopped
200g (7oz/generous
    ¾ cup) full-fat
    natural yoghurt
Juice of ½ lemon
1 tbsp sugar
1 tbsp mint sauce
    (from a jar)
½ tsp ground cumin

The best masala chips are from Paddy's Marten Inn in Leicester – my favourite 'Desi pub': once British boozers, that have been taken over by Asian owners. It's the most ingenious idea ever because cold beer and British curries are best friends! The Leicester masala chips are not, as you might expect, made with dried spices. Instead they are drenched in a wet, sticky, slightly sweet sauce, packed with spice. I've tried others in cities like Birmingham – but they're never as good. You can either make your own chips for this recipe, or just buy a packet of good chips from the supermarket.

If using shop-bought chips, skip the chip cooking steps and simply cook the chips according to the packet instructions.

Peel the potatoes and cut into chips, around 5mm (¼in) thick. Rinse in a bowl of cold water to remove excess starch, then pat dry with kitchen paper.

In a deep pan, or deep-fat fryer, heat the sunflower oil to 140°C (280°F) – use a thermometer to monitor the temperature, and never leave hot oil unattended. Once hot, fry the chips in batches for 6 minutes, making sure not to overcrowd the pan, until cooked through but not coloured. Drain and place on a tray lined with kitchen paper. Allow to cool and place in the freezer for 30 minutes – this will help remove moisture from the chips and crisp them up. This step can be completed a day in advance if you wish; just keep the chips uncovered in the fridge.

To make the yoghurt dip, add all of the ingredients to a bowl and mix thoroughly. Pour into a serving dish and set aside.

For the sauce, combine both types of chilli sauce with the ketchup and spice powders. Heat the oil in a small pan and, when hot, fry the ginger and garlic for 2–3 minutes until golden. Add the sauce to the pan and warm through. Keep warm.

To finish the chips, reheat your pan of oil or deep-fat fryer – this time to 180°C (350°F). When hot, fry the chips in batches until crisp and golden. They will take just 2–3 minutes to crisp up. Place the hot chips into a wide bowl, season with salt and toss through the warm sauce, so that they are completely covered.

Garnish the chips with the chopped chives and serve with the yoghurt dip on the side. Warning: these are highly addictive!

LE WELSH COMPLET

MAKES 4 WELSH

4 slices sourdough bread
4 thick slices good-quality
  smoked ham
4 eggs
1 tbsp vegetable or
  sunflower oil

Cheese sauce:
2 tbsp Dijon mustard
2 tbsp chilli sauce
  (such as Sriracha)
120ml (4fl oz/½ cup)
  blonde beer
300g (10½oz) Double
  Gloucester cheese,
  grated
300g (10½oz) mild
  Cheddar cheese, grated
6 green finger chillies,
  finely chopped

To serve:
Worcestershire sauce
Chips

Le Welsh may sound like a curious thing, but it is the French version of Welsh rarebit! Complet refers to the beautifully friedegg which is placed on top of the melted cheese and ham, completing this hearty meal. I'm adding green chillies to my Welsh and it makes perfect sense, because in India you'll find the popular snack of chilli cheese toast. Actually, in Mumbai there is a very famous version, called kejriwal, which sees fried eggs being placed onto the chilli cheese toast – almost like, but not as good as an Indian Le Welsh!

Le Welsh is made with a slightly orange cheese and after much testing, I found that Double Gloucester melts very evenly, has the right flavour profile and creates the perfect orange pigment. Preheat your grill (broiler) to 250°C (480°F).

Toast the slices of bread and place each slice into an individual gratin dish (or use one large dish for all) and top with a slice of ham.

For the sauce, combine the mustard, chilli sauce and beer in a pan set over a very low heat. When hot, add the cheeses and chillies. Allow to melt very gently, stirring. Gentle heat is important as it will prevent it from splitting and releasing its fat and you will be left with a smooth, thick sauce. At this point, pour an equal amount of sauce over each slice of ham-topped toast.

Place the gratin dishes under the hot grill for 2–3 minutes, until bubbling and dark brown on top. Remove from the oven and allow to rest while you fry the eggs.

Heat a large non-stick frying pan over a medium–high heat. When hot, add the oil and crack the eggs into the pan. Fry until cooked the way you prefer.

Top each Welsh with a fried egg and a splash of Worcestershire sauce. Serve with plenty of chips on the side.

SAMBHAR SOUP WITH CORIANDER & BASIL PISTOU

SERVES 4

200g (7oz) red split lentils
½ tsp ground turmeric
¼ tsp asafoetida
2 garlic cloves, finely grated
3 tbsp oil
1 tsp black mustard seeds
½ cumin seeds
2 sprigs fresh curry leaves
1 medium red onion,
    finely sliced
3 green finger chillies, halved
2 tbsp tamarind paste
1 tsp jaggery or brown sugar
1 tsp Kashmiri chilli powder
2 medium tomatoes, diced
2 carrots, peeled and cut
    into 1cm (½in) dice
1 courgette (zucchini),
    cut into 1cm (½in) dice
½ fennel bulb, cut into
    1cm (½in) dice
100g (3½oz) green beans,
    cut into 2cm (¾in) pieces
Salt

Sambhar masala:
½ tsp chilli flakes
1 tsp desiccated (dried
    shredded) coconut
1 tsp cumin seeds
2 tsp coriander seeds
½ tsp fenugreek seeds
2 tsp chana dal or yellow
    split peas

Pistou:
A bunch of fresh coriander
    (cilantro)
A bunch of basil leaves
1 garlic clove
1 green finger chilli
A pinch of salt and pepper
60ml (2fl oz/¼ cup) olive oil
Zest of 1 lemon

This is a classic South-Indian sambhar, but made with ingredients that you'll find in your local supermarket. Sambhar is a light lentil and vegetable soup; it's a staple of South India, where you'll find it served with idli (steamed rice and lentil dumplings), dosas (crisp rice pancakes) or simply with rice. If making this in the autumn or winter, this recipe would work equally well with roots such as butternut squash, parsnip, celeriac (celery root) or turnip. You don't have to do anything different – just cook the soup until the vegetables are cooked through.

Rinse the lentils under running water, then add them to a large pot with the turmeric, asafoetida, garlic and 1.2 litres (40fl oz/5 cups) water. Bring to the boil, then simmer for 30 minutes. Periodically skim off any scum which floats to the surface. Take an immersion hand blender and pulse the lentils for a few seconds leaving some texture – you don't want to completely purée the lentils.

While the lentils are cooking, warm a large pan over a medium heat. When hot, add the oil and the mustard and cumin seeds. Allow the spices to sizzle in the hot oil for 30 seconds to release their aroma, then add the curry leaves, onion and green chillies. Fry for 10 minutes until the onions are lightly golden, then add the tamarind paste, jaggery, chilli powder and all the vegetables and stir well. Cook for 5–7 minutes to soften the vegetables. If the pan becomes dry just add a splash of water.

To make the sambhar masala, set a non-stick frying pan over a moderate heat. Add all the ingredients and toast for around 2 minutes until the coconut is lightly golden. Grind to a fine powder in a spice grinder and set aside.

Add the vegetable mixture and the masala to the pot of simmering lentils and cook for a further 20 minutes, or until the vegetables are tender. It should be a nice soupy consistency, so add water as required at this stage to adjust. Season with salt to taste.

While the soup is cooking, make the pistou. Pound together all the pistou ingredients in either a small food processor or using a mortar and pestle until you are left with a nice green pesto.

To serve, ladle the soup into bowls and stir in a spoonful of pistou.

SOUTH-INDIAN POLENTA CHIPS WITH PEANUT CHUTNEY

SERVES 4–6

525ml (18fl oz/2¼ cups)
   vegetable stock, made
   from bouillon powder
150g (5½oz) quick-cook
   polenta (Valsugana is best),
   plus extra for dusting
A bunch of fresh coriander
   (cilantro), finely chopped
softened butter, for greasing
3 tbsp ghee, plus extra for
   drizzling

Temper:
3 tbsp oil or ghee
1 tsp black mustard seeds
1 tsp cumin seeds
2 sprigs fresh curry leaves
½ tsp chilli flakes
2cm (¾in) piece of ginger,
   finely grated
2 green finger chillies,
   finely chopped
½ tsp ground turmeric
¼ tsp asafoetida
30g (1oz) cashew nuts, halved

Peanut chutney:
2 tbsp oil
½ tsp black mustard seeds
A pinch of chilli flakes
¼ medium red onion, sliced
1cm (½in) piece of ginger,
   grated
2 garlic cloves,
   roughly chopped
1 green finger chilli,
   roughly chopped
2 tbsp desiccated (dried
   shredded) coconut
75g (2½oz) blanched,
   unsalted peanuts,
   toasted until golden
½ tsp salt

To temper the chutney:
3 tbsp ghee
½ tsp black mustard seeds
1 sprig of fresh curry leaves
1 dried red chilli or a pinch
   of chilli flakes

SouthIndian idli is one of my all-time favourite dishes. These are light and airy steamed dumplings, which are best served with a spoonful of ghee and a creamy peanut or coconut chutney. One night I had a vision of South-Indian polenta chips served with a peanut chutney, just as you might do with idli! This really was a stroke of genius and polenta isn't a million miles away from the semolina (rava) idli you get in India. Take a chip and dip it into this wonderful peanut chutney.

Warm a large non-stick pan over a medium-low heat. When the pan is hot, add all the temper ingredients and toast until the cashews are lightly golden.

To make the polenta, add the vegetable stock to the pan with the temper and bring to a simmer. Add the polenta and coriander and cook for 8 minutes, stirring until you have a thick paste. Grease a 20cm (8in) square cake tin (or similar-sized roasting tin) with butter. Pour the polenta into the tin and set aside. Once cool, place in the fridge to firm up for 30 minutes.

Preheat your oven to 180°C fan/400°F/Gas 6.

To make the chutney, warm a frying pan over a medium heat. When hot, add the oil, mustard seeds and chilli flakes. Fry until the mustard seeds begin to crackle, then add the onion and cook for 5–6 minutes, until softened. Add the ginger, garlic, green chillies and coconut and cook for 2–3 minutes. Remove from the heat and transfer to a blender jug with the toasted peanuts, salt and 150ml (5fl oz/scant ⅔ cup) water. Blend to a smooth, thick paste and transfer to a serving bowl. Warm the same pan over a medium heat. When hot add the ghee, mustard seeds, curry leaves and chilli for tempering. Fry for 30 seconds, then pour over the chutney.

To bake the polenta chips, run a knife around the edge of the tin and unmould the polenta. Cut into chunky chips, about 1cm (½in) thick and 6cm (2½in) long. Coat the chips in a dusting of polenta and brush off any excess. Place the chips into a large metal roasting tin and coat with 3 tablespoons of ghee. Place in the centre of the oven and bake for 25–30 minutes, until crisp and golden, turning halfway through the cooking.

Serve the chips warm with a good drizzle of extra ghee and the peanut chutney for dipping.

WARM SALAD OF MALAI CHICKEN

SERVES 4

500g (1lb 2oz) chicken thighs
30g (1oz/2 tbsp) butter, melted
1 tsp chaat masala

Chicken marinade:
100g (3½oz/scant ½ cup)
    Greek yoghurt
1 tbsp cornflour (cornstarch)
30ml (1fl oz/2 tbsp) double
    (heavy) cream
30g (1oz) medium Cheddar
    cheese, grated
3 green finger chillies,
    finely chopped
1 tbsp chopped coriander
    (cilantro)
3 garlic cloves, finely grated
2cm (¾in) piece of ginger,
    finely grated
1 tsp salt
½ tsp black pepper
Juice of ½ lemon

Croutons:
2 thick slices crusty bread
3 tbsp olive oil
Salt and pepper

Dressing:
3 tbsp vegetable oil
1 tbsp white wine vinegar
1 tbsp lemon juice
1 tsp Dijon mustard
1 garlic clove
3 green finger chillies
30g (1oz) coriander (cilantro)
20g (²/₃oz) mint leaves
1 tbsp Greek yoghurt
1 tbsp mayonnaise

Salad:
100g (3½oz) fine green beans
½ red onion, finely sliced
3 tbsp red wine vinegar
1 tsp caster (superfine) sugar
2 Cos or Romaine lettuce, torn
½ cucumber cut into batons
A large handful of mint, torn
A large handful of coriander
    (cilantro) leaves, torn
50g (1¾ oz) Parmesan
    cheese, shaved

A delicious warm salad, or salade tiède *is the sort of fare that you might find on the blackboard of a classic French bistro. Slices of chicken with crispy skin, tossed with fresh, bitter leaves, al dente green beans and crunchy croutons – all covered in a luxurious dressing, piquant with mustard. There's not a lot that can beat this combination – except perhaps, by adding malai chicken to the mix?*

Malai translates as 'cream' and these marinated chicken kebabs are as famous to north India as Tandoori chicken is to Britain. Rather than being slathered in an in-your-face, orange-stained marinade, malai chicken is all about delicate creaminess – with only the gentlest suggestion of green chilli – and when combined with the salad I described earlier, you've got something that is undeniably delicious!

....

Cut the chicken thighs in half. Mix together all the ingredients for the marinade in a bowl and add the chicken thighs. Leave covered in the fridge for 1–24 hours.

Bring a small pan of salted water to the boil. Cook the green beans for 4 minutes; drain and plunge into a bowl of cold water, under a running tap. When cool, pat dry with kitchen paper. Put aside.

For the croutons, cut the bread into 2cm (¾in) dice. Drizzle with the olive oil, season and fry in a large frying pan until golden.

Start the salad by putting the red onion in a small bowl with the red wine vinegar and sugar and leaving it to steep for 20 minutes.

To cook the chicken: preheat the grill (broiler) to 250°C (480°F). Line the bottom of a grill tray with foil and place the chicken thighs on a rack suspended over the tray. Grill for around 4–6 minutes on each side, until lightly charred and sizzling. Immediately brush with melted butter and sprinkle with chaat masala. Allow to rest whilst you make the dressing.

For the dressing, add all the ingredients, except the yoghurt and mayonnaise, to a blender jug and blitz until smooth. Mix in the yoghurt and mayo and season with salt and pepper.

In a large salad bowl, toss together the beans, lettuce, cucumber, herbs and pickled onion with the croutons, dressing and two-thirds of the Parmesan cheese. Arrange the chicken pieces over the top with the remaining Parmesan and enjoy.

TUNA, MANGO & CRISPY NOODLE SALAD

SERVES 4

1 tbsp coriander seeds,
   lightly crushed in a
   mortar and pestle
1 tbsp black sesame seeds
1 tsp ground black pepper
2 thick tuna steaks
1 tbsp vegetable or
   sunflower oil, for frying
20g (²/3oz) shop-bought
   crispy fried onions

Salad:
4 spring onions (scallions),
   finely sliced
1 carrot, peeled and
   julienned
½ cucumber, seeds
   removed and julienned
6 radishes, finely sliced
1 small red onion,
   very finely sliced
1 very ripe mango, cut
   into 7mm (⅛in) dice
Zest of 2 limes
1 large handful fresh
   coriander (cilantro),
   roughly chopped
1 large handful fresh mint,
   roughly chopped

Crispy noodles:
80g (2¾oz) fine rice
   vermicelli noodles
150ml (5fl oz) vegetable oil

Dressing:
2cm (¾in) piece of
   ginger, finely grated
2 garlic cloves, finely grated
1 tbsp tamarind paste
Juice of 2 limes
3½ tbsp olive oil
3 green finger chillies,
   finely chopped
1 tsp brown sugar
A pinch of salt

This is a salad which will wake up and excite your taste buds. Here we have a patchwork of flavours and textures: crunchy, sweet, fresh, spicy, tangy, sweet and sour – the list is endless. The combination of the seared tuna with this lively salad is a glorious thing. Tuna is best when seared very briefly in an extremely hot pan, and is still pink in the middle. If making this salad during the mango season, which runs from April to July, try to find speciality mangoes – they are so lovely and sweet.

For the tuna, mix together the coriander seeds, sesame seeds and black pepper. Pat the tuna steaks dry with kitchen paper and rub the spices into both sides of the tuna. Set aside on a plate, in the fridge until ready to sear.

For the salad: mix together all the ingredients. Season with salt and stir to combine.

For the crispy noodles: break the vermicelli noodles into 5cm (2in) pieces. Warm the oil in a wok over a high heat. When the oil reaches 200°C (400°F) – check this with a probe thermometer – add the noodles to the oil in batches and fry for around 10 seconds until crisp and puffed up. Make sure you allow the oil to come back up to temperature between batches. Remove the noodles from the oil and allow to drain on a plate lined with kitchen paper.

For the dressing: whisk together all the ingredients in a bowl and set aside.

To sear the tuna steaks, heat a large frying pan over a high heat. When very hot, add the 1 tablespoon of oil to the pan. When the oil starts to smoke, add the tuna steaks and sear for 30 seconds on each side. Remove the tuna from the pan and season with a pinch of salt, then carve into thin slices.

When you are ready to eat, add the dressing to the salad. Spread the crispy noodles out over a large serving platter – you can break them up a little. Arrange the dressed salad over the noodles, top with the seared tuna and finish with the crispy fried onions.

MELON, CITRUS, BURRATA & AVOCADO SALAD

SERVES 4

2 grapefruits
2 oranges
1 ripe cantaloupe melon
2 avocados
¾ tsp coriander seeds
¾ tsp fennel seeds
¾ tsp caraway seeds
¾ tsp chilli flakes
¾ tsp black peppercorns
Seeds from 3 green
   cardamom pods
2 burrata balls
2 green finger chillies,
   seeds removed and
   thinly sliced
A large handful of mint
   leaves, torn

Dressing:
Juice of 2 limes
50ml (1¾oz/3½ tbsp)
   cold pressed rapeseed
   (canola) oil
A pinch of saffron
1 tsp sugar
A pinch of salt and
   black pepper

In the summer, there's no fruit better than the Cantaloupe melon – I can get through one a day at the height of the season. I'm not a great fan of the melon and ham combo, I have to say. I'd much rather make a delicious salad and this one's a banger – it's full of refreshing flavours and contrasts which will keep you coming back for more and more.

To prepare the fruit, cut off the top and bottom of the grapefruits and oranges. One at a time, place them on a chopping board and slice off the peel and pith with a small knife, running it from top to bottom to remove it in strips. Once peeled, segment all the oranges and grapfruits and set aside.

Peel and dress the melon and chop it into 3cm (1¼in) pieces. Cut the avocados in half, remove the stones and scoop out the flesh, leaving the skin behind. Cut into 3cm (1¼in) pieces.

Add all the spices to a mortar and pestle, crush lightly and set aside.

For the dressing, whisk together all the dressing ingredients.

To serve, arrange the fruit on a large serving platter. Top with the burrata and sprinkle with the spices, green chillies and mint leaves. Finally, drizzle over the dressing.

KOLKATA FISH CUTLETS WITH MUSTARD KASUNDI

SERVES 4

300g (10½oz) fillets of flaky
white fish (such as cod,
haddock or pollock)
Vegetable oil, for drizzling
and frying
2 medium potatoes,
peeled and quartered
2 green finger chillies,
finely chopped
1 tsp Kashmiri chilli powder
A small bunch of coriander
(cilantro), finely chopped
½ tsp salt
½ tsp ground turmeric
2 garlic cloves, finely grated
2cm (¾in) piece of ginger,
finely grated

Coating:
100g (3½oz/¾ cup) plain
(all-purpose) flour
2 eggs, beaten
150g (5½oz/3 cups) dried
breadcrumbs

Kasundi:
100g (3½oz) wholegrain
mustard
Juice of 1 lime
A pinch of salt
3 green chillies, finely chopped
½ tsp ground turmeric
50ml (1¾fl oz/3½ tbsp)
vegetable oil
1cm (½in) piece of ginger
½ tsp ground cumin

Carrot salad:
3 large carrots
2 banana shallots,
finely chopped
2cm (¾in) piece of
ginger, finely grated
3 green finger chillies,
finely chopped
1 tsp ground cumin
Juice of 2 limes
Leaves from 4 sprigs
mint, finely chopped
A small bunch of coriander
(cilantro), chopped
3½ tbsp extra virgin olive oil
½ tsp salt

*Fried cutlets are hugely popular in Kolkata thanks to the British,
who wanted almost everything they ate to be breadcrumbed and
fried. The tradition has stuck and you'll find all manner of them
all over the city. The most famous are the fish cutlets similar to a
fishcake with a hint of chilli and spice and they are served with the
local condiment, Kasundi. This is a bright yellow sauce, made from
a paste of mustard seeds, green chillies and lime juice and is just
the ticket, with a fried fish cutlet!*

Preheat your oven to 180°C fan/400°F/Gas 6. Wrap the fish
fillets in foil and add a splash of oil and a pinch of salt. Place onto
a baking tray and cook in the oven for 10 minutes. Remove the
fish from the foil and allow to cool.

Put the potatoes in a small saucepan, cover with water and
add a pinch of salt. Bring to the boil and simmer for 15 minutes,
or until tender. Mash the potato until there are no large lumps.

Flake the fish into a bowl. Add the mashed potato with all
of the other ingredients for the cutlets and mix thoroughly.
Divide the mixture into eight balls and form into rectangular
fishcakes, around 7mm (⅛in) thick.

To coat the cutlets, set out three bowls: one each for the flour, eggs
and breadcrumbs. Dredge the fishcakes through the flour, so that
they are lightly dusted, then coat in beaten egg. Turn the fishcakes
in the breadcrumbs, so that they are completely coated, then place
the crumbed fishcakes onto a tray and set aside in the fridge.

To make the Kasundi, add all of the ingredients and 2 tablespoons
of water to a food processor or blender and blitz until smooth.
Place in a serving bowl.

For the carrot salad, grate the carrots and mix together with
the remaining ingredients. Place into a serving dish.

To fry the fishcakes, heat a large frying pan over a medium
heat. Add oil to a depth of 1cm (½in) and, when hot, add the fish
cutlets. Fry on each side for 3–4 minutes, until lightly golden on
both sides. They may start to inflate – this is perfectly normal.
Place onto kitchen paper before serving to absorb any excess oil.
Serve with the kasundi and the carrot salad.

MUSHROOM GALOUTI KEBABS

SERVES 4-6

Masala:
1 whole mace blade
4 green cardamom pods
4 cloves
1 tsp white peppercorns

Kebabs:
60ml (2oz/4 tbsp) ghee or
   sunflower oil, plus 2 tbsp
   to fry the finished kebabs
15 cashew nuts
1 tsp cumin seeds
1 onion, finely diced
500g (1lb 2oz) chestnut
   (cremini) mushrooms,
   thinly sliced
2cm (¾in) piece of ginger,
   finely grated
4 garlic cloves, finely grated
2 green chillies, finely
   chopped
1 tsp Kashmiri chilli
   powder
1 tsp garam masala
½ tsp ground cinnamon
2 tbsp gram (chickpea)
   flour
Small handful of fresh
   coriander (cilantro),
   finely chopped
Salt

To serve:
Small handful of mint
   leaves, torn (optional)
½ red onion, finely sliced
1 lime, cut into wedges
Mint and Coriander
   Chutney (page 232)

These little kebabs are like mini burger patties and you'll find the original, which are made of either goat meat or buffalo, in the famous Tunday Kababi shop in the historic city of Lucknow in northern India. Galouti *translates as 'melt in the mouth' and the recipe was supposedly written in the 16th century for the Nawab of Lucknow who had no teeth! The poor chap wanted to enjoy a kebab like everyone else, but one he didn't have to chew! Today, the galouti kebab is one of the legendary street foods of Lucknow, and you'll see them being fried in huge wide pans, hundreds at a time. The mushroom version is a popular vegetarian alternative, which I think is just as good as the original. The intense mushroom nuttiness gives a fantastic meatiness and deliciously soft texture.*

To make the masala, add the whole spices to a spice grinder and blitz to a fine powder. Set aside

For the kebabs, place a frying pan over a medium heat. Add the 60ml (2oz/4 tbsp) ghee or oil and, when hot, add the cashew nuts. Fry the cashews for 2 minutes until lightly golden, then remove them from the pan with a slotted spoon and set aside, leaving the oil in the pan. Add the cumin seeds and onion to the pan and fry over a medium heat for 15 minutes, or until golden brown. Add the mushrooms, ginger, garlic and green chillies and continue to cook for a further 10 minutes. By this time, the mushrooms should have released all of their water and should be golden and the mixture quite dry. Add your ground masala powder along with the chilli powder, garam masala and cinnamon. Stir through for 1 minute, then remove from the heat and allow to cool.

Once cool, put the mushroom mixture in a food processor or blender and add the cashews, gram flour, fresh coriander and a generous pinch of salt. Blitz to a smooth paste.

To cook the kebabs, warm a non-stick frying pan over a medium-low heat. Grease your hands with oil and shape the kebab mixture into little patties, around 5-6 cm (2-2½in) in diameter. Add 2 tablespoons of ghee or oil to the pan and fry the kebabs for 3-4 minutes on each side until lightly golden.

Garnish with piles of mint leaves and red onions, then serve with lime wedges and the Mint and Coriander chutney.

GAZPACHO-RASAM WITH WATERMELON

SERVES 4

500g (1lb 2oz) very
  ripe tomatoes
3 tbsp olive oil
2 tsp black mustard seeds
2 tsp cumin seeds
½ tsp asafoetida
2 sprigs fresh curry leaves,
  leaves picked
4 garlic cloves, finely grated
2 tsp Kashmiri chilli
  powder
3 green finger chillies,
  finely chopped
500ml (17fl oz/2 cups)
  good-quality tomato
  juice (Cawston Press
  is a good one)
1½ tsp brown sugar
Juice of 2 limes
1 handful of chopped
  fresh coriander
Salt

Rasam seasoning:
1 tsp cumin seeds
¾ tsp fenugreek seeds
1 tsp black peppercorns

To serve:
¼ watermelon
A small handful of
  fresh coriander
A generous drizzle of
  extra virgin olive oil
Freshly milled
  black pepper

This is a deliciously refreshing cold soup with a spicy and tangy South-Indian twist. The combination of mustard seed, curry leaf, chilli and lime really awaken this classic tomato soup!

Cut the tomatoes into chunks, place in a bowl and season with 1 tablespoon of the olive oil and a generous pinch of salt. Mix well, then allow to macerate for an hour. After this time, put the tomatoes and any juices which have been released into a blender, blend to a smooth purée and set aside.

For the rasam seasoning, add the cumin, fenugreek and black pepper to a spice grinder (or use a mortar and pestle) and grind to a fine powder.

In a medium saucepan, heat another 2 tablespoons of oil over a medium heat. Add the black mustard seeds and cumin and fry for 1 minute to release their oils. Add the asafoetida, curry leaves and garlic to the pan and fry for 2 minutes. Add the chilli powder, green chillies, tomato juice, sugar, lime juice, 250ml (9fl oz/1 cup) water, the rasam seasoning and your blended tomato purée to the pan. Turn the heat up to high and bring to the boil. Simmer for 3 minutes, then turn the heat off. Season with salt and add the fresh coriander. Allow to cool before placing in the fridge.

To serve, peel the skin off the watermelon quarter with a sharp knife, then cut it into 2cm (¾in) cubes.

Divide the chilled soup between four bowls. Add 4–5 pieces of watermelon to the centre of each bowl. Top with a sprinkling of fresh coriander, a generous splash of olive oil and a twist of freshly ground black pepper.

MIDWEEK STAPLES

Midweek dinners can be troublesome. I know how hard it is to return home from a tiring day's work with the prospect of cooking looming overhead like a thundering storm cloud in a threatening sky. Cooking can be a therapeutic pastime, allowing us to forget about all our troubles – a clear division between work and relaxation. Pour yourself a glass of wine and luxuriate in the fun of cooking. Transport yourself to whichever faraway destination takes your fancy! Cooking at short notice can also be a chore that you could do without. You come home and slump yourself on the sofa, no idea about exactly what to cook and little chance of inspiration. A deep, long sigh, followed by a raid of the fridge and cupboards. Eventually, you settle for a jar of pasta sauce which has been lurking right at the back of the cupboard because you know the resulting meal will be mediocre. There is another idea, which is to start flicking through the delivery options on your phone, looking for an easy way out – something that will really hit the spot.

I have to say that I've never been one for takeaways – we never had them growing up, and that sticks with me today. I did, however, fall victim to many wistful midweek meals. My parents were always busy during the week, and although they used to dedicate lots of time to cooking inventive weekend feasts, midweek food was plain and bland in comparison. My mum had her go-to suppliers of choice. Bernard was on speed-dial and he would bring with him his frozen shortcuts – a saviour for the busy parent: Turkey Drummers, Twizzlers or Dinosaurs! Another of these reliable chums was an old sea dog, who went by the name of Captain Birdseye. He would come in the dark of night, telescope underarm, flogging bags of loot: cut-price fish fingers, potato waffles and chicken dippers. It's not that we didn't enjoy these noble treats – it all just became quite repetitive and boring. Everything was served with mash, which I grew to hate because we had it on an almost daily basis and Mum would never add enough butter to it. It was a kind of health mash – not the delicious, excessively buttery stuff that James Martin would whip up. An endless carousel of mash with peas and broccoli. Mash, peas, broccoli. Repeat.

Friday comes and ahhhh, the relief! Every Friday, a fish-and-chip van would pull up in our village and blare its klaxon to exclaim its arrival. As soon as I heard it, I would run – it was my job to queue up and order the chips. We would rarely order fish from the van – just chips – as earlier in the day, my dad would have been to

Leicester Fish Market to buy the haddock, which my mum would then fry in beer batter to have with the soggy, vinegar-soaked chips from the van. Of course, we also had tins of Batchelors mushy peas and the greatest home-made tartare sauce. The ritual of fish Friday really was the best! My maternal grandfather, Pa, as he was known to me and my brother was an expert cook and lover of food. His weakness was the Great British Fish and Chips! Pa used to love telling me and my brother stories about when he first came to the UK from India in the 1960s. On a Friday, he would go to the local chippy and, for one shilling, he would gorge on two humongous pieces of cod, fried in dripping. They would come with so many chips that one ordinary person couldn't possibly have eaten them all. He would brag about how he was friendly with the person who worked in the shop and how he would get an extra-large portion. He really was the fish and chip king (perhaps also the king of hyberbole) and genetically, I also have the same fish and chip lover's gene. It's a dish that you simply cannot beat and one that unites our island nation.

So, to save YOU, from having to put yourself, your kids and loved ones through the same pain that was inflicted on me as a child – a smörgåsbord of midweek beige – I bring you this chapter of easy-to-follow recipes which provide you with dishes to wake up your tastebuds. I have spent time ensuring that the ingredients can be found in just about every supermarket – many of which may already be hiding in your store cupboards. These recipes can be cooked quickly, with minimum fuss, which is of paramount importance when trying to sustain yourself during a hectic week. Having used a variety of cookbooks, I can say that many books may look fantastic and feature aspirational photography. But, if every time I want to follow a recipe, I have to visit a specialist shop or fly to Modena in search of an extremely rare 100-year-aged balsamic vinegar, the book will just start to gather dust. The best books feature recipes that are realistic and in-line with the expectations of an everyday cook. Most people want to be able to cook a balanced meal, which bursts with flavour – and not have to go further than their local supermarket to source the ingredients. And this is what I aim to achieve. On the pages that follow are a variety of speedy but vibrant dishes, using spice to enhance everyday, seasonal ingredients. But more importantly, recipes which aim to delight!

PUNJABI CAULIFLOWER CHEESE

SERVES 4

1 large head of cauliflower, washed and cut into small florets, large stalks removed
A handful of chopped fresh coriander (cilantro)
2 tbsp dried panko breadcrumbs (optional)
Salt and black pepper
Green salad, to serve

Masala:
3 tbsp vegetable or sunflower oil, or ghee, plus extra for drizzling
3 garlic cloves and
2cm (¾in) piece of ginger, grated to make a paste
3 green finger chillies, finely chopped
1 fresh plum tomato, grated
½ tsp ground turmeric
2 tsp garam masala
1 tsp ground cumin
1 tsp ground coriander
1 tsp salt

Chilli-cheese sauce:
20g (⅔oz/1½ tbsp) unsalted butter
20g (⅔oz/3 tbsp) plain (all-purpose) flour
300ml (10½fl oz/ 1¼ cups) whole milk
200g (7oz) mature Cheddar cheese, grated
3 green finger chillies, finely chopped
1 heaped tsp chaat masala

Introduced by the British 200 years ago, the cauliflower (gobi) was seamlessly adopted into the colourful cuisine of India and to this day it is a fundamental part of the Indian diet. There are so many exciting and delicious Indian recipes for preparing this, otherwise, pretty humble vegetable. This recipe plays on a fusion of a classic Punjabi aloo gobi – but I'm swapping potato for a chilli-cheese sauce – because, who doesn't love a proper cauliflower cheese?!

....

Preheat the oven to 180°C fan/400°F/Gas 6.

Bring a large pan of salted water to the boil. Add the cauliflower florets and cook for 5 minutes until tender. Drain and allow to cool.

To make the masala, add the oil or ghee to a large pan set over a medium heat. When hot, add the garlic, ginger and green chillies. Fry for 2–3 minutes until lightly golden. Add the tomato and ground spices and stir for a further 2 minutes. If the mixture starts to stick to the pan, simply add a splash of water. Turn the heat off and add the cauliflower and fresh coriander. Stir to mix so that everything is properly coated in the masala. Season with the salt and black pepper.

To make the cheese sauce, melt the butter in a saucepan. Add the flour and cook over a medium heat for 2–3 minutes, stirring all the time. Whisk in the milk and bring to a gentle simmer, continuing to whisk in order to remove any lumps. Turn the heat down to low and allow to cook for 3 minutes to thicken the sauce slightly. You will be left with a silky smooth béchamel sauce. Finally, remove from the heat, add the Cheddar cheese and stir to make sure that the cheese melts evenly. When melted, stir in the chillies and season with a pinch of salt and pepper and the chaat masala.

Tip the cauliflower into an ovenproof gratin dish and pour over the cheese sauce. Sprinkle with the panko breadcrumbs, if using, and drizzle over some oil or ghee. Bake in the centre of the oven for 15–20 minutes, until bubbling and golden. Serve with a fresh green salad.

KERALA STEAK FRY

SERVES 4

2 large pieces of onglet
    steak or 4 thick-cut
    ribeye steaks also work
    very well (use ribeyes
    with the bone in for
    even more flavour),
    at room temperature
1–2 tbsp coarsely crushed
    black pepper
2 tbsp vegetable oil
Butter, for frying
Salt
Fries, to serve

Sauce:
3 shallots, finely chopped
2cm (¾in) piece of ginger,
    finely grated
2 garlic cloves, finely grated
1 green finger chilli,
    finely chopped
3 tbsp desiccated (dried
    shredded) coconut
3 sprigs fresh curry leaves
500ml (17fl oz/2 cups)
    good-quality beef stock
    (fresh stock from the
    chiller aisle rather than
    a cube, if possible)
1 tsp ground black pepper
1 tsp ground coriander
1 tsp Kashmiri chilli
    powder
1 tsp garam masala
100ml (3½fl oz/scant
    ½ cup) coconut cream

Beef in Kerala, you may be surprised to learn, is a most cherished dish – especially among the Christian Syrian population. They love it fried in coconut, black pepper, curry leaves and green chillies, which really works wonders with the beef. So I'm taking these wonderful flavours of Kerala and infusing them into a classic French-style sauce to pour over a bloody good steak. All you need to finish the meal is a bottle of hearty red and some fries! Some of the world's best black pepper is grown in Kerala – which is known as the spice garden of India. You'll find it in good supermarkets, known as Tellicherry black pepper. Crush it fresh in a mortar and pestle, for the ultimate peppered steak.

Pat the steaks dry, then season both sides with salt and the coarse pepper. Set a large frying pan over a high heat and add the oil. The pan should be very hot, as you want to create a really nice golden sear on the steaks. When the oil starts to smoke, place the steaks in the pan, making sure that there is plenty of room in the pan – if your pan isn't large enough, sear the steaks in batches. Cook for 2 minutes each side for rare, 2–3 minutes for medium and 4 minutes for well done – turning them every 30 seconds, to ensure an even cooking. Cooking times will vary, according to the thickness of your steaks. For the last couple of minutes of cooking, throw a couple of knobs of butter into the pan. When it starts to foam, baste the steaks with the hot juices. When the steaks are cooked, transfer them to a warm dish. Cover with foil and allow to rest.

To make the sauce, use the same pan as there will be lots of amazing flavour and rendered beef fat. Add the shallots, ginger, garlic, chillies, coconut and curry leaves and fry for 2 minutes over a medium–high heat. Add the beef stock and ground spices to the pan and reduce, on the highest heat, for 4–5 minutes, until reduced by half in volume. Add the coconut cream and remove from the heat. Pour the sauce over the steaks to coat, then carve and serve with chips.

ROASTED VEGETABLE CHAAT

5 tbsp duck fat, vegetable oil or sunflower oil
8 Jerusalem artichokes, whole
8 baby potatoes (Albert Bartlett Apache work brilliantly), whole
4 parsnips, halved
4 carrots, halved
Salt and pepper

Sweet chutney:
80g (2¾oz/5½ tbsp) tamarind paste
80g (2¾oz) dates
1 tsp jaggery or soft brown sugar
½ tsp Kashmiri chilli powder
½ tsp ground cumin
A pinch of salt

Yoghurt:
400g (14oz/1¾ cups) natural full-fat yoghurt
1 tbsp icing (confectioners') sugar

To garnish:
Green Chutney (see page 233)
A bunch of finely chopped coriander (cilantro)
¼ red onion, finely diced
2 tsp ground cumin

All over India, you'll find limitless variations of chaat. A base of potatoes or savoury papdi biscuits are topped with a sweet and tangy tamarind chutney and a second, spicier vibrant chutney of mint, coriander and green chillies. Creamy, very slightly sweetened yoghurt is drizzled over, which cools everything down. The idea is to create an explosive symphony of vibrant textures and flavours; the ultimate voyage for the senses!

Preheat your oven to 200°C fan/425°F/Gas 7. Pour the fat into a large roasting tin and add the vegetables. Season with salt and pepper and mix together everything with your hands. Place the tin on the top shelf of the preheated oven and roast for 25 minutes. After this time, give the tray a shake and turn the vegetables over so they get an all-round roasting. Return the tray to the oven and continue to cook for a further 20 minutes, or until evenly cooked and golden.

While the vegetables are roasting, make the chutneys. For the sweet chutney, add all of the ingredients to a small pan with 250ml (9fl oz/1 cup) water. Bring to a simmer, cover with a lid and cook gently for 20 minutes. By this time, the dates will be very soft and falling apart. Blend, either using a stick or jug blender, to make a smooth purée, then transfer to a bowl to cool.

For the sweet yoghurt, whisk together the yoghurt and icing sugar and refrigerate until required.

When the vegetables are ready, remove them from the tray and place onto a plate lined with kitchen paper to remove any excess fat. Season with plenty of salt. Spoon the yoghurt onto the bottom of a serving platter and arrange the roasted vegetables over the yoghurt. Drizzle the two chutneys over the top, followed by the fresh coriander, diced onion and ground cumin.

KOLKATA TACOS

SERVES 4

4 lamb leg steaks
(approx. 500g/1lb 2oz)
3 eggs
12 mini flour tortillas
Vegetable oil, for frying
2 medium red onions,
thinly sliced
1 tsp chaat masala
Salt
Green Chutney
(see page 233)

Lamb marinade:
2 tbsp Greek yoghurt
1 tbsp ketchup
1 tbsp Kashmiri
chilli powder
1 tsp salt
1 tsp garam masala
½ tsp ground black pepper
1 tsp ground cumin
Juice of ½ lime

Onion garnish:
1 red onion, thinly
shredded
A pinch of salt
A pinch of sugar

The people of Kolkata have just the thing for a late-night, post-drink snack – their famous rolls! Take a porotta *(paratha as you may know it, but in Kolkata it's* porotta*), a slightly flaky flatbread and fry it on a hot* tawa *(griddle) – either plain or egg-fried. It's loaded with griddled onions, peppers and spicy marinated lamb or chicken. Seasoned with lime juice and topped with raw shredded onion, you roll it up and eat it there and then on the street. My rolls are the taco variety. They are easy to make, fun to build and even better to eat!*

Combine all the ingredients for the lamb marinade. Add the lamb and marinate for up to a day in the fridge. If you don't have time to marinate, don't worry – you can cook them straightaway. Remove the lamb from the fridge 30 minutes before you want to start cooking, so that it comes up to room temperature.

For the onion garnish, season the red onion with the salt and sugar and set aside.

Crack the eggs into a wide dish and beat until combined. Dip the tortillas in the egg, making sure that they are coated on both sides. Warm a frying pan over a medium heat, add a splash of oil and fry the tortillas for a couple of minutes on each side, until lightly coloured. Wrap the tortillas in a clean tea towel and keep warm.

Warm the same frying pan over a high heat. When hot, add a tablesoon of oil. When it starts to smoke, add the red onions. Fry for 3–4 minutes, until softened. Season with salt and keep warm.

Warm a griddle pan over a high heat. When very hot, brush with a tablespoon of oil and sear the lamb steaks for 2–3 minutes on each side, so that they are pink in the centre. If you prefer your lamb well done, cook for a couple of minutes extra on each side. Allow the lamb to rest for a couple of minutes before slicing into thin strips and mixing with the softened onions. Season with the chaat masala.

To build the tacos, add some of the lamb mixture to a tortilla. Add a spoon of green chutney and a little of the onion garnish. Enjoy!

SEEKH DOG

MAKES 6 SEEKH DOGS

6 of the best brioche
   hot-dog buns you
   can buy
Ketchup
60g (2oz) shop-bought
   crispy fried onions

Kebabs:
400g (14oz) minced
   (ground) lamb
2 garlic cloves, finely grated
2cm (¾in) piece of ginger,
   finely grated
2 tsp garam masala
1 tsp ground cumin
1 tsp salt
1½ tsp chilli powder
   (Kashmiri chilli powder
   is best)
½ tsp freshly ground
   black pepper
1 tbsp butter

Relish:
2 large pickled gherkins
A small handful of fresh
   coriander (cilantro)
2 green finger chillies
2 tbsp mint sauce
¼ white onion, grated
Salt and black pepper

I am delighted to admit that I have the unhealthiest of obsessions with Indian kebabs. The smoky hit you get from meat charring slowly over hot coals is so unbelievably addictive! Juicy, succulent and melt-in-the-mouth textures combine with a gentle aromatic warmth of spices which permeate the meat from within. There's no denying that proper kebabs are a real crowd-pleaser. My favourite has to be the seekh kebab: long skewers, covered in a thin layer of lamb mince. They are gently spiced with garam masala and green chillies, then seared over hot coals. Seekh kebabs are great wrapped up in hot naan bread, so naturally they make a terrific hot dog.

To make the seekh kebabs, mix all the kebab ingredients except the butter in a large bowl. Use your hands to massage the mixture, making sure that everything is thoroughly combined. Divide the mixture into four equal pieces and roll them into long sausages, around 25cm (10in) in length (longer than your hot dog-buns as they will shrink during cooking). Keep in the fridge whilst you prepare the relish.

For the relish, finely chop the gherkins, coriander and green chillies. Mix together in a bowl with all of the other relish ingredients and set aside.

It's best to cook the kebabs on a charcoal or gas barbecue. Thread them onto skewers, which will help you turn them over on the grill, and cook for 2–3 minutes, turning during cooking and brushing with butter, until caramelised on all sides. Or you can cook them in a frying pan: heat a large frying pan on a medium–high heat and add the butter. When hot, add the kebabs. Fry for 2–3 minutes on each side, or until the kebabs are nicely caramelised on all sides. Remove from the pan and keep warm.

Toast your hot-dog buns until lightly golden. Spread ketchup on both sides of the bun, followed by a generous bed of the relish. Top with a seekh kebab and finish with a hearty sprinkling of crispy fried onions for that quintessential hot-dog flavour!

SAAG GOATS' CHEESE TART

SERVES 4

50g (1¾oz/3½ tbsp)
   butter, plus extra
   for greasing
2 tsp cumin seeds
1 large onion, thinly sliced
2cm (¾in) piece of ginger,
   finely grated
3 garlic cloves, finely grated
3 green finger chillies,
   chopped
750g (1lb 10oz) spinach
   leaves, washed
1 tsp ground cumin
2 tbsp dried fenugreek
   leaves (kasoori methi)
1 tsp garam masala
1 x 150g (5½oz) goats'
   cheese log
3 medium eggs
200ml (7oz/generous
   ¾ cup) double
   (heavy) cream

Pastry:
200g (7oz/1½ cups) plain
   (all-purpose) flour
80g (2¾oz/⅓ cup)
   unsalted butter, cold
A generous pinch of salt
Or
1 x 500g (1lb 2oz) block
   of ready-made
   shortcrust pastry

The combination of spinach, cheese and pastry is one that so many cultures have adopted. I've enjoyed spinach and goats' cheese tarts in France, spinach and ricotta-filled tortellini in Italy and spinach spanakopita in Kefalonia. In Punjab, Northern India, spinach and paneer curries are a great staple, and it's this combination that I've based my recipe on. A favourite dish that my grandmother would make was sarson ka saag – a hearty dish that many Punjabi households will cook during the winter months. Spinach is slowly cooked with mustard greens and fenugreek to a thick paste with plenty of butter. It's indulgent and proper comfort food to warm up the spirit! Since goats' cheese may not be to everyone's taste, it can be replaced with ricotta or feta.

Start by making the pastry. Blitz the flour, butter and salt in a food processor, until it resembles fine breadcrumbs. Add 2 tablespoons of water and pulse until the dough forms a ball. Wrap in cling film and flatten it out to a thickness of 2cm (¾in). Chill for 30 minutes.

Warm a large, deep pot with a lid over a medium heat. When hot, add the butter and the cumin seeds. Allow the cumin to sizzle for 30 seconds, to release their aroma. Add the onion and cook for 10 minutes, until lightly golden. Add the ginger, garlic and green chillies and cook for a further 3 minutes. Add the spinach to the pot and cover with a lid. Leave to wilt over a medium heat for 5 minutes. Add the ground cumin and fenugreek and continue to cook for a further 25 minutes, with the lid off, stirring from time to time. You should be left with a relatively dry spinach paste. Sprinkle with garam masala and plenty of salt; set aside to cool.

Preheat your oven to 180°C fan/400°F/Gas 6, and place a heavy baking sheet inside to heat up. Lightly grease a 23cm (9in) loose-based tart tin with a little butter.

Roll the pastry out to a thickness of 3mm (⅛), large enough to line the tart tin. Place the pastry inside the tart tin, pushing it into the sides, then trim the excess pastry around the edge of the tin.

Spread the spinach filling into the tart case. Cut the goats' cheese into rounds and arrange on top. Whisk together the eggs and cream and pour this into the tart tin.

Place the tart on the preheated baking sheet and bake for 1 hour, until golden.

AMRITSARI FISH WITH MUSHY PEAS & TARTARE SAUCE

SERVES 4

1 tsp Kashmiri
    chilli powder
1 tsp ground cumin
1 tsp garam masala
1 tsp salt
1 tsp ground coriander
1 tsp dried mango powder
    (amchoor)
1 tsp garlic granules
1 tsp ginger powder
½ tsp ground turmeric
1 tsp ajwain (carom) seeds
4 skinless haddock or
    cod fillets (about
    600g/1lb 5oz)
Vegetable or sunflower
    oil, for frying
Lemon wedges, to serve

Batter:
150g (5½oz/1 cup plus
    2 tbsp) self-raising flour
50g (1¾oz/½ cup)
    cornflour (cornstarch)
A generous pinch of salt
275ml (9½fl oz/scant 1 cup)
    cold sparkling water

Peas:
1 tbsp vegetable or
    sunflower oil
1 tsp cumin seeds
2cm (¾in) piece of
    ginger, finely grated
2 garlic cloves, finely grated
3 green finger chillies,
    finely chopped
2 x 300g (10½oz) tins
    mushy peas
Juice of 1 lime
A handful of chopped
    fresh mint

Fish and chips is a dish that you simply cannot beat. My mother's side of the family moved to the UK from Punjab in India – not far from the Holy City of Amritsar. As well as being home to the Sikh faith and the magnificent Golden Temple, the city is also a well-known temple for food lovers who visit from across India. You can find the famous Amritsari fish at a sports bar at the legendary Makhan Fish and Chicken Corner where they have been expertly frying fish since 1962. The fish is spiced in a delicate Punjabi blend of aromatic spices, heavy on ajwain, which has a similar earthiness to dried thyme. It is then fried in a thin chickpea batter – finished with sharp lemon juice. This is perfect finger food, which disappears in seconds. So here we have my Amritsari fish, served in true British style with spicy minted mushy peas and proper tartare sauce! Serve with chips, for a proper fish-and-chip feast.

Ajwain is available in some supermarkets, but if you can't find it, simply replace with an equal quantity of dried thyme. If you don't feel like making the tartare sauce, then a shop-bought alternative will be absolutely fine.

....

For the fish, add all the spices to a bowl and mix to combine. Dip the fish fillets in the spices so that they are thoroughly coated in the masala. Keep aside on a plate.

To make the batter, whisk together both types of flour and the salt in a large bowl. Slowly add the sparkling water, so that you are left with a smooth, runny batter, the same consistency of single (light)cream. Allow to rest in the fridge.

For the peas, heat the oil in a saucepan, over a low–medium heat. When hot, add the cumin seeds, ginger, garlic and green chillies. Fry for 2–3 minutes, until lightly golden. Add the mushy peas to the pan and stir to combine. Add the lime juice, cover with a lid and allow to warm gently for 10–15 minutes. Keep warm, and add the fresh mint when ready to serve.

Recipe continued overleaf

Tartare sauce:
3 tbsp mayonnaise
1 tbsp natural yoghurt
½ tsp Dijon mustard
Juice of ½ lemon
1 large handful of
    chopped dill
1 tbsp chopped capers
½ banana shallot,
    finely diced

Seasoning:
½ tsp salt
½ tsp chilli powder
½ tsp dried mango
    powder (amchoor)

For the tartare sauce: add all of the ingredients to a bowl, add a pinch of salt and pepper and stir to combine. Keep refrigerated.

To fry the fish, warm a deep, heavy-based pan. Fill it with oil to a depth of 6–7cm (2½–2¾in), making sure that it comes no more than halfway up the sides of the pan. (You can also use a deep-fat fryer). I recommend that you use a temperature probe to monitor the temperature and never leave the hot oil unattended. When the oil is at approximately 180°C (350°F), dip each piece of fish in the batter, allowing the excess to run off, so that it is coated in a thin, even layer of batter. Gently lower the fish into the hot oil and agitate the pan as soon as you have done so – this stops the fish from sticking to the bottom of the pan. Fry in batches of no more than two pieces at a time, for 2–3 minutes on each side, until crisp and golden brown. When cooked, remove the fish with a slotted spoon and place onto a plate lined with kitchen paper to absorb the excess oil.

Combine all the ingredients for the seasoning and dust the fish with it. Serve with the mushy peas, tartare sauce and lemon wedges.

LAAL MAAS SPAGHETTI & MEATBALLS

SERVES 4

300g (10½oz) venison
or other ready-made
meatballs, or 300g
(10½oz) minced
(ground) venison,
rolled into 12
equally-sized balls
Vegetable or sunflower
oil, for drizzling
Salt and black pepper

Sauce:
3 tbsp ghee or vegetable oil
4 cloves
2 bay leaves
1 medium red onion,
finely diced
4 garlic cloves
15 dried red Kashmiri
chillies soaked in 200ml
(7fl oz/generous ¾ cup)
of hot water for 20
minutes (use this water
to make the paste), or
2 heaped tbsp Kashmiri
chilli powder
250g (9oz/1 cup) natural
yoghurt

To serve:
500g (1lb 2oz) spaghetti
or pasta of choice
100g (3½oz) Parmesan
cheese, grated
10 basil leaves

In case you're wondering, Laal Maas is a mighty hunters' curry from the princely state of Rajasthan. The ingredients are very simple: dried red chillies, yoghurt and game meat. 'Laal' refers to the vibrant ruby-red colour which the chillies add to the dish and 'Maas', the game meat which was historically used. It sounds extremely hot but it's not as fiery as you might imagine it to be; the dish is mainly about showcasing the natural sweetness of the red chillies. I love the idea of turning this famous dish into spaghetti and venison meatballs – keeping up with the game tradition. If you don't like the idea of venison, it can also be made with lamb or beef.

Preheat your oven to 200°C fan/425°F/Gas 7. Place the meatballs in a roasting tin. Season with plenty of salt and pepper and drizzle with a glug of oil. Roast for 15–20 minutes, until they are golden, giving them a turn halfway.

To make the sauce, set a heavy-based pan over a medium heat. When hot, add the ghee or oil, the cloves and bay leaf. Let the spices sizzle in the oil for 30 seconds to release their aroma. Add the red onion and fry for 10–15 minutes, until golden brown.

Meanwhile, blend the garlic, Kashmiri chillies (or powder) and yoghurt, for a couple of minutes to make a smooth red paste. Add the paste to the onion with the chilli soaking water (or the same amount of tap water, if you used chilli powder) and bring to a simmer. Turn down the heat, cover with a lid and cook for 20 minutes. Add the meatballs to the pan with their juices and simmer for a further 5 minutes with the lid on.

During this time, cook the pasta according to the packet instructions. When the spaghetti is tender, add it to the Laal Maas with a pair of tongs. Add a few tablespoons of the pasta water to the pot, and stir to coat the pasta for a minute or two, until you have a silky sauce. Grate over some Parmesan, garnish with basil leaves and serve.

BENGALI MUSTARD FISH WITH ROASTED BUTTERNUT SQUASH & LENTIL SALAD

SERVES 4

½ butternut squash,
  peeled and cut into
  2cm- (¾in-) thick slices
2 tbsp oil
2 large fillets pollock,
  halibut or cod
  (400–500g/14oz–1lb 2oz
  total), patted dry with
  kitchen paper
Salt and pepper

Mustard paste:
4 heaped tbsp wholegrain
  Dijon mustard
Juice of ½ lime
2 tbsp coconut cream
3 tbsp desiccated (dried
  shredded) coconut
½ tsp salt
6 green finger chillies
2 tbsp extra virgin olive oil
  (or mustard oil)
2 tsp ground turmeric

Lentil salad:
1 x 400g (14oz) tin cooked
  green lentils, rinsed
1 banana shallot,
  finely chopped
A handful of mint,
  finely chopped
A handful of coriander
  (cilantro), finely chopped
2cm (¾in) piece of ginger,
  finely grated
6 tbsp olive oil
Juice of 1 lime, plus extra
  wedges to serve
½ cucumber, diced
1 carrot, finely grated

Mustard fish wrapped in banana leaf is the jewel in the crown of Bengali cuisine. Using an old-fashioned grinding stone, a paste is made of black and yellow mustard seeds, green chillies and turmeric. It is then smeared on the local 'bhetki' (barramundi) river fish, before being wrapped in a banana leaf and steamed to perfection. I tasted this dish at the famous 6 Ballygunge Place and it didn't disappoint. The mustard marinade melds with the fish and adds an earthy, mildly sweet flavour, with a gentle warmth of mustard. Not only is it a wonderful way to eat fish, but this dish really is the emblem of Bengali heritage and culture.

Preheat the oven to 180°C fan/400°F/Gas 6. Place the squash on a baking tray. Drizzle with oil, season with salt and pepper and roast for 35 minutes until tender.

To make the mustard paste, add all the ingredients to a food processor or blender, and grind to a smooth, thick paste, adding a splash of water if required.

Lay out a large piece of foil and place a slightly smaller piece of baking parchment over the top. Smear the centre of the baking parchment with half of the mustard paste and place the fish fillets, side by side, on top, then cover with the remaining paste in an even layer. Wrap the fish tightly in the baking parchment and follow with the foil, making sure to seal all the sides. Place the parcel on a baking sheet and bake for 20 minutes, then allow the fish to rest for 5 minutes before unwrapping.

Meanwhile, make the salad. In a large bowl, mix together all of the salad ingredients and season with salt and pepper. Spread over a large serving dish and carefully place the fish on top. Arrange the butternut squash around, along with some lime wedges, and enjoy.

GRILLED COURGETTES
WITH CUMIN, MINT & MOZZARELLA

SERVES 4

4 courgettes (zucchini)
   (mix with some
   yellow ones, if you
   can find them)
2 tbsp olive oil

Dressing:
60ml (2fl oz/4 tbsp)
   olive oil
1 tsp ground cumin
1 tsp ground coriander
½ tsp fennel seeds,
   crushed to a powder
   in a mortar and pestle
   or spice grinder
1cm (½in) piece of ginger,
   finely grated
Zest and juice of 1 lemon
Salt and pepper

Fried garlic:
Vegetable oil, for frying
2 garlic cloves, thinly sliced

Garnish:
2 green finger chillies,
   finely chopped
A bunch of mint
   leaves, torn
2 balls of mozzarella
   (buffalo mozzarella
   is best)

Around 2002, my dad invested in a tiny storm-damaged cottage in Normandy, which would become the starting base of all of our French, summer holiday, camping adventures. We had bought a little cast-iron, gas plancha-type BBQ from a supermarket and we cooked everything on that.

Courgettes were, and still are, a favourite of mine. When grilled, I think courgettes are at their most delicious – when you get some really nice char marks going and they become deliciously soft on the inside. This recipe is no exception – serve with simply grilled sardines, or lamb chops and you've got a dish that was very typical of the summer evening meals we would enjoy in our little paradise in Normandy!

For the dressing, whisk together all the ingredients and season with salt and pepper. Set aside.

For the garlic, pour oil to a depth of 2cm (¾in) into a small pan and place over a medium heat. When hot, add the slices of garlic and fry for approximately 4 minutes, until golden brown. Remove from the oil and drain on kitchen paper. Set aside.

Slice the courgettes into 1cm- (½in-) thick slices, on the diagonal. Add to a bowl and mix with the olive oil and a generous pinch of salt and pepper. Preheat a griddle pan over a high heat. When hot, add the courgette slices and grill for around 3–4 minutes on each side, so that they become nicely charred. (They can also be cooked on a barbecue if you wish.) Arrange on a serving dish.

Scatter the fried garlic, green chillies and mint leaves over the courgettes. Rip off chunks of the mozzarella and place those around the dish. Finish by spooning over the dressing, so that the courgettes can soak up all of the lovely flavours!

BANGERS & MASALA MASH WITH SORPOTEL GRAVY

SERVES 4

8 top-quality pork sausages

Masala mash:
1kg (2lb 4oz) potatoes (Maris Piper or King Edward)
100g (3½oz/7 tbsp) salted butter
2 tsp cumin seeds
2 tsp black mustard seeds
2 sprigs fresh curry leaves
2cm (¾in) piece of ginger, finely grated
3 garlic cloves, finely grated
200ml (7fl oz/generous ¾ cup) whole milk, warm
Zest of 1 lemon
4 green finger chillies, finely chopped
A large handful of fresh coriander (cilantro), finely chopped
2 tsp chaat masala
Salt and pepper

Gravy:
20g (⅔oz/1½ tbsp) unsalted butter
1 large onion, thinly sliced
20g (⅔oz/2⅓ tbsp) plain (all-purpose) flour
500ml (17fl oz/2 cups) chicken stock
80g (2¾oz/⅓ cup) natural yoghurt
1 heaped tbsp brown sauce

Spice paste for gravy:
1 heaped tbsp Kashmiri chilli powder
½ tsp ground turmeric
1 tsp cumin seeds
1 tsp black mustard seeds
1 tsp fennel seeds
3 cloves
1cm (½in) cinnamon stick
4 garlic cloves, peeled
2cm (¾in) piece of ginger, peeled
50ml (1¾fl oz/3½ tbsp) red wine vinegar
2 tsp brown sugar

The best accompaniment to sausages and mash has to be gravy – lots of it! So, I present to you the Sorpotel curry from the Indian state of Goa. Sorpotel involves braising pork in an intense spice paste made from red chillies, Goan spices and vinegar and I personally can't think of a better gravy than this spicy one of Goan inspiration to enjoy with my bangers and masala mash.

For the gravy, warm a large deep pan over a medium–high heat. When hot, add the butter and onion and fry for 10–15 minutes, until golden brown. While the onion is cooking, add the spice paste ingredients to a blender and process to a smooth purée.

When the onion is golden, add the flour and stir for a minute. Add the spice paste, chicken stock, yoghurt and brown sauce and whisk together. Cover with a lid and simmer over a gentle heat for 20 minutes while you make the mash.

Peel and chop the potatoes into 4–5cm (1½–2in) chunks. Boil in a pan of salted water for 15 minutes, until tender. Drain the potatoes then mash with a potato ricer or masher.

Melt 2 tablespoons of the butter in a small pan over a medium heat. Add the cumin seeds, mustard seeds, curry leaves, ginger and garlic. Fry for 2–3 minutes, until lightly golden. Add the rest of the butter, allowing it to melt over a very gentle heat. Pour the melted butter and warm milk over the mash, along with the lemon zest, green chillies, chopped coriander and chaat masala. Fold through and season with salt and plenty of black pepper.

Heat the oil a large frying pan over medium heat. Fry the sausages for around 15 minutes, turning them periodically, until golden.

To serve, add a generous dollop of mash to a plate, top with sausages and serve with plenty of gravy over the top.

BUTTER GARLIC CRAB LINGUINE

SERVES 4

500g (1lb 2oz) linguine
   or fusilli pasta
120g (4¼oz/½ cup)
   unsalted butter
10 garlic cloves,
   finely chopped
5 green finger chillies,
   finely chopped
200g (7oz) white crab meat
100g (3½oz) brown
   crab meat
Zest and juice of 1 lemon
2 tsp freshly ground
   black pepper
1 tsp garlic granules
1 heaped tbsp crème
   fraîche
A bunch of fresh
   coriander (cilantro),
   finely chopped
Salt
Lemon wedges, to serve

If you are visiting Mumbai and you want to eat seafood, you'll no doubt be signposted to Trishna – it's on the well-trodden tourist route and it deserves its reputation. The lip-smacking butter garlic crab was a highlight for me. Crab linguine is a very familiar dish to us all, but I'm adding a little Mumbai twist and believe me, this buttery crab sauce is a delight not to be missed. Crab meat is available in supermarkets and takes the hassle out of having to cook and pick out your own crab. This dish is extremely quick and will only take as long as you need to boil the pasta.

Bring a large pot of salted water to the boil. Add the pasta and cook, according to the packet instructions.

Place a large deep pan on a medium heat. Add the butter and allow it to melt. Add the garlic and green chillies and cook for 3 minutes until softened and lightly golden. Add the crab meat and all the remaining ingredients and warm through gently.

When the pasta is al dente, add it to the crab with a pair of tongs. Add a ladle of pasta water and continue to cook for 1 minute, stirring to get a nice glossy sauce. Check the seasoning and add a pinch of salt if required.

Serve in pasta bowls with wedges of lemon.

NANNY'S KEEMA PASTA

SERVES 4

15g (½oz/1 tbsp) butter
1 tbsp ghee or vegetable oil
1 black cardamom pod
½ tsp cumin seeds
3 cloves
1cm (½in) cinnamon stick
1 bay leaf
1 medium onion,
    finely diced
2cm (¾in) piece of ginger,
    finely grated
3 garlic cloves, finely grated
500g (1lb 2oz) minced
    (ground) lamb (10% fat
    is best)
1 tomato, grated
2 green finger chillies,
    halved
½ tsp salt
¼ tsp ground turmeric
500g (1lb 2oz) conchiglie
    or farfalle pasta
1 tsp garam masala
100g (3½oz) frozen peas
grated pecorino (or
    Parmesan) cheese,
    to serve

My grandfather, Pa, was the expert cook of the family. His signature was his famous keema: a dish of lamb mince, slowly braised, until soft and juicy, in a subtle blend of aromatic Punjabi spices. The glory of Pa's keema was the unadulterated simplicity – the less-is-more attitude. The pure taste of the meat stole the show, only delicately enhanced by the spices he used. The keema was served simply, with Nanny's piping hot buttered chapattis. The next day came the exciting bit: leftovers! The keema would be transformed into something even more legendary, keema pasta! Just like a kind of Punjabi lamb bolognese, covered in loads of grated cheese – what a superb idea Nanny had.

Place a large, heavy-based pan over a medium-high heat. When hot, add the butter, ghee, cardamom, cumin, cloves, cinnamon and bay and allow the spices to sizzle in the hot oil for 1 minute. Add the onion and fry for 10–15 minutes, until golden and caramelised. Add the ginger and garlic and fry for a further 2 minutes. If the mixture starts to stick, add a splash of water to deglaze the pan.

Add the lamb mince to the pan, breaking up the chunks with a whisk. Cook until browned. Stir in the grated tomato, green chillies, salt, turmeric and 100ml (3½fl oz/scant ½ cup) water. Bring to a simmer, cover with a lid, turn the heat to medium-low and cook gently for 20 minutes.

With 10 minutes to go, cook the pasta, according to the packet instructions. Add the garam masala and frozen peas to the keema and cook for a further 5 minutes.

Drain the pasta when al dente and add to the keema, with a spoon or two of pasta water. Stir the pasta to make sure that it's all evenly coated, then serve with plenty of grated pecorino.

TAMIL NADU FISH PIE

SERVES 6

2 tbsp vegetable or
    sunflower oil
½ tsp fenugreek seeds
1 tsp fennel seeds
1 tsp black mustard seeds
1 tsp black peppercorns
2 onions, diced
3 garlic cloves, finely grated
2cm (¾in) piece of ginger,
    finely grated
6 green finger chillies,
    finely chopped
3 sprigs fresh curry leaves
25g (1oz/3 tbsp) plain
    (all-purpose) flour
½ x 400g (14oz) tin
    chopped tomatoes
2 tbsp tamarind paste
160ml (5¼fl oz/⅔ cup)
    coconut cream
½ tsp ground turmeric
1 tsp ground coriander
2 tsp Kashmiri chilli
    powder
200g (7oz) fillets firm
    white fish (eg. cod,
    haddock or pollack)
200g (7oz) undyed
    smoked haddock
200g (7oz) salmon fillets
3 medium eggs, hard-
    boiled, peeled and halved
cooked frozen peas,
    to serve

Mash:
6 Maris Piper or King
    Edward potatoes,
    peeled and cut into
    small chunks
100g (3½oz/7 tbsp) butter
2 tsp black mustard seeds
100ml (3½fl oz/scant
    ½ cup) whole milk
Salt

On a visit to the temple city of Madurai in late 2022, I ordered this Kuzhambu curry in a simple roadside eatery and I was blown away with the deep intensity of flavour. I enjoyed it so much that it has become the essence of my Tamil Nadu fish pie. Of course, any classic fish pie must include boiled eggs, which add a lovely richness with this spicy, tangy gravy.

Warm the oil in a large pan over a medium–high heat. When hot, add the fenugreek, fennel and mustard seeds and the peppercorns. Allow the spices to sizzle in the hot oil for a minute, to release their aroma. Add the onions and fry for 10 minutes until softened. Add the garlic, ginger, green chillies and curry leaves and stir for another 2 minutes. Stir in the flour and cook for a further minute. Add the chopped tomatoes, tamarind paste, coconut cream and ground spices to the pot. Cover with a lid and simmer on a medium heat for 15 minutes. Remove from the heat and transfer to an ovenproof gratin dish.

Preheat the oven to 180°C fan/400°F/Gas 6.

For the mash, place the potatoes into a large pan of well-salted water. Bring to the boil, then simmer for 15 minutes, until tender. Drain in a colander and mash, either using a masher or potato ricer. In a small pan, melt the butter with the mustard seeds. As soon as the mustard seeds start to crackle and pop, remove the pan from the heat and add the milk. Mix the mashed potatoes with the butter and milk. Season with plenty of salt and set aside

To finish the pie, cut the fish into chunks. Add the fish and boiled eggs to the pie filling, making sure that everything is distributed evenly. Top with an even layer of the mashed potatoes and place into the oven. Bake for 40 minutes, by which time the mash should be golden. Allow the pie to rest for 10–15 minutes before serving with peas.

PUNJABI BARNSLEY LAMB CHOPS

SERVES 4

4 Barnsley lamb chops
 or 8 lamb cutlets from
 a rack of lamb

Marinade:
150g (5½oz/scant ⅔ cup)
 Greek yoghurt
1 tbsp vegetable oil
3 garlic cloves, finely grated
2cm (¾in) piece of ginger,
 finely grated
2 tsp dried fenugreek
 leaves (kasoori methi)
1 tsp salt
½ tsp ground turmeric
1 tsp garam masala
½ tsp ground coriander
½ tsp ground cumin
2 heaped tsp Kashmiri
 chilli powder
Juice of ½ lemon

To serve (all optional):
Ratatouille (page 128)
1 red onion, thinly shaved
Mint and Coriander
 Chutney (page 232)
Sautéed Potatoes
 Persillade (page 134)

This recipe works very well when served with my Ratatouille (see page 134). Just omit the croutons and goats' cheese from the ratatouille if opting for these spectacular lamb chops. 'Barnsley' refers to the specific cut of lamb chop which, for a Yorkshireman is, of course, the best. You can also use lamb cutlets: just remember to serve two per person as they are much smaller. The chops can either be grilled in the oven or outside on a barbecue.

....

Mix together the ingredients for the marinade until thoroughly combined. Add the lamb chops or cutlets to a wide dish and coat with the marinade. Allow to marinate in the fridge for anywhere between 30 minutes and 24 hours. Remove the chops from the fridge 30 minutes before cooking so that they come up to room temperature.

Preheat the grill (broiler) on your oven to 250°C (480°F).

Line the bottom of the grill pan with foil and place the lamb chops on a rack suspended over the pan, spacing them out nicely. Grill for around 4–6 minutes on each side, until lightly charred and sizzling.

Remove from the oven and serve with your choice of the Ratatouille, red onion, Mint and Coriander Chutney or the Sautéed Persillade Potatoes.

PISTAWALA CHICKEN PIE

SERVES 4

Pastry:
200g (7oz/1½ cups) plain
(all-purpose) flour,
plus extra for dusting
80g (2¾oz) cold
unsalted butter
1 sheet ready-rolled
all-butter puff pastry
Egg wash made from 1 egg
yolk, mixed with 1 tbsp
of milk

Filling:
50g (1¾oz/3½ tbsp)
unsalted butter, plus
extra for greasing
4 green cardamom pods,
lightly crushed
3 cloves
1 tbsp cumin seeds
1 large onion, diced
6 medium chestnut
(cremini) mushrooms,
quartered
8 chicken thighs, each
fillet cut into 4 pieces
(about 650g/1lb 7oz)
3 garlic cloves
2cm (¾in) piece of ginger
Juice of 1 lemon
3 green finger chillies
1 small handful fresh
coriander, stalks and all
(10g/⅓oz approx.)
½ tsp ground turmeric
150g (5½oz/scant ⅔ cup)
natural yoghurt
30g (1oz/4 tbsp) plain
(all-purpose) flour
70g (2½oz) shelled
pistachio nuts, chopped
150ml (5fl oz/scant ⅔ cup)
chicken stock, made with
2 chicken stock pots
Salt and pepper

Mark my words, this is not your bog-standard chicken pie. It is based on a pistawala murgh – *a creamy chicken dish made from a paste of pistachios, fresh coriander and green chillies. Personally, I love the base to be made from shortcrust pastry and the top from puff because puff never cooks properly under the wet filling and usually turns out very soggy. I really enjoy the contrast in textures of the two types, giving you the ultimate pastry experience – because, let's face it, a pie is all about the pastry!*

Start by making the pastry: blitz the flour, butter and a good pinch of salt in a food processor until it resembles fine breadcrumbs. Add 2 tablespoons of water and pulse until the dough forms a ball. Wrap the pastry in cling film (plastic wrap) and flatten it out to a thickness of 2cm (¾in). Chill for 30 minutes.

For the filling, heat a large pan over a medium-high heat. Add the butter and, when melted, add the cardamom, cloves and cumin. Allow the spices to sizzle in the butter for 30 seconds, then add the onion and mushrooms and fry until soft and golden – about 7–10 minutes. Add the chicken and cook for 3–4 minutes until browned.

During this time, make the spice paste. Put the garlic, ginger, lemon juice, green chillies, fresh coriander, turmeric and yoghurt into a blender and blitz to a smooth green paste.

Add the plain flour to the pan with the chicken, stirring to coat everything for a minute or two. Add the paste, pistachios and stock and bring to a simmer. Turn the heat down to medium-low, and cook for 25 minutes. Season with ½ teaspoon of salt and some black pepper, then remove from the heat and allow to cool.

Preheat the oven to 180°C fan/400°F/Gas 6 and put a baking tray in the oven to heat up. Grease a pie dish with softened butter.

Remove the pastry from the fridge. Roll out on a lightly dusted surface until you have a circle about 3mm (⅛in) thick and large enough to line the pie dish. Place the pastry inside the pie dish, leaving the excess overhanging the sides. Pour the filling into the dish and top with the sheet of ready-rolled puff pastry. Crimp the edges with the back of a fork, then trim off any excess pastry with a small knife. Egg wash the pastry and season with sea salt. Place onto the baking tray and bake in the centre of the oven for 45 minutes, until a deep golden brown.

RADIO RESTAURANT AFGHANI CHICKEN CURRY

SERVES 4

600g (1lb 5oz) skinless
   chicken thighs
5 tbsp ghee or oil
3 green cardamom pods
3 cloves
1cm (½in) cinnamon stick
1 medium red onion, diced
¼ green pepper, deseeded
   and cut into 5mm
   (¼in) dice
1 tomato, deseeded
   and finely diced
Salt
Buttered naan bread
   or Khameeri Roti
   (see opposite), to serve

Spice paste:
30g (1oz) fresh coriander
   (cilantro)
130g (4½oz/generous
   ½ cup) full-fat natural
   yoghurt
3 green finger chillies
4 garlic cloves
2cm (¾in) piece of ginger
Juice of 1 lime
2 tbsp dried fenugreek
   leaves (kasoori methi)
1 tbsp ground coriander
1 tsp ground black pepper
40g (1½oz) blanched
   almonds

Mumbai can be very much a city dominated by trendy modern food habits – you'll find as many cocktail bars here as in central London. But, having said that, there are still plenty of old-school hidden gems in this megalopolis – you just have to know where to find them. My absolute favourite has to be Radio Restaurant. It was once a grand music hall that played host to sophisticated opera concerts. Not any more, it doesn't! Located in the bustling Crawford Market, the grand entrance is hidden amongst numerous textile stalls and opens onto the market, almost like a railway station concourse. Walk inside the cavernous dining hall to discover 10-metre high ceilings with huge cracks where chunks of plaster have fallen off, from years of neglect. It is very dimly lit and a hazy mist of kebab smoke lingers in the air. In one of the old chartreuse-coloured leatherette booths we sat down to one of the greatest curries I've ever experienced: tender chunks of chicken, in an unappetising, dark greenish, grey gravy. Forget what it sounds like; it has the most incredible flavour of garlic, coriander and dried fenugreek. It's rich, but at the same time bright, earthy and spicy: just the kind of curry that you want to eat – perfect in every way! And the naan was superlative: fluffy, lightly charred and glistening with ample melted butter. A local chap who was sitting opposite asked if I was enjoying my meal? I suppose he was surprised that he found a tourist like me braving his local haunt. He was really curious about how satisfied I was. There are no two ways about it – this chicken curry was the ultimate and I'm kindly recreating it so you, too, can enjoy a bit of the Radio Restaurant magic!

Season the chicken thighs with 1 teaspoon of salt and set aside in a bowl.

To make the spice paste, add all the spice paste ingredients to the jug of a blender or stick blender with 125ml (4fl oz/½ cup) of water. Blend to a smooth, green-coloured paste. Pour over the chicken. This can now marinate in the fridge for up to a day, although it can also be cooked straightaway.

Place a heavy-based lidded casserole over a medium-high heat. Add the ghee or oil and, when hot, add the cardamom, cloves and cinnamon stick and let them sizzle for 30 seconds to release their aroma. Add the onion and green pepper and fry for 10–15 minutes, until golden.

Add the spice paste-coated chicken to the casserole, along with 250ml (9fl oz/1 cup) water. Bring to a simmer, cover with the lid and cook gently for 30 minutes, stirring every now and then.

Add the tomato and cook for another 15 minutes. You want the sauce to be quite thick and cling to the chicken. If it's too thin, cook it for a little longer with the lid off to reduce it; if it's too thick, just add a splash of water.

Check for seasoning and serve with buttered naan or my Khameeri Roti.

KHAMEERI ROTI

MAKES 6

400g (14oz/3 cups)
    strong white bread flour,
    plus extra for dusting
250ml (9fl oz/1 cup)
    lukewarm milk
7g (¼oz) instant
    dried yeast
1 tsp salt
½ tsp sugar
Butter, for serving

Here is a recipe for a Mughlai flatbread called khameeri roti to serve with the curry. It is very similar to naan, but with the addition of yeast, which makes it soft and fluffy. Serve with plenty of butter!

Mix together all the ingredients in the bowl of a stand mixer fitted with a dough hook. Knead the dough on medium speed for 10 minutes, or knead by hand until you have a smooth dough.

Divide the dough into six equal pieces, then roll them into six tight balls. Dust a large roasting tin with flour and place the balls inside, spaced well apart. Cover with a light sprinkling of flour then with cling film (plastic wrap). Allow to prove for 40 minutes–1 hour until doubled in size.

Preheat the grill (broiler) function of your oven to 250°C (480°F).

Heat a heavy-based ovenproof frying pan over a high heat.

To shape the khameeri roti, place a dough ball on a lightly dusted work surface. Push the dough outwards from the centre with your fingertips, gently stretching it into a 16cm (6¼in) circle. Turn the roti over and brush with cold water. Place it into the very hot pan, water side down. Cook for 2 minutes before placing the pan under the grill for a further 2 minutes – this will colour the top of the bread.

Repeat with the other dough balls to make six roti, and serve with a knob of butter brushed over the surface of each.

TANDOORI BUTTER TROUT
WITH GINGER & LIME GREENS

SERVES 4

3 tbsp oil
4 trout fillets (or salmon or
    tuna, if you wish), about
    140g (5oz) per fillet
2 Little Gem (Baby Bibb)
    lettuces, halved
    lengthways
8 tenderstem broccoli
    spears
100g (3½oz) frozen peas
Salt and pepper

Tandoori butter:
125g (4½oz/½ cup)
    salted butter
Zest and juice of ½ lemon
A bunch of coriander
    (cilantro), chopped
2cm (¾in) piece of ginger
4 garlic cloves, peeled
½ tsp ground cumin
1 tsp dried fenugreek leaves
    (kasoori methi)
2 tsp Kashmiri chilli
    powder
1 tsp garam masala
¼ tsp ground turmeric
½ tsp black pepper
6 green chillies

Dressing:
5 tbsp olive oil
1cm (½in) piece of
    ginger, finely grated
1 garlic clove, peeled
    and finely grated
2 green chillies,
    finely chopped
Juice of 1 lime

Strictly speaking, this dish isn't a tandoori recipe as I'm not cooking any element of it in a tandoor. This is only because we don't usually have them at home. One thing that we certainly do all have, though, is a love of tandoori grilled meat or fish. So here are the flavours of your favourite tikka spice rub, forced into a flavoured butter. It's great when melted over pan-fried, barbecued or even steamed fish – a really quick and easy way of getting a whack of tandoori spice into your everyday home cooking, with the added advantage that butter makes everything taste better! It also works exceptionally well with scallops, prawns, corn on the cob, or even melted over a steamed lobster. And do switch the trout for salmon or tuna, if you prefer. The choice is yours – I'm just here to inspire. The butter can be kept wrapped in the fridge for up to a week.

To make the butter, add all of the ingredients to a food processor and blitz until smooth. Lay a double layer of cling film (plastic wrap) on your worktop and spread the butter in the centre, in a long line. Wrap the butter in the cling film, in a nice tight sausage shape and place in the fridge to harden.

Make a quick dressing by whisking the olive oil with the ginger, garlic, green chillies, lime juice and a pinch of salt.

Place a large frying pan over a medium–high heat. When hot, add 1 tablespoon of the oil. Season the fish fillets with salt and pepper, then add them to the pan, skin side down. Leave to cook for around 6 minutes – you will see the colour of the flesh change as it cooks, moving upwards through the fish. When the colour has changed almost to the top, turn the fillets over and remove the pan from the heat and set aside whilst you cook the veg. Cut a few rounds of the butter and place onto the fillets of fish, so they melt gently as the fish rests. (You can also barbecue the fish, if you prefer.)

Warm a large pan with a lid over a high heat. Add the remaining 2 tablespoons of oil and, when almost smoking, add the lettuce, cut sides down, followed by the broccoli. Allow the veg to colour for a couple of minutes, then add the frozen peas and 3½ tablespoons water. Immediately cover the pan and cook for 3 minutes, until the broccoli is tender. Drain the veg, then pour the dressing over. Serve with the fish fillets, and a couple more slices of butter.

MUGHLAI HACHIS PARMENTIER

SERVES 4

50g (1¾oz/3½ tbsp)
   butter (or 4 tbsp ghee)
1 black cardamom pod
5 green cardamom pods
4 cloves
1 bay leaf
8 black peppercorns
2cm (¾in) cinnamon stick
2 onions, diced
500g (1lb 2oz) minced
   (ground) beef or lamb
   (10% fat is best)
2cm (¾in) piece of ginger,
   finely grated
3 garlic cloves, finely grated
2 carrots, grated
100g (3½oz/scant ½ cup)
   natural full-fat yoghurt
100ml (3½fl oz/scant
   ½ cup) beef or
   lamb stock
2 tsp Kashmiri chilli
   powder
2 tsp ground coriander
1 tsp ground nutmeg
1 tsp garam masala
100g (3½oz) mature
   Cheddar cheese, grated
Salt and pepper

Mash:
6 large Maris Piper or
   King Edward Potatoes
100g (3½oz/7 tbsp) butter
100ml (3½fl oz/scant
   ½ cup) whole milk
2 green finger chillies,
   finely chopped
A handful of fresh
   coriander (cilantro),
   chopped

Hachis Parmentier is France's answer to the cottage pie. We're talking slow-cooked mince, suspended in a thick, flavoursome gravy, topped with heavenly, buttered mash!

I'm taking the Hachis Parmentier on a trip to Old Delhi, to really zhuzh up the traditional cottage pie-feel of the dish with the mutton Quorma of Old Delhi, which is the real authentic Quorma. It bears no resemblance whatsoever to the overly sweet, coconut-based concoction you might find in a British-Indian restaurant. The Quorma is characterised by simmering meat in a stock of fried onions and yoghurt. One of the best examples of this dish can be found in Karim's of Old Delhi. Their Quorma is an expertly-made dish of wonderful depth and simplicity; a perfect marriage for my Hachis Parmentier.

....

Melt the butter in a large heavy-based casserole over a medium heat. When hot, add the black and green cardamom, cloves, bay, peppercorns and cinnamon and allow to sizzle for 1 minute to release their aroma. Add the diced onions to the pan and cook for 15 minutes, until they are golden brown.

Add the beef or lamb and fry for 10 minutes until it has all coloured, breaking it up as much as you can – this can be achieved easily by using a whisk. Add the ginger, garlic, carrots, yoghurt, stock and ground spices. Bring to a simmer and season with salt. Turn the heat down to medium and cook with the lid on for 35 minutes, when the meat should be soft and tender. Transfer to an ovenproof gratin dish.

Meanwhile, make the mash topping. Peel and chop the potatoes into small chunks. Put in a saucepan, cover with water and add a generous amount of salt. Bring to the boil, then simmer for 15 minutes or until the potatoes are tender. Drain and mash.

Add the butter and milk to a small saucepan and warm through over a gentle heat. When warm, stir the milk and butter through the mash. Finally, add the green chillies and coriander and season with salt and pepper. Set the mash aside.

Recipe continued overleaf

Salad:
1 Cos lettuce
A selection of peppery
    salad leaves: rocket
    (arugula), chicory,
    radicchio and/or
    watercress work well
Radishes, thinly sliced

Dressing:
1 tsp Dijon mustard
4 tbsp walnut or olive oil
1 tbsp red wine vinegar
1 garlic clove, crushed

Preheat the oven to 180°C fan/400°F/Gas 6.

Top the meat filling with an even layer of mash. Grate the Cheddar over the top and bake in the hot oven for 40 minutes until bubbling and golden.

For the salad, chop the Cos lettuce and mix with the other leaves and sliced radishes. Whisk together the dressing ingredients until slightly thickened and pour over the leaves. Gently toss together at the last minute, just before serving.

Allow the Hachis Parmentier to rest for 10–15 minutes, then serve with the salad.

STUFFED PEPPERS PULAO

SERVES 4

4 red peppers
Oil or ghee, for drizzling
2 tsp garam masala
300g (10½g/1¼ cups)
   Greek yoghurt
A small bunch of fresh
   coriander (cilantro),
   chopped
Salt and pepper

Rice:
2 tbsp oil or ghee
2 tsp cumin seeds
3 green cardamom pods
1 bay leaf
2cm (¾in) cinnamon stick
4 cloves
1 medium (or ½ a large)
   red onion, sliced
2cm (¾in) piece of ginger,
   finely grated
3 garlic cloves, finely grated
2 green chillies, finely
   chopped
150g (5½oz/scant 1 cup)
   basmati rice
75g (2½oz) frozen peas
Zest of 1 lemon
1 tsp salt

Garlic and chilli oil:
40ml (1½fl oz/2½ tbsp)
   olive oil
2 garlic cloves, crushed
1 tsp cumin seeds
2 tsp chilli flakes
Juice of ½ lemon

Stuffed peppers crop up all along the Mediterranean – Greece, Spain Turkey, France. They are almost always stuffed with either meat or rice. Here, I'm opting for the rice variety and I can't think of a better rice stuffing than my grandparents' recipe for Punjabi peas pulao. It's a simple, everyday pulao that they would cook during the week and it's just the best way to cook rice. All the flavours from the spices are soaked up by the rice. These peppers are as fun to eat as they are to make and they always bring a lot of joy to the table.

Preheat the oven to 200°C fan/425°F/Gas 7.

Cut the tops off the peppers and keep them to one side – these will be used as the lids after stuffing the peppers. With a small knife, cut the seeds out of the insides, then turn upside-down and tap to remove them all. Season the inside with a drizzle of oil or ghee, garam masala and salt and pepper.

For the rice, warm a saucepan with a lid over a medium–high heat. When hot, add the oil or ghee and the whole spices. Allow the spices to sizzle in the hot oil for a minute, to release their aroma. Add the sliced onion and cook for 10–15 minutes, until golden brown. Next, add the ginger, garlic and green chillies and cook for a further 2 minutes. Add the rice and stir to coat in the oil for a few seconds, before adding 300ml (10½fl oz/1¼ cups) water. Add the peas, lemon zest and salt. Bring to the boil, stir once and cover with a lid. Turn the heat down to low and cook for 8 minutes, then remove from the heat. The rice will now be just over half-cooked, with still quite a lot of water. Give it all a stir then stuff the rice into the peppers – the rice will finish cooking inside them. Top the peppers with their lids, pop them into a deep baking dish and drizzle with some ghee or oil and a sprinkling of salt. Place into the oven and bake for 40 minutes, until tender and charred.

For the garlic and chilli oil, warm the olive oil in a pan and add the crushed garlic, cumin seeds and chilli flakes. Fry gently for 2–3 minutes – you don't want the oil to get too hot, or it will burn. Pour into a bowl and add the lemon juice.

When ready to serve, smear a large serving dish with the yoghurt. Spoon over the garlic and chilli oil and grind over a healthy amount of black pepper. Place the cooked peppers onto the plate and finish with a sprinkling of chopped coriander.

BUTTER CHICKEN & CHIPS

SERVES 4

1 free- range chicken,
    around 1.5kg (3lb 5oz)
    (cornfed are very good
    in flavour)
A bunch of fresh
    coriander (cilantro)
½ lemon
2cm (¾in) piece of
    ginger, sliced
3 garlic cloves, crushed
3 green chillies, halved
60g (2oz/4 tbsp) unsalted
    butter, softened
Salt and pepper
Green beans or salad,
    to serve

Sauce:
2 tbsp ghee or oil
3 green cardamom pods
2cm (¾in) cinnamon stick
1 bay leaf
3 cloves
3 garlic cloves, finely grated
2cm (¾in) piece of ginger,
    finely grated
1 x 400g (14oz) tin
    good-quality plum
    tomatoes
30g (1oz) cashew nuts
2 tsp Kashmiri chilli
    powder
2 green finger chillies,
    halved
75g (2½oz/5 tbsp)
    unsalted butter
1 tsp garam masala
1 tsp dried fenugreek leaves
    (kasoori methi)
1 tsp soft brown sugar
30ml (1fl oz/2 tbsp) single
    (light) cream

Chips:
4 large Maris Piper or
    King Edward Potatoes,
    approx 1kg (2lb 4oz)
3 tbsp oil or duck fat
2 unpeeled garlic cloves
3 sprigs thyme

Roast chicken and chips is a very French tradition. Perfectly roasted golden chicken, with crisp, blistering and salty skin, smothered in herbs and melted butter and accompanied with a silky rich béarnaise sauce. My two golden rules are: don't overcook your chicken or undercook your chips – simple as! An hour after your chicken has hit the oven, you've got yourself a legendary meal.

Rather than going to the trouble of a béarnaise sauce, I've got a trump card up my sleeve. This sauce is another butter-laden sauce – the Old Delhi butter sauce perfected by the Gulati Restaurant in Delhi: it's hot, tangy, smoky and buttery – probably the best you'll find anywhere on this earth. Until you make it to Delhi, I hope you enjoy my chicken and chips.

The butter sauce can be made well ahead of time and simply reheated in a pan. Smoking dishes with charcoal is a technique used in India for adding a layer of smoky depth. If you have a lump of charcoal handy, I recommend that you give this a go, to add some charred flavours to the sauce.

....

Remove the chicken from the fridge and cut off any string which may be trussing it together. Fill the cavity with the coriander, lemon half, ginger, garlic and chillies. Season the whole bird with plenty of salt and pepper and rub with the softened butter so that the whole chicken is covered. Place into a roasting tin and leave to come up to room temperature for 15–20 minutes. Meanwhile, preheat the oven to 220°C fan/475°F/Gas 9. Place the chicken in the centre of the oven and roast for 20 minutes. Baste the chicken with the hot buttery juices, then reduce the oven temperature to 180°C fan/400°F/Gas 6. Return the chicken to the oven for a further 45 minutes, basting every 15 minutes.

For the chips, cut the potatoes into wedges around 7mm (⅜in) thick. Rinse them in a bowl of cold water to remove excess starch, then pat dry with kitchen paper. Place the chips into a large roasting tin in a single even layer (use two tins if you can't achieve this in one) and coat with the oil or duck fat. Throw in the garlic and season with plenty of salt and pepper. Set aside.

For the butter sauce, heat a pan over a medium heat and add the ghee or oil. When hot, add the whole spices. Allow the spices to sizzle in the hot oil for 1 minute, to release their aroma, then add the ginger and garlic and fry for 2 minutes until lightly coloured.

Recipe continued overleaf

Add the tinned tomatoes, cashew nuts, chilli powder and green chillies, along with 150ml (5fl oz/scant ²/₃ cup) of water. Bring to a simmer, cover with a lid and cook gently for 20 minutes.

Remove from the heat and discard as many of the whole spices as you can find. Blend with a stick blender to a smooth, silky sauce. If at this point, you would like to pass the sauce through a sieve, for an even smoother finish, do so but it is not absolutely necessary.

The next step is optional: if you have a piece of charcoal, set it alight. When it is white-hot, use tongs to put it inside a little heatproof bowl. Place the bowl into the pan, so that it is floating in the sauce. Pour 1 tablespoon of melted butter over the charcoal. At this point there will be lots of smoke. Cover the pan tightly with a lid and leave to smoke for 3 minutes, then remove the bowl with the charcoal and discard the contents.

Whisk the rest of the butter into the sauce, a little at a time, followed by the garam masala, kasoori methi and sugar. Season with salt and cover with a lid. Set aside until later.

With 15 minutes of cooking time left for the chicken, place the tray of potatoes on the top shelf of the oven to cook for 45 minutes to an hour, until golden, making sure that you turn them halfway. Sprinkle with thyme for the last 5 minutes.

To check that the chicken is cooked, insert a skewer into the thickest part of the leg – if the juices run clear, with no pink blood, it is ready. Leave to rest, covered in foil for 30 minutes, while the potatoes finish cooking.

Warm the sauce and, if it's become a little thick, just add a splash of water. Stir in the cream and keep warm.

Carve the chicken and serve with the chips and plenty of the sauce on the side, along with green beans or a salad.

CHAPLI DOUBLE CHEESEBURGER

SERVES 4

Burgers:
100g (3½oz) beef bone
  marrow (optional)
600g (1lb 5oz) minced
  (ground) beef (20% fat)
2 tsp red chilli flakes
3 garlic cloves, grated
2cm (¾in) piece of ginger,
  finely grated
2 tbsp coriander seeds,
  gently crushed in a
  mortar and pestle
½ tsp ground turmeric
3 green finger chillies,
  finely chopped
1 tsp ground cumin
A bunch of coriander
  (cilantro), chopped
¼ red onion, finely diced
1 tbsp gram flour, or 2 tsp
  cornflour (cornstarch)
1 medium egg
1 tsp salt
Vegetable or sunflower oil,
  for brushing

Kashmiri burger sauce:
3 tbsp mayonnaise
2 tbsp ketchup
2 tsp Kashmiri
  chilli powder

Chutney:
1 large gherkin,
  finely chopped
A bunch of coriander
  (cilantro), chopped
½ red onion, finely diced
Juice of ½ lemon
1 tbsp finely chopped
  pickled jalapeños

To build:
8 cheese slices
4 brioche burger buns
2 tomatoes, thinly sliced
1 Little Gem (Baby Bibb)
  lettuce, thinly sliced

There are very few British Indian restaurants that I rank higher than Akbars. Based in Bradford, they have been proudly serving West Yorkshire's greatest curries since 1995. The experience is a no-frills, no-nonsense approach to Pakistani classic cuisine. There is a starter that I always order whenever I visit: the chapli kebab – a thin, crisp-fried beef patty, with a dominant lemony flavour which comes from a generous seasoning of crushed coriander seeds. You might bite into seeds which burst in your mouth, releasing their delicious zesty aroma. In Pakistan, the kebabs are often enriched with bone marrow, which slowly melts as they are fried – I'm salivating at the thought. These burgers are delicious and inspired by the great Akbars! I've seen bone marrow available in my local supermarkets and butchers will often have it if you ask – it is definitely an ingredient which is worth seeking out for this recipe.

If using bone marrow, scoop the soft marrow from the bones, using the back of a spoon and roughly dice it.

To make the patties, combine the beef and bone marrow with the remaining ingredients except the vegetable oil and some grinds of black pepper. Give this a good mix with your hands, then divide into eight balls, flattening each ball into a thin burger, around 5mm (¼in) thick.

To make the burger sauce, mix the mayonnaise, ketchup and chilli powder in a bowl and refrigerate until needed.

For the chutney, mix the ingredients and decant into a small serving dish.

Brush the burgers with oil on both sides and season with salt and pepper. Heat a large frying pan over a high heat and fry the burgers in batches for 2 minutes on each side. As soon as you flip the burgers, top each with a slice of cheese. You want the burgers to develop a nice caramelised golden crust. (They can also be cooked on a barbecue, for a wonderful smoky flavour.)

To build the burgers, toast the buns, spread some chutney on the bottom of each bun and burger sauce on the top halves. Place two patties in each bun and top with a slice of tomato and some lettuce.

HARIYALI ROASTED CELERIAC

SERVES 4

1 large celeriac, peeled and
  cut into 8 large chunks
1 pack halloumi, sliced
  into 6 slices

Marinade:
50g (1¾oz) spinach
30g (1oz) fresh mint
30g (1oz) fresh coriander
  (cilantro)
3 green finger chillies
2 tsp dried fenugreek
  leaves (kasoori methi)
Juice and zest of 1 lemon
1 tsp garam masala
1 tsp ground cumin
½ tsp ground turmeric
½ tsp black pepper
1 tsp salt
125g (4½oz/½ cup)
  Greek yoghurt

Crispy kale:
250g (9oz) kale
2 tbsp vegetable oil
Salt and pepper

Dressing:
60g (2oz/4 tbsp)
  unsalted butter
1 tbsp capers
2 garlic cloves, crushed
1 tsp cumin seeds
Juice of ½ lemon

Hariyali is a green marinade originally from the Punjab, although popular throughout Northern India. The vibrant green colour comes from a paste of spinach, mint and coriander which is usually rubbed over a chicken and roasted in a tandoor, but I think that celeriac is a much more exciting idea; it has the intensity of earthy, meaty flavours, which come alive when roasted and add a nutty depth. A dressing of butter, lemon, garlic and capers adds another dimension to the fresh and herby yoghurt-roasted celeriac.

To make the marinade, bring a pan of salted water to the boil. Cook the spinach, mint and coriander for 1 minute. Drain immediately and plunge into a bowl of cold water – this helps keeps the vibrant green colour. When cold, remove the herbs and squeeze out as much water as you can. Blend with the chillies, fenugreek, lemon juice and zest, ground spices, salt and one-quarter of the yoghurt, to make a smooth green paste. Add this purée to the remaining yoghurt and rub all over the celeriac and halloumi. (The celeriac and halloumi pieces can be marinated up to a day in advance.)

Preheat the oven to 200°C fan/425°F/Gas 7. Put the celeriac in a large roasting tin, lined with baking parchment. Roast for 20 minutes, then add the halloumi to the tin and roast for a further 20–25 minutes, until everything is nicely charred.

On another large tray, mix the kale with the oil and a pinch of salt and pepper. Place into the oven for the last 15–20 minutes of cooking time. Turn the kale halfway – it should be nice and crispy when cooked.

Remove everything from the oven – the celeriac should be lovely and tender in the centre. You can check by inserting a skewer – it should slide in easily. Allow the vegetables to rest while you make the dressing.

In a small pan, melt the butter over a medium heat. Cook until it is dark and nutty, but not burnt – it should take about 10–12 minutes. Remove from the heat and add the capers, garlic, cumin seeds and lemon juice, taking care as it might splutter. Allow everything to sizzle in the pan for a minute or so, before transferring to a bowl.

To serve, cover a large serving dish with the crispy kale. Arrange the celeriac and halloumi over the top and dress with spoonfuls of the delicious brown butter.

KERALAN FISH IN BANANA LEAF

SERVES 4

2 whole sea bass or sea
  bream, scaled and gutted
  or 4 fillets of sea bass
  or sea bream
2 tsp ground turmeric
2 tsp Kashmiri chilli powder
Juice of 1 lime
1 tsp salt
60ml (2oz/4 tbsp) coconut
  oil, plus extra if needed
Sautéed Potatoes Persillade
  (page 134), to serve
  (optional)

Masala:
8 shallots, finely sliced
4 sprigs fresh curry leaves
3cm (1¼in) piece of ginger,
  finely grated
6 garlic cloves, finely grated
4 green chillies, finely
  chopped
1 tsp ground turmeric
1 tsp chilli powder
2 tsp freshly ground
  black pepper
2 tsp ground coriander
2 fresh tomatoes, diced
200ml (7fl oz/generous
  ¾ cup) coconut milk
A handful of chopped
  fresh coriander
Juice of 1 lime

There is one dish that you must try if you ever visit the tropical region of Kerala – it's the meen pollichathu, *or fish in banana leaf. The local freshwater karimeen fish is spread with a thick, red-hot masala and steamed in a banana leaf. It's such an ingenious way of cooking. Don't start worrying about finding banana leaves. You can, if you wish, (they are available from most Asian supermarkets) but this dish is more about the idea of steaming the fish in a parcel – it's a brilliant way of infusing and locking the flavours together. Foil and parchment are a good alternative. If you opt for the banana leaf, remember to temper the leaves over a flame for a few seconds, which makes them more pliable and stops them splitting. Traditionally, the whole fish is used, which I recommend. Fish cooked on the bone always has more flavour, but if you object to bones you can use fillets. This dish also works very well with whole mackerel or trout.*

....

Pat the fish dry with kitchen paper and rub with the turmeric, chilli powder, lime juice and salt. Heat the coconut oil in a large frying pan and over a high heat. When very hot, add the fish to the pan and fry for 3 minutes on each side. If using fillets, fry for 2 minutes, but only on the skin side. Carefully remove using a fish slice and set aside on a baking tray.

For the masala, add the shallots and curry leaves to the same pan, over a medium–high heat, and fry for 3–4 minutes until softened. Add a splash more coconut oil if the pan is dry. Add the ginger and garlic and fry for a further 2 minutes. Add the chillies, all of the spices, tomatoes and coconut milk. Cook for another 5 minutes, or until you're left with a thick and quite dry, spreadable paste. Stir the fresh coriander through and season with lime juice.

Preheat your oven to 180°C fan/400°F/Gas 6. To make the fish parcels, place a large piece of baking parchment (or a banana leaf) on top of a similar-sized sheet of foil and spread one-quarter of the masala paste in the centre. Top with one of the fish, and add another one-quarter of masala paste, so that it is covered. Wrap the fish up tightly in the baking parchment. Repeat with the foil and crimp the edges. Repeat to make the second parcel. Place the parcels on a baking tray and bake for 8 minutes. Allow to rest for 5 minutes before opening and serving, with sautéed potatoes, if you like.

INDO-CHINESE CHILLI CHICKEN WITH HAKKA NOODLES

SERVES 4

2 tbsp rice vinegar
3 tbsp soy sauce
1 tsp Kashmiri chilli powder
1 tsp salt
2 garlic cloves, finely grated
80g (2¾oz) cornflour (cornstarch)
350g (12oz) chicken thighs, cut into 3cm (1¼in) pieces
100g (3½oz/¾ cup) plain (all-purpose) flour
Vegetable oil, for frying
1 red onion, sliced into 1cm (½in) lengths
1 green pepper, sliced into 1cm (½in) lengths
2 garlic cloves, finely grated
2cm (¾in) piece of ginger, finely grated, plus a 10g (⅓oz) piece, cut into matchsticks to serve
4 green finger chillies, thinly sliced
1 heaped tbsp chilli sauce (such as Sriracha)
1 heaped tbsp ketchup
2 tbsp light soy sauce
1 tsp brown sugar
Juice of 1 lime
½ tsp ground cumin
1 tsp cornflour (cornstarch), mixed with 2 tbsp water

Noodles:
2 tbsp vegetable oil
3 spring onions (scallions), finely sliced, white and green parts kept separate
½ carrot, grated
2 garlic cloves, finely grated
1cm (½in) piece of ginger, finely grated
250g (9oz) egg noodles, cooked according to the packet instructions
2 tbsp hot chilli sauce
1 tbsp light soy sauce
A small bunch of coriander (cilantro), chopped

Kolkata was the birthplace of Indo-Chinese cuisine. Kolkata's large population of Chinese settlers adapted their food to suit the local Indian palate. We're talking classic Chinese dishes, but pumped full of green chillies and handfuls of Indian spice, which combine to make a fiery fusion of flavours! You may have tried Indo-Chinese food in the UK, but trust me, nothing compares to what you'll taste in Kolkata. These were some of the spiciest dishes that I've ever tasted; not for the faint-hearted, but each so distinctive. You'll never have Chinese food like it, anywhere!

In a large bowl, mix together the vinegar, soy sauce, chilli powder, salt, garlic, cornflour and 2 tablespoons water. You should have a nice thick but runny paste. Add the chicken and coat in the paste.

Tip the flour onto a tray and dust the chicken pieces in it, giving each piece a shake to remove any excess. Fill a non-stick frying pan 2cm (¾in) deep with oil and set over a medium–high heat. When hot, fry the chicken pieces in batches for 2–3 minutes until golden. Set aside on a plate lined with kitchen paper.

To make the noodles, warm a large non-stick wok over a high heat. When hot, add the oil. As the oil starts to smoke, add the spring onion whites, carrot, garlic and ginger and stir-fry the vegetables for 1 minute. Add the cooked noodles and the chilli and soy sauces. Stir-fry the noodles for 2–3 minutes until piping hot, stirring as you go. Keep warm in a serving dish whilst you finish the chicken.

To finish the chicken, add 2 tablespoons of oil to the same pan you cooked the noodles in. Fry the onion and pepper over a high heat for 1 minute, until very slightly softened. Add the garlic, ginger and green chillies to the pan and stir-fry for a further minute. Add the chilli sauce, ketchup, soy sauce, sugar, lime juice and cumin with 4 tablespoons of water. Give everything a good stir, then add the cornflour and water mixture – this will thicken the sauce.

Add the chicken pieces to the pan, making sure to coat well in the sauce. Cook for a further 2 minutes, until the sauce is glossy and thick, and sticks to the chicken. Garnish the chicken with the ginger matchsticks and spring onion greens. Garnish the noodles with the fresh coriander and serve them together.

RATATOUILLE

SERVES 4

Ratatouille:
1 red (bell) pepper, core
   and seeds removed,
   roughly chopped
5 ripe tomatoes, halved
1 medium onion,
   thinly sliced
210ml (7½fl oz/scant
   1 cup) olive oil, plus
   a glug for the garlic
1 whole garlic bulb
1 large aubergine
   (eggplant), cut into
   2cm (¾in) dice
1 large courgette
   (zucchini), cut into
   2cm (¾in) dice
2cm (¾in) piece of
   ginger, finely grated
2 tsp chilli flakes
1 tsp ground cumin
1 tsp ground coriander
1 tsp garam masala
Juice of ½ lemon
Salt and pepper

Croutons:
4 slices sourdough bread
4 tbsp black olive tapenade

*Goats' cheese garnish
   (optional):*
125g (4½oz) soft
   goats' cheese
1 tsp ground cumin
½ tsp ground black pepper

Ratatouille is plagued with an awful reputation. I've tasted countless versions that bear no resemblance to the original Provençal recipe of intensely sweet vegetables that have been fried in excessive amounts of top-quality olive oil. I'm doing justice to this fine French classic and my version actually tastes of the sunshine flavours that its supposed to be brimming with! I've added a gentle hint of spice, which really complements these intense Mediterranean dish.

....

Preheat the oven to 180°C fan/400°F/Gas 6.

Place the pepper, tomatoes and sliced onion onto a baking tray, drizzle over 2 tablespoons of oil and a good pinch of salt. Cut the top 1cm (½in) from the garlic bulb, place on a piece of foil and drizzle over a glug of oil. Wrap it up in the foil and add to the tray with the veg. Roast the vegetables for 40–45 minutes, until nice and soft and just starting to caramelise. Set aside.

Warm the remaining olive oil in a saucepan over a medium heat. When hot, add the aubergine and fry for 10–12 minutes until golden brown. Remove the aubergine with a slotted spoon and place on some kitchen paper to absorb any excess oil. Repeat with the courgette, frying until they are also golden brown.

Remove most of the oil from the pan, leaving behind 3 tablespoons (the leftover oil can be kept and reused for cooking). Fry the ginger and chilli flakes over a medium heat for 2 minutes until lightly coloured. Add all the cooked vegetables to the pan, along with the ground spices, and cover with a lid. Cook gently for 10 minutes over a gentle heat, to meld all the flavours, then season to taste.

Remove the garlic from the foil and squeeze the roasted pulp from the bulb with the back of a large knife. Stir the garlic through the vegetables, along with the lemon juice.

For the croutons, heat a good splash of the olive oil (use what you removed from the vegetables) in a large frying pan and fry the bread on both sides, until crunchy and golden. Remove from the pan and spread each slice with 1 tablespoon of tapenade.

If adding the goats' cheese, mix the cheese with the ground cumin and black pepper until well combined.

To serve, pile the ratatouille over the croutons, dot over some goats' cheese and enjoy.

SPRING VEGETABLE AVIYAL

SERVES 4

300g (10½oz) Jersey
  Royals or other new
  potatoes, washed
100g (3½oz) fresh coconut
  flesh, or 2 tbsp coconut
  cream mixed with 3 tbsp
  desiccated (dried
  shredded) coconut
3 tbsp Greek yoghurt
100g (3½oz) fine beans,
  tops cut off
100g (3½oz) baby corn,
  halved
200g (7oz) frozen peas
8 asparagus spears, woody
  base removed and halved
1 tbsp coconut oil
1 courgette (zucchini), cut
  into batons, 1cm (½in)
  thick x 4cm (1½in) long
1 tsp ground turmeric
1 tsp ground cumin
4 green finger chillies,
  finely chopped
Leaves from 1 sprig fresh
  curry leaves (optional,
  although recommended)
Juice of 1 lime
Salt

Taking a boat to cruise along the pure and serene backwaters of Kerala is a magical experience. These inland waterways were once used as transport networks, connecting the tiny villages with ports to transport goods. It's a fascinating place. The boats stop to enjoy lunch and an array of Keralan specialities are served: beef fry, roasted prawns, pineapple pickle, okra fry, yellow dal. But the one dish that stood out to me most was the aviyal. *This is a very simple dish of local vegetables: bitter gourd, beans, drumstick (a kind of stringy, fibrous bean) and carrots, which are dressed in a paste of yoghurt, coconut and green chillies. It can be made in just a few minutes but the results are tremendous. Rather than using the traditional Keralan vegetables which are difficult to find, I am using a medley of others, which sing with coconut and yoghurt freshness. This dish is fantastic to accompany fish fried simply in a pan. Feel free to add any vegetables of your choice.*

....

Put the potatoes in a pan, cover with water and add a generous amount of salt. Bring to the boil and simmer for 20–25 minutes until tender. Drain and cut in half.

If using a whole coconut, use a hammer or something heavy to crack it open. Scoop out the flesh with a spoon and whizz in a food processor to make a paste. If you are using creamed coconut, simply mix it with the desiccated coconut. Mix the coconut with the yoghurt and stir together.

Bring a large deep pan of salted water to the boil. Add the fine beans and baby corn and cook for 2 minutes, then add the peas and asparagus and cook for a further 3 minutes. Drain the vegetables and immediately plunge into ice-cold water. Drain when cooled.

Warm a large frying pan over a medium–high heat. When hot, add the coconut oil and fry the courgette batons for 3–4 minutes, until softened. Add the potatoes and all of the other vegetables to the pan, along with the turmeric, ground cumin, green chillies and curry leaves (if using). Stir in the coconut and yoghurt paste and warm through for 3 minutes. Season with 1 teaspoon salt and transfer to a serving dish. Finish with the lime juice.

SHIMLA PIPERADE WITH HAKE & AIOLI

SERVES 4

2 tbsp olive oil
1 tsp cumin seeds
1 tsp fennel seeds
1 tsp caraway seeds
½ tsp fenugreek seeds
1 red pepper, deseeded and
    cut into 1cm (½in) slices
1 green pepper, deseeded
    and cut into 1cm
    (½in) slices
2 medium onions, cut
    into 1cm (½in) slices
2cm (¾in) piece of ginger,
    finely grated
3 garlic cloves, grated
2 tbsp tomato purée (paste)
100g (3½oz) green olives
1 tsp ground cumin
1 tsp ground coriander
2 tsp Kashmiri chilli
    powder
½ tsp garam masala
400g (14oz) waxy
    potatoes, halved
A generous pinch of saffron
    soaked in 350ml (12fl oz/
    1½ cups) of warm water
    for 10 minutes
4 hake fillets
    (600g/1lb 5oz total)
Juice of ½ lemon
Finely chopped
    coriander (cilantro)
Salt and pepper

Aioli dressing:
3 tbsp good-quality
    mayonnaise
1 tsp Dijon mustard
Juice of ½ lemon
2 garlic cloves, finely grated
50ml (1¾fl oz/3½ tbsp)
    extra virgin olive oil

Dishes of capsicum, very similar to piperade, are seen all over India. Take the jalfrezi for example; it's virtually identical, but with the addition of Indian spices. Peppers were first introduced to India by the British and were grown in the hill station of Shimla – where the Raj spent their summers. Hence why, in India, peppers are sometimes called Shimla mirch (mirch *meaning 'chillies'). Like Keith Floyd's famous piperade, I love the flavour of an Indian capsicum curry.*

Preheat your oven to 180°C fan/400°F/Gas 6.

Warm a large pan over a medium–high heat. When hot, add the oil and the cumin, fennel, caraway and fenugreek seeds. Let the spices sizzle in the hot oil for 30 seconds, to release their aroma. Add the sliced peppers, onions, ginger and garlic and stir-fry for 10 minutes until the vegetables have softened. Stir in the tomato purée, olives, ground spices and a pinch of salt. Add the potatoes to the pan along with the saffron water. Mix well.

Transfer the mixture to an ovenproof gratin dish. Season with more salt and pepper and roast in the oven for 35 minutes.

Remove the dish from the oven. Season the fish with plenty of salt and pepper on both sides. Place the fish into the gratin dish and return to the oven for a further 15 minutes.

To make the aioli dressing, simply whisk together all the ingredients in a large bowl and pour into a serving dish.

Remove the gratin dish from the oven, finish with a spritz of lemon juice over the fish and some chopped coriander, and serve with a drizzle of aioli.

HYDERABADI AUBERGINE SALAN

SERVES 4

3 medium aubergines
(eggplants)
Sunflower or vegetable
oil, for drizzling

Paste:
75g (2½oz) peanuts
3 tbsp desiccated (dried
shredded) coconut
1 tbsp white sesame seeds
1 tsp fenugreek seeds
2 tsp Kashmiri chilli
powder
½ tsp ground turmeric
3 garlic cloves
2cm (¾in) piece of ginger
4 green finger chillies
2 fresh tomatoes
1 tbsp tamarind paste
1 tsp muscovado sugar
1 tsp salt

To finish:
60ml (2fl oz/4 tbsp)
sunflower or
vegetable oil
2 dried red chillies
or 1 tsp chilli flakes
2 tsp black mustard seeds
2 tsp cumin seeds
1 sprig fresh curry
leaves (optional)
1 medium onion,
finely diced

To serve:
Lime juice
Chopped coriander
(cilantro)
Steamed basmati rice

The cuisine of Telangana, the area surrounding the city of Hyderabad, plays with a thrilling contrast of flavours – from nutty, sweet and tangy to fiery chilli heat. Aubergine salan, or 'Baingan ka Salan' is a dish that I'm instantly drawn to. The soft aubergine marries beautifully with the flavours of peanut, coconut and tamarind. Every time I taste this dish, my palate is swept away on an electrifying rollercoaster ride of tastes and aromas.

Preheat the oven to 200°C fan/425°F/Gas 7.

Slice the aubergines in half lengthways and score the inside of the flesh in a criss-cross pattern. Drizzle with plenty of oil, season with salt and pepper and place on a baking tray, cut side up. Bake for 40 minutes. After 40 minutes, change the oven setting to the grill (broiler) function and set to 250°C (480°F). Grill the aubergines for 5–6 minutes, until nicely browned on top.

While the aubergines are cooking, toast the peanuts, coconut, sesame seeds and fenugreek seeds in a frying pan over a medium heat for 5–10 minutes, until lightly golden in colour. Add them to a blender with the remaining paste ingredients and 300ml (10½fl oz/1¼ cups) of cold water and blend to a smooth paste.

For the curry, heat the oil in a saucepan over a medium–high heat. When hot, add the chillies or chilli flakes, mustard seeds and cumin seeds. Let the spices sizzle for 30 seconds, to release their aroma. Add the curry leaves (if using) along with the onion and fry for 10–15 minutes, until golden.

Add the paste to the pan and bring to a simmer. Cover with a lid, turn the heat down to low and cook for 30 minutes, stirring frequently. If, after 30 minutes, the sauce has become dry, slacken it with some water – it should be a nice medium-thick consistency.

To serve, cover the bottom of a serving platter with some sauce and top with the roasted aubergines. Drizzle the remaining sauce over the top and garnish with a spritz of lime juice and some chopped coriander. Serve with steamed basmati rice.

SAUTÉED POTATOES PERSILLADE

SERVES 4 AS
A SIDE DISH

700–800g (1lb 9–1lb 12oz)
   waxy small potatoes,
   Ratte, Jersey Royals
   or Charlottes work well
4 tbsp ghee or oil
2 tsp mustard seeds
2 tsp cumin seeds
½ tsp red chilli flakes
1 shallot
2 green finger chillies
A bunch of fresh
   coriander (cilantro)
2cm (¾in) piece of
   ginger, finely grated
3 garlic cloves, finely grated
Zest and juice of 1 lime
Salt

One of my favourite accompaniments are classic sautéed potatoes. This very simple French side dish goes extremely well with practically anything. As a teenager, I went through a phase of cooking these potatoes with almost everything I ate! Persillade is French for a parsley and garlic sauce, and it is made from finely chopping shallots with parsley, garlic and lemon zest. This recipe, though, uses the same idea, but with an Indian-style makeover.

Wash and scrub the potatoes and place into a medium-sized pan. Cover with water, season with a generous amount of salt and bring to the boil. Cook for 25 minutes, or until tender, then drain. Cut the potatoes into 3cm (1¼in) chunks while still hot.

Heat a large non-stick frying pan over a medium heat. Add the ghee or oil and when hot, add the mustard seeds, cumin seeds and chilli flakes. Let the spices sizzle in the hot oil for a minute, to release their aroma.

Add the potatoes to the pan and cook for around 20–25 minutes over a medium heat, stirring every few minutes, until the potatoes are crispy and golden.

While the potatoes are cooking, finely chop the shallot, green chillies and coriander. Mix together with the ginger, garlic and lime zest. When the potatoes are cooked, remove the pan from the heat and stir the persillade through, making sure that the potatoes are covered in all of the delicious flavours. Season with salt and finish with lime juice.

CELERIAC REMOULADE

½ celeriac, peeled
100g (3½fl oz/scant
   ½ cup) good-quality
   mayonnaise
50g (1¾oz/3½ tbsp)
   natural yoghurt
1 tsp wholegrain mustard
1 tsp Dijon mustard
Zest and juice of ½ lemon
1 tsp garlic granules
A packet of chives,
   finely chopped
½ tsp ground black pepper
½ tsp salt

I will always buy a tub of celeriac remoulade from the supermarket in France to bring home – I love it so much and the French love remoulade just like the British love tubs of coleslaw. This is a brilliant and simple salad to enjoy for lunch with cured meats or smoked fish and I recommend that you make it to accompany the Mackerel Rillettes on page 146.

Cut the celeriac into fine matchsticks – the best way is to use a mandoline with the fine julienne comb fitted, or a food processor with the correct attachment will also do the job well.

Mix the remaining ingredients together in a large bowl. Add the celeriac and mix well. Refrigerate until required.

WEEKEND
BLOW-OUTS

I will spend the whole week collecting recipe ideas and the weekend is my time to put them into action. A labour of love: I want to make things that take all day to cook; only then am I satisfied. I find immense pleasure in taking the time to carefully prepare something, leisurely tending the dish in between cups of coffee, flicking through books and intermittently watching classic Peter Sellers films. The smells develop from the kitchen, changing every hour, and fills the whole house with life. I take pleasure in boring tasks such as stirring a pot over the course of a few hours, taking in its transformation. I've always had extravagant projects in mind. When I was 12, I taught myself how to make croissants. I spent the days before preparing myself: I raided my parents' collection of vintage cookbooks and compiled every recipe I could find which mentioned the word croissant, working out every process in detail. The weekend came and I spent almost 24 hours immersing myself in the never-ending process of making, laminating, shaping, proving and baking the magical dough into the perfect croissant.

This is the type of cook I am. It may be mad, but the weekend is really the only time we have to engage in these types of experiments. I will meticulously plan each detail and formality of my weekend meal and go out in search of the best ingredients – and wines to match the food – and it's the only time in the week that I'll religiously enjoy a cheese course. Polished wine glasses and cutlery, cloth napkins and a smart shirt – this is what a proper weekend means to me: a no holds barred, slap-up meal, a proper blow-out!

Take Aslam's fish on page 164 for example. I love to draw comparisons between the great cuisines of India and France and there are many more similarities than you might at first imagine. I've always found beurre blanc sauce magnificent: a piece of fish, poached or grilled to perfection, served with the most luxurious, glossy sauce, made almost entirely from butter, but with a hint of acidity from white wine and zesty lemon. The butter is held and hidden within the sauce by emulsification, which creates the most magical sauce ever!

Fly 10 hours east and we reach the Jama Masjid in Old Delhi. The bustling street beside the great mosque is named 'Matia Mahal', which is home to some Delhi street-food gems! Aslam's is a restaurant which has become SO popular, that they now have two locations right opposite each other in the same street. They are constantly packed full of diners, many of whom have travelled halfway across India to taste their delights. Just two dishes are served: chicken or fish – marinated in spice, then grilled on a white-hot inferno of charcoal embers, right on the street for all to watch. It's real drama to feel the heat and take in the wafts of smoke. After grilling, the meat or fish is seasoned with handfuls of sharp acidic chaat masala and slathered in a serious helping of yoghurt and cream. An insane amount of melted butter is then poured over, hot from the pan.

I had watched videos of this famous place on the internet, dreaming of how it might taste and when I got the chance to try it I discovered new octaves of flavour! The combination of butter, cream, yoghurt and zesty chaat masala works together with the smoky undertones of the meat to create a sauce of mind-blowing elegance and refreshing complexity. It was then that I realised that Aslam's shares its DNA with the French beurre blanc!

The recipes I have written in this chapter focus on slightly more luxurious ingredient centrepieces that you might associate with a special occasion or the weekend – when we want to enjoy something more restauranty. These are the kinds of things that I want to eat at the weekend, whether it's cooking for myself or entertaining family and friends. Although, these recipes are not complicated, the processes are more involved. But it is these projects, like slow-cooking or barbecuing over smoking hot charcoal which will bring you the most cooking pleasure and make these recipes really worthwhile, because time and care are my two secret ingredients for the perfect meal.

OYSTERS WITH COCONUT WATER, GINGER, CHILLI & LIME

SERVES 4 AS A STARTER

1 tbsp vegetable oil
16–20 fresh curry leaves
16–20 oysters
Crushed ice
A few lemon or
 lime wedges

Dressing:
2 shallots, very finely
 chopped
2 green finger chillies,
 thinly sliced
1 tbsp finely chopped fresh
 coriander (cilantro)
3cm (1¼in) piece of ginger,
 very finely diced
200ml (7fl oz/generous
 ¾ cup) coconut water
60ml (2fl oz/¼ cup)
 lime juice

In France, the world is quite literally your oyster! We would come off the ferry in St Malo, near the town of Cancale – home to one of the largest oyster-farming regions and see nothing BUT oysters! Restaurants packed full of people ordering grand seafood platters – eating oysters by the bucketload.

This recipe is a really vibrant way to enjoy them on a hot summer's afternoon, with an ice bucket of sparkling wine. Oysters can be kept for up to 3 days in the bottom of the fridge.

You will need an oyster knife and tea towel to shuck the oysters. Oysters are best ordered online from reputable seafood specialists. Personally, I love Lindisfarne oysters, which you can buy direct. I also have a habit of buying Jersey oysters, which are also delicious.

Combine all the ingredients for the dressing in a small bowl.

Warm the oil in a small pan over a medium heat. When hot, fry the curry leaves for a couple of minutes, until crisp and translucent. Place them on a piece of kitchen paper to absorb the excess oil.

To shuck the oysters, fold the tea towel into thirds along the length, so that you have a long thin towel. Place it on your worktop and place an oyster on the tea towel, the pointed end (hinge) facing towards you. Pick up the other end of the tea towel and fold it over the oyster. Whilst holding the oyster down with the tea towel in one hand, take the oyster knife with your other hand and place it into the hinge. Apply some downwards pressure, wiggling the knife and twist – make sure that the tea towel is protecting your hand, incase it slips, so you don't cut yourself on the sharp shell. You should feel the top of the oyster shell release. Run the knife along the top shell of the oyster and lift off. Repeat with the other oysters, making sure that you remove any shards of broken shell.

Place the crushed ice into a nice serving dish and put the oysters on the ice to keep them cold. Top each oyster with a fried curry leaf and add a good spoonful of the dressing. Decorate the platter with some lemon or lime wedges and serve.

GARAM MASALA CHICKEN LIVER PARFAIT WITH FIGS

SERVES 6

1 shallot, finely diced
2 garlic cloves, finely grated
1 bay leaf
100ml (3½fl oz/scant
    ½ cup) port
100ml (3½fl oz/scant
    ½ cup) red wine
200g (7oz) chicken livers
2 large eggs, at room
    temperature
1 tsp Kashmiri chilli
    powder
½ tsp ground ginger
200g (7oz/generous
    ¾ cup) unsalted butter,
    melted, plus 150g
    (5½oz/scant ⅔ cup),
    to finish
1 tsp salt
Toast and cornichons,
    to serve

Masala:
4 black peppercorns
½ tsp cumin seeds
½ tsp coriander seeds
3 cloves
½ star anise
1 black cardamom pod
2 green cardamom pods
½ piece of mace
2cm (¾in) cinnamon stick

Confit figs:
8 figs
1 tbsp tamarind purée
100ml (3½fl oz/scant
    ½ cup) port
80g (2¾oz/7 tbsp) sugar
2 lemon slices
1 star anise
3 cloves
2cm (¾in) cinnamon stick
1 bay leaf

I love a French bistro classic and, to me, there's not much better than a really good home-made paté, washed down with a glass of Beaujolais. My recipe has an exciting spicy twist!

Preheat the oven to 120°C fan/275°F/Gas 1, and find yourself a deep ceramic or cast-iron terrine, approximately 20 x 10cm (8 x 4in), or 6 ovenproof ramekins.

Add the shallot, garlic, bay leaf, port and wine to a saucepan. Cook over a medium heat until it has reduced and you are left with 50ml (1¾fl oz/3½ tablespoons) of liquid. Strain through a fine sieve into a bowl and allow to cool. Discard whatever is left inside the sieve.

To make the masala, grind the whole spices in a spice grinder until you are left with a fine powder. Add this to a blender with the, chicken livers, eggs, chilli powder and ginger and blitz until smooth. Tip into a bowl and add the cooled reduction.

Using a stick blender, blend the chicken liver and egg mixture on a medium speed. Slowly drizzle in the melted butter, keeping the stick blender running all the time to emulsify. Season with the salt and carefully pour the paté mixture into the terrine or ramekins.

Place the dish(es) into a deep roasting tin and pour in boiling water so that it comes halfway up the sides of the terrine or ramekins – this will ensure even cooking. Bake for 30–40 minutes for the large terrine and around 20–25 minutes if using ramekins. The paté is ready when it is firm to the touch in the centre, but with a slight wobble. If you have a temperature probe, the internal temperature should be approximately 70°C (158°F) in the centre. Remove the terrine from the water and leave to cool. When cool, melt the 150g of butter and pour it on top of the paté to finish. Transfer to the fridge for at least 8 hours, or overnight.

To prepare the figs, place them into a pan in which they fit snugly in a single layer. Add the other ingredients and top up with water to just cover. Place the pan over a medium heat and bring to a simmer. Reduce the heat to low and cook for around 1½ hours, adding a splash of water if the pan looks dry, until you are left with a thick syrupy glaze. Remove from the heat and allow to cool.

Remove the paté from the fridge and enjoy spread onto crusty toasted bread, with the confit figs and a couple of cornichons.

BAIGNAN BHARTA DIP

SERVES 4-6

4 medium aubergines
4 tbsp vegetable oil
1 tsp cumin seeds
3 green cardamom pods
2cm (¾in) cinnamon stick
3 cloves
½ tsp red chilli flakes
3 garlic cloves, finely grated
2cm (¾in) piece of ginger,
   finely grated
1 green chilli,
   finely chopped
1 fresh tomato, diced
¼ tsp ground turmeric
½ tsp garam masala
1 tsp ground cumin
1 tsp ground coriander
Salt

Crispy chickpeas:
½ x 400g (14oz)
   tin chickpeas
2 tbsp vegetable oil
1 tsp Kashmiri
   chilli powder
½ tsp ground cumin
½ tsp salt

Dressing:
70ml olive oil
Juice of 1 lemon
2 garlic cloves, finely grated

To serve:
A bunch of fresh coriander
   (cilantro), chopped
Vegetables of your choice
   for dipping, such as
   steamed asparagus,
   radishes, cucumber,
   quartered Little Gem
   (Baby Bibb) lettuces,
   cherry tomatoes, spring
   onions (scallions), olives
Slices of sourdough bread
   brushed with olive oil

Aubergines are glorious when roasted over an open fire. The skins blacken and blister, leaving behind the most concentrated, smoky purée. This is actually a very traditional method of cooking in Punjab when making a simple baignan bharta, *aubergine curry. A tempering of spices are fried and added to the aubergine, which brings a soothing warmth. You can also roast the aubergines on your BBQ.*

This dip is great to have as a snack or starter before a meal. It's delicious served with spears of vegetables or on toasted bread.

Preheat your oven on the grill (broiler) function as high as it will go. Rub the aubergines with 1 tablespoon of the oil and place on a baking tray lined with foil. Place the aubergines under the grill. Allow to roast for 25 minutes. Turn the aubergines and return to the grill for another 25–30 minutes. By this time they will be completely burnt and very soft. Allow to cool before peeling the skin and scooping out the soft pulp. If there is still some excess water, just drain the flesh in a colander.

Put the remaining oil in a saucepan over a medium heat. When hot, add the whole spices and chilli flakes and let them sizzle in the hot oil for a minute to release their aroma. Add the garlic, ginger and green chilli to the pan and fry for a further 2–3 minutes. Add the fresh tomato and ground spices and cook for a further minute or so. As soon as the mixture becomes dry, add the aubergine pulp and cook for 2 more minutes. Remove from the heat, remove the whole spices and allow to cool. Season with plenty of salt.

Preheat your oven to 180°C fan/400°F/Gas 6.

Rinse the chickpeas with cold water and pat dry with kitchen paper. Line a roasting tin with baking parchment and add the chickpeas, oil, spices and salt then stir to coat. Bake for 15–20 minutes until golden, making sure to stir halfway through cooking. Allow to cool.

To serve, spread the aubergine onto a plate and sprinkle with the chickpeas and fresh coriander. Whisk together the dressing ingredients and spoon over the aubergine. Serve with the vegetables and bread for dipping.

MACKEREL RILLETTES

**SERVES 4
AS A STARTER**

2 fresh mackerel fillets,
 approx 150g (5½oz)
A splash of vegetable
 or sunflower oil
150g (5½oz) hot
 smoked mackerel
1 tbsp capers
4 cocktail gherkins
 or cornichons
50g (1¾oz/3½ tbsp)
 duck or goose fat
 (or melted butter)
50g (1¾oz/3½ tbsp)
 crème fraîche
50g (1¾oz/3½ tbsp)
 natural yoghurt
A small bunch of fresh
 coriander (cilantro),
 finely chopped
3 green finger chillies,
 finely chopped
1 tsp ground cumin
1 tsp coriander seeds,
 gently crushed
1 tsp garam masala
½ tsp ground black pepper
1 shallot, finely chopped
Zest of 1 lemon
100g (3½oz/7 tbsp)
 unsalted butter,
 for the top
Salt and pepper

To serve:
Buttered sourdough
 toast, to serve
Celeriac Remoulade
 (page 135), to serve

Rillettes is something you'll only really find in France. You may occasionally see the odd tub of it sold in posh British supermarkets, but it is rarely worth buying. The best rillettes are always from the specialist charcuterie shops who have perfected their craft. 'Daniel' in the beautiful Norman town of Villedieu-les-Poêles was the most memorable of these charcuteries I have ever visited.

Hot smoked mackerel makes remarkable rillettes because of its strong, oily flavour and fatty texture. It also really stands up to the robust flavours of the spice that I'm packing into this recipe. It makes a wonderful starter, best heaped onto toasted sourdough bread with some celeriac remoulade on the side.

Preheat your oven to 180°C fan/400°F/Gas 6.

Pat the fresh mackerel dry with some kitchen paper, then wrap it in a parcel of foil, adding a splash of oil and some salt and pepper. Bake at the top of the oven for 10 minutes, then remove and allow to cool. Once cool, flake both the fresh cooked and hot smoked mackerel into a bowl.

Finely chop the capers and cornichons and add them to the fish, along with all of the other ingredients, except the butter for the top. Mix well with the back of a fork, to break up the fish.

Divide the rillettes evenly amongst four ramekins and smooth the tops flat with the back of a spoon. Pour the melted butter over the top of each ramekin. Season with salt and pepper and refrigerate for a couple of hours. Serve with lots of buttered sourdough toast and celeriac remoulade.

CHICKEN 65 LOLLIPOPS WITH GARLIC-CHILLI DIPPING SAUCE

MAKES 12

12 chicken wings
Oil, for frying
Green tops of 2 spring
    onions (scallions),
    finely sliced, to garnish

Marinade:
1 tbsp Kashmiri
    chilli powder
1 tsp salt
½ tsp ground black pepper
½ tsp ground cumin
3 garlic cloves, finely grated
2cm (¾in) piece of ginger,
    finely grated
1 tbsp natural yoghurt
1 tbsp lemon juice
2 tbsp cornflour
    (cornstarch)
1 tbsp rice flour
    (if you can't find this,
    replace with extra
    cornflour/cornstarch)

Garlic-chilli dipping sauce:
1 tbsp vegetable or
    sunflower oil
3 garlic cloves,
    finely chopped
3 green finger
    chillies, sliced
2 sprigs fresh curry leaves
1 tbsp sweet chilli sauce
1 tbsp Sriracha hot sauce
1 tbsp ketchup
½ tsp ground black pepper

Chicken wings are the perfect finger food to enjoy with a couple of cold beers on a weekend afternoon – and the hotter they are, the more addictive they are! Chicken 65 (famously invented in 1965) is just the ticket: deep-fried chicken in a crisp spicy batter, laden with garlic and chilli from the South-Indian city of Chennai.

Remove the wings and tips from the chicken wings with a sharp knife, leaving behind the drumette. With a small knife, cut around the central bone at the bottom of each drumette, scraping the meat downwards and exposing the bone to form a lollipop. Repeat with the other chicken wings.

For the marinade, mix together all of the ingredients, except both types of flour. Add the chicken lollipops to the marinade, cover and leave in the fridge for 45 minutes. Remove the chicken from the fridge and mix in the corn- and rice flours.

To make the sauce, place a saucepan over a medium heat. When hot, add the oil and the garlic, green chillies and curry leaves. Fry for 2–3 minutes, until the garlic is lightly golden. Add the remaining ingredients, warm through and transfer to a small bowl.

Pour oil to a depth of 5–6cm (2–2½in) into a deep pan and heat it to 170°C (325°F). Be very careful and use a digital probe to monitor the temperature (or you can use a deep-fat fryer). When the oil is hot, add the chicken lollipops in batches and fry for 4–5 minutes until golden. Remove with a slotted spoon and transfer to a plate lined with kitchen paper to absorb any excess oil.

Serve scattered with the spring onions, with the sauce on the side.

KOLKATA SCOTCH DIMER DEVIL

**MAKES 4
SCOTCH EGGS**

4 medium whole eggs,
    plus two beaten
100g (3½oz/¾ cup) plain
    (all-purpose) flour
100g (3½oz/1 cup)
    panko breadcrumbs
Kasundi Mustard (page 66)
    or ketchup, to serve

Stuffing:
250g (9oz) minced
    (ground) lamb
    (10% fat is best)
¼ medium red onion,
    finely diced
1 tbsp ginger garlic paste
    made from finely grating
    2 garlic cloves and
    2cm piece of ginger
½ tsp ground turmeric
½ tsp dried mango
    powder (amchoor)
    or chaat masala
½ tsp ground cumin
½ tsp ground coriander
¾ tsp garam masala
1 tsp Kashmiri chilli
    powder
2 tbsp ketchup
1 tsp salt

The Scotch egg is a snack of distinction and loved by all. It is said to have been invented by Fortnum & Mason in 1738, as a luxurious travelling snack for the gentry to enjoy on long stagecoach journeys. There is an alternative story, however, which I much prefer. They say that it was actually a British adaption of the Indian Mughlai dish of nargisi kofta *– a boiled egg, wrapped in minced mutton and served in a pool of delicate and intricately spiced sauce. Kolkata has its own version known as the Dimer Devil. Just like our Scotch egg, it's a boiled egg wrapped in spiced minced goat meat, rolled in breadcrumbs and deep-fried. It must be one of the original fusion dishes! The current trend is to serve Scotch eggs with runny yolks, but I much prefer it the original way, with my eggs hard-boiled.*

Gently place the whole eggs in a small saucepan, cover with water and bring to the boil. Once boiling, turn the heat down to a simmer and cook for 7 minutes. Immediately remove the eggs from the water and plunge them into a bowl of cold water. When cold, gently tap the eggs on your work surface to crack the shells and peel. Rinse to remove any tiny bits of shell, then keep in the fridge.

To make the coating, mix all of the ingredients together with your hands and massage until thoroughly incorporated. Divide into four equal-sized balls. Flatten out a ball of the lamb mince in your hand and mould it around an egg so that it is completely enveloped in an even layer. Repeat to cover all the eggs.

Put the flour in one shallow bowl, the beaten eggs in another and the breadcrumbs in a third bowl. Roll each Dimer Devil first in the flour, dusting off any excess, then in the beaten egg mixture, making sure that it is completely coated. Drop the eggs into the breadcrumbs and roll around to cover completely.

Preheat your oven to 180°C fan/400°F/Gas 6. Pour oil to a depth of 5–6cm (2–2½in) into a deep pan and heat it to 180°C (350°F). Be very careful and use a digital probe to monitor the temperature (or you can use a deep-fat fryer). When the oil is hot, gently place two Dimer Devils in the pan and fry for 3–4 minutes, turning over halfway through cooking, until golden all over. Cook the remaining two eggs in the same way, then transfer them to a baking tray. Place the eggs in the preheated oven for 6 minutes to finish cooking through.

Allow to cool, then serve with the mustard, or plenty of ketchup!

GOAN VINDALOO PULLED PORK BUNS
WITH FENNEL & APPLE SLAW

SERVES 6–8

1 pork shoulder joint
   (about 1.25kg/2¾lb)
1 onion, finely sliced
300ml (10½fl oz/1¼ cups)
   chicken or pork stock
6–8 brioche burger buns

Spice rub:
2 tsp coriander seeds
1 tsp black peppercorns
4cm (1½in) cinnamon stick
6 cloves
1 star anise
1 tsp fennel seeds
1 tsp cumin seeds
2 tsp salt

Spice paste:
6 garlic cloves
3cm (1¼in) piece of ginger
20 dried red Kashmiri
   chillies, soaked in boiling
   water for 20 minutes
   (or 3 tbsp Kashmiri
   chilli powder)
125ml (4½fl oz/½ cup)
   cider vinegar or white
   wine vinegar
2 tbsp dark muscovado sugar

Slaw:
¼ white cabbage
½ fennel bulb
1 red onion
1 carrot
1 apple
3cm (1½in) piece of ginger
Juice and zest of 1 lemon
A bunch of fresh coriander
   (cilantro), chopped
3 tbsp Greek yoghurt
3 tbsp mayonnaise
1 tsp Dijon mustard

The king of Goan cuisine is the famous pork vindaloo. In the UK, eating it has become a sort of party trick which will leave you in a pool of sweat! But the British iteration bears no resemblance to the original dish – which was introduced to Goa by the Portuguese, who ruled this part of India for hundreds of years. Traditionally, vindaloo is an aromatic curry, not overly hot, made from a paste of vinegar, spices and dried red chillies. It is cooked with pork until vibrant in colour and acidic from vinegar. It is wonderful when marinated over a shoulder of pork and slow-cooked for hours. Served in a brioche bun with a slaw, this is perfect weekend family food.

Preheat your oven to 140°C fan/325°F/Gas 3.

To make the spice rub, place all the spices into a spice grinder and blitz to a fine powder, then mix in the salt. Pat the pork joint dry with some kitchen paper, then rub the spice mix all over it.

For the spice paste, add the ginger, garlic, soaked red chillies (or Kashmiri chilli powder), vinegar and sugar into a blender and blitz until smooth. Smear the paste all over the pork.

Add the sliced onion to a large ovenproof cast-iron pot with lid and place the pork joint on top. Pour in the stock, cover and cook in the middle of the oven for 3½ hours. Alternatively, if you have a barbecue with a smoker, you can cook the pork slowly in an uncovered roasting tin. Close the lid of the barbecue and cook for 3–4 hours, until the meat is falling apart.

While the meat is cooking, make the slaw. Very finely shred the cabbage, fennel and red onion using a mandoline, a sharp knife, or the slicing blade on a food processor. Use a coarse grater to grate the carrot, apple and ginger. Mix everything together in a large bowl and add the lemon juice and zest and chopped coriander.

In a separate bowl, combine the yoghurt, mayonnaise and mustard, and season with plenty of salt and pepper. Coat the shredded veg with the dressing. Keep covered in the fridge until ready to serve.

After 3½ hours of slow cooking, the meat should fall apart. With two forks, shred the meat, then mix it with the cooking juices. Toast the buns, fill with the pork and serve with slaw on the side.

GOAN-PORTUGUESE SEAFOOD RICE

SERVES 4

3 tbsp oil or ghee
1 medium onion,
    finely diced
700ml (24fl oz/3 cups)
    good-quality fish stock
    (see page 233)
1 tbsp tamarind paste
125ml (4fl oz/scant ½ cup)
    coconut milk
250g (9oz) paella rice
250g (9oz) monkfish fillets,
    cut into 4 pieces
8 whole tiger prawns
300g (10½oz) mussels
    and/or clams, cleaned
    and rinsed in a bowl of
    cold water, or under a
    running tap to remove
    any grit
Lemon wedges, to serve
Chopped coriander
    (cilantro), to serve

Spice paste:
100g (3½oz) grated fresh
    coconut, or 50g (1¾oz)
    desiccated (dried
    shredded) coconut
5 cloves
3cm (1¼in) cinnamon
    stick
3 garlic cloves, finely grated
2cm (¾in) piece of ginger,
    finely grated
2 tbsp tomato purée (paste)
2 green finger chillies,
    finely chopped
1 tbsp Kashmiri chilli
    powder
1 tsp ground cumin
1 tsp ground coriander
½ tsp ground black pepper
1 tsp ground turmeric

Spain has its paella and Portugal has the lesser-known 'Arroz de Marisco'. I always support the underdog – it's much more fun that way – so I'm with Portugal on this one.

Goa and Portugal have much history in common. The Portuguese ruled this tiny coastal region for hundreds of years. Consequently, the Portuguese had a great influence on the food of Goa, and wider India. Before the Portuguese arrived, chillies didn't exist in India and now we know India as the land of chilli! As a chef of Goan-Portuguese diplomacy, I've created an Indo-Portuguese seafood rice. I'm using the classic Goan fish curry, Xec Xec – made from a paste of coconut, red chillies, tomato and tamarind – as a medium for simmering the rice, which will soak up all of these Goan flavours.

For the spice paste, warm a dry frying pan over a medium heat. Add the coconut and toast until lightly golden. Tip it into the jug of a blender, add the remaining spice paste ingredients and 100ml (3½fl oz/scant ½ cup) of water. Blend to a smooth paste.

Place a large, deep pan over a medium heat. When hot, add the oil or ghee. Add the onion and fry for 10–15 minutes, or until golden. Add the spice paste and cook for 5–6 minutes, until almost dry.

Add the fish stock to the pan along with the tamarind paste and coconut milk. Bring to a gentle simmer, add the rice and then cook for 15 minutes, stirring from time to time.

Add the fish and seafood to the pot and simmer gently with the lid on for a final 10 minutes – making sure that the clams and/or mussels have opened fully before removing from the heat. Discard any clams or mussels that haven't opened. The rice should be perfectly cooked and there should still be a good amount of unabsorbed broth.

Place the pan in the centre of the table and decorate with lemon wedges and some freshly chopped coriander.

MANIPURCHETTA WITH APPLE CHUTNEY

SERVES 6–8

1 tbsp fennel seeds
1 tbsp cumin seeds
2 tsp red chilli flakes
2–2.5kg (4½–5½lb) piece of belly pork, with the skin on, boneless (tell your butcher that you are planning on rolling it)
10 green finger chillies, finely sliced
30g (1oz) fresh coriander (cilantro), finely chopped
4cm (1½in) piece of ginger, finely grated
10 garlic cloves, finely grated
Zest of 2 limes
2 fennel bulbs
2 medium onions
250ml (9fl oz/1 cup) white wine
Salt and pepper
Roast potatoes, to serve

Apple chutney:
1 tbsp ghee or oil
½ tsp cumin seeds
½ tsp ajwain seeds
½ tsp fennel seeds
2cm (¾in) cinnamon stick
2 shallots, finely sliced
2cm (¾in) piece of ginger, finely grated
2 Granny Smith apples, peeled, cored and cut into 7mm (⅜in) dice
60g (2oz/heaped ¼ cup) granulated sugar
1 green chilli, slit in half
¼ tsp ground turmeric
2 tbsp vinegar

There was always turkey or goose on the menu for Christmas dinner in our house, until I tasted a proper porchetta, or porceddu. *The dish is usually associated with Tuscany, but it is also a delicacy of the beautiful island of Sardinia. Traditionally, its preparation is a very communal affair; the inhabitants of a village will celebrate spit roasting a pig, which is carefully cooked over a fire made from aromatic myrtle wood, bay leaves and rosemary. There's lots of singing and jubilance, as well as quaffing of the local wine. It's just a brilliant excuse for an exuberant Italian party, where you'll spend at least 7 hours eating around a long table. I was staying in a wonderful eco-tourism resort up in the hills in a very remote part of the island, when I enjoyed this traditional banquet. The pork, so simply cooked with oil, garlic, herbs and olive oil, with a generous amount of salt, was the best I can ever remember. I always say that the best food is created when you take the best ingredients and let them shine – which was so true of this feast.*

If you travel to the north eastern states of India, you will find a cuisine which is very similar to that found in Italy. The people in this region rely on the pure, unadulterated flavours of the ingredients which grow around them – which include the famous Naga chillies, some of the hottest in the world! Unlike other cuisines of India, which use lots of complex spice powders, the food here is more straightforward and you'll taste the ingredients in their truest form. The region of Manipur is famous for its pork dishes, which use belly pork, often cooked with a combination of nothing more than ginger, garlic, green chillies and fresh coriander. This is a great combination of ingredients for a slow-cooked Indian Manipur-Porchetta. The 'Manipurchetta' has a ring to it, I hope you'll agree. You saw it here first.

This recipe makes a great pork Sunday roast. It isn't very labour-intensive, but make sure that you tie the belly pork up, either a day or two in advance, so that the pork skin has time to dry out and crisp up properly when cooked.

In a spice or coffee grinder, blitz the fennel seeds, cumin seeds and chilli flakes to a fine powder.

Pat the pork skin dry with some kitchen paper and, with a sharp knife, prick the skin all over. Season the skin and flesh with a generous amount of salt and pepper.

Turn the belly over, so it's skin side down. Rub the meat with the spice powder and cover with the sliced green chillies, chopped coriander, ginger, garlic and lime zest. Roll up the belly from the longest side, to form a tight giant stuffed sausage. Tie very tightly at 3–4cm (1¼–1½in) intervals with butcher's string and place on a baking tray. Leave in the fridge, uncovered, for 24–48 hours – this will dry the skin out and help to produce some lovely crackling.

The next day, preheat the oven to 200°C fan/425°F/Gas 7. Cut the fennel bulbs and onions in half and place in the bottom of a roasting tin. Place the porchetta on top of the vegetables, so they act like a trivet. Roast in the middle of the oven for 30 minutes.

After 30 minutes, reduce the oven temperature to 150°C fan/337°F/Gas 3. Pour the white wine into the roasting tin and continue to cook for 4 hours. Add a splash of water to the tin every hour or so, if it dries out.

To make the apple chutney, place a saucepan over a medium heat. When hot, add the ghee or oil and the whole spices. Allow them to sizzle in the hot oil for 30 seconds, to release their aroma. Add the shallots and ginger and cook for 4 minutes, until softened. Add the remaining ingredients along with 150ml (5fl oz/scant ⅔ cup) water. Cook for 25–30 minutes, stirring every few minutes, until the apples are soft and you are left with a thick chutney. You can crush the apples against the side of the pan a little. If the pan starts to dry out, simply add a splash of water. Season with salt and transfer to a serving bowl. Allow to cool.

Remove the porchetta from the oven and allow to rest for at least 2 hours, before carving into thin slices.

To serve, place a couple of thin slices of porchetta onto a plate with some of the roasted fennel and onions. Serve with the roasting juices from the tin, apple chutney and some perfect roast potatoes.

SALMON CAFREAL COULIBIAC

SERVES 6

A large side of salmon (about
    1–1.5kg/2lb 4oz–3lb 5oz),
    skin removed
1 sheet ready-rolled,
    all-butter puff pastry
1 x 500g (1lb 2oz) block
    all-butter puff pastry
Plain (all-purpose) flour,
    for dusting
1 egg yolk mixed with
    1 tbsp of whole milk,
    for the egg wash
Salt and pepper

Stuffing:
3 tbsp vegetable oil
2 medium red onions,
    finely diced
2cm (¾in) piece of
    ginger, finely grated
3 garlic cloves, finely grated
1 x 250g (9oz) pouch of
    precooked basmati rice
3 green finger chillies,
    finely chopped
Zest of 1 lemon, finely grated
3 hard-boiled eggs, (cooked
    in boiling water for 10
    minutes and chilled in
    cold water)
A bunch of fresh
    coriander (cilantro)

Sauce:
1 tsp coriander seeds
½ tsp fennel seeds
½ tsp cumin seeds
½ tsp black peppercorns
2 cloves
3 green finger chillies
30g (1oz) fresh coriander
    (cilantro), stalks and all,
3 garlic cloves
2cm (¾in) piece of ginger
1 tbsp brown sugar
Juice of 1 lime
2 tbsp white wine vinegar
A pinch of salt
50ml (1¾fl oz/3½ tbsp)
    double (heavy) cream

This is a dish with real wow-factor. My dad would often make a salmon coulibiac, stuffed with fresh herby flavours. I've added a Goan Cafreal sauce – a vibrant sauce of spices blended with vinegar, coriander and green chillies. It sure packs a punch and cuts through the buttery pastry brilliantly with a chilled glass of Riesling.

To make the stuffing, heat the oil in a frying pan over a medium heat. When hot, add the onions and sauté for 10–15 minutes, until softened and golden brown. Add the ginger and garlic and cook for a further 2–3 minutes, then transfer to a bowl and allow to cool. When cool, stir in the basmati rice, green chillies and lemon zest. Mix thoroughly and set aside. Finely chop the boiled eggs and fresh coriander and combine in a bowl.

Cut the side of salmon in half, into two equal pieces. Unroll the pastry sheet onto the baking sheet. Spread one-third of the rice mixture onto the pastry, roughly the same size as the pieces of salmon. Place one piece of salmon onto the rice and season with salt and pepper. Cover with another third of the rice and all of the coriander and egg. Place the second piece of salmon on top, season with salt and pepper and cover with the remaining rice.

Dust the block of puff pastry in flour and roll out to a thickness of around 5mm (¼in) so that you have a rectangle large enough to cover the fish completely. Place the pastry over the top and seal well with the edge of the pastry base. Trim the excess pastry with a knife and crimp the edges. Place into the fridge for 30 minutes.

Preheat the oven to 180°C fan/400°F/Gas 6 and line a baking sheet with baking parchment.

After 20 minutes, brush the pastry with egg wash and score the top lightly with a sharp knife in a criss-cross pattern, making sure not to score right through the pastry. Place into the centre of the preheated oven and bake for 35–40 minutes, until golden.

For the sauce, blitz the whole spices in a spice grinder until you have a fine powder. Add the spice powder to the other sauce ingredients, except the cream, and 3 tablespoons water in a blender and blitz until smooth. Add the sauce to a pan and cook over a medium-low heat with the lid on for 20 minutes. Finish the sauce by stirring through the cream. Keep warm.

Carve the coulibiac into generous slices and serve with the sauce.

MURG MUSALLAM WITH GHEE RICE

SERVES 4

2 poussins (French hens)
   or a 1.5kg (3lb 5oz)
   chicken
½ tsp saffron
1 tbsp kewra water
   (or rosewater)
2 tsp Kashmiri
   chilli powder
60g (2oz) blanched
   almonds, chopped
10g (⅓oz) white poppy
   seeds (optional)
2cm (¾in) piece of ginger
3 garlic cloves
40g (1½oz) shop-bought
   crispy fried onions
1 tsp salt
200g (7oz) Greek yoghurt
2 eggs, hard-boiled for
   8 minutes and peeled
4 tbsp ghee
A handful of coriander
   (cilantro), chopped,
   to serve

Masala:
6 cloves
8 green cardamom pods
1 tsp cumin seeds
2 black cardamom pods
½ nutmeg

Rice:
4 green cardamom pods
4 cloves
2cm (¾in) cinnamon stick
1 bay leaf
400g (14oz/2¼ cups)
   basmati rice
3½ tbsp ghee
A large pinch of saffron
   mixed with 5 tbsp whole
   milk (allow to steep for
   2 hours in the fridge)

Everyone looks forward to a roasted chicken at the weekend – so you may as well serve the one enjoyed by Moghul royalty!

Firstly, remove the skin from the poussins or chicken: start at the top of the bird and peel the skin off the breast, then work your way down to each leg. The skin will then pull off each drumstick; have a little knife on hand to cut any sinews. Grind the saffron in a mortar and pestle and add to the kewra or rosewater. Rub this all over the birds, then chill while you prepare the other ingredients.

To make the masala, grind all the spices together in a coffee or spice grinder to a fine powder. Add the masala to the bowl of a food processor, along with the chilli powder, half the almonds, the poppy seeds (if using), ginger, garlic, crispy onions, salt, yoghurt and 5 tablespoons water and process to make a smooth paste.

Smear the birds with all of the yoghurt paste and place a boiled egg in the cavity of each poussin or both inside the chicken. Allow to marinate for around 30–40 minutes at room temperature.

Warm a large cast-iron pot with a lid (large enough to hold the poussins or chicken) over a medium–high heat. When hot, add the ghee and the bird(s). If there is any remaining marinade, pour this over the top. Tilt the pan and baste the ghee over the top of the chicken or poussins. Cover, turn the heat down to medium and cook for 20–25 minutes if using poussin and 50 minutes–1 hour for a chicken.

Whilst the birds are cooking, prepare the rice. Bring a large pot of water to the boil with a tablespoon of salt and the green cardamom, cloves, cinnamon stick and bay leaf. Once boiling, add the rice and cook for 5 minutes, until al dente. Strain the rice and spices in a colander, then tip into a saucepan with a lid in an even layer. Sprinkle the rice with the ghee and saffron-infused milk. Cover and cook over a low heat for 20 minutes.

When the poussin or chicken is cooked, remove the lid, baste over more of the ghee and juices and allow to rest in the warm pot.

Allow the rice to rest for 5 minutes, before spooning it onto a serving platter. Garnish with the fresh coriander. Sit the birds on the bed of rice, garnish with the remaining chopped almonds and serve with the sauce of cooking juices on the side.

LAMB ROGAN CHOPS

SERVES 6

2 best end racks of lamb,
 French trimmed
2 tbsp oil
Salt and pepper
Gratin Aloo Boulangère
 (page 179), to serve

Rogan josh sauce:
500g–800g (1lb 2oz–1¾lb)
 lamb bones
150ml (5fl oz/scant ⅔ cup)
 vegetable or sunflower
 oil, plus a drizzle for
 the lamb
2 medium red onions,
 finely sliced
1 tsp Kashmiri chilli
 powder
8 garlic cloves
5 dried Kashmiri chillies,
 soaked in 150ml (5fl oz/
 scant ⅔ cup) boiling
 water for 20 minutes
80g (2¾oz/5½ tbsp) ghee
6 green cardamom pods
2 black cardamom pods
4cm (1½in) cinnamon
 stick
4 cloves
125g (4½oz/½ cup)
 natural full-fat yoghurt
2 tsp ground ginger
A pinch of saffron
1 tsp salt
½ tsp green cardamom
 powder (made from
 finely grinding 4 green
 cardamom pods in a
 mortar and pestle)

Lamb rogan josh is a staple on most British-Indian restaurant menus, but you'll rarely taste a version which is authentic as they all contain tomatoes. Here is my (tomato-less) take on this classic.

....

Preheat your oven to 180°C fan/400°F/Gas 6. Place the lamb bones in a large roasting tin, drizzle with oil and roast in the oven for 45 minutes until well browned.

Heat the 150ml oil in a pan. When hot, add the onions and fry for 10–15 minutes, until golden brown, stirring occasionally. With a slotted spoon, remove them from the oil and drain on a plate lined with kitchen paper. When the onions have cooled, add them to a blender with the chilli powder, garlic and the dried Kashmiri chillies along with their soaking water. Blend to a smooth purée.

Place a large deep pan over a medium heat. When hot, add the ghee and the whole spices and sizzle for 30 seconds. Add the onion and chilli paste and fry well for 6–8 minutes. Add the lamb bones to the pan with the yoghurt, ginger, saffron and salt. Top up with enough water to cover, give the pot a good stir and bring to a simmer. Cover with a lid and cook gently for 2 hours.

After 2 hours, remove and discard the lamb bones. Cook the sauce, uncovered, allowing it to reduce over a medium heat until you have a nice sauce consistency, but not too thick. Finish with the green cardamom powder. Check the seasoning for salt and keep warm.

Reheat the oven to 180°C fan/400°F/Gas 6, and place a large frying pan over a medium–high heat. Season the lamb racks all over with salt and pepper. When the pan is hot, add the oil and place the lamb, fat side down, into the pan. Fry for 6–8 minutes, on the skin side, to render the fat until golden. Turn the lamb over and brown on all remaining sides for 2 minutes per side, not forgetting the ends.

Place the lamb on a rack suspended over a baking tray and roast in the oven for 12–15 minutes. A digital thermometer is useful to check the cooking: push it into the centre of the lamb and take a reading. As a guide: 57°C (135°F) is medium rare, 62°C (144°F) is medium, and 70°C (158°F) is well done. Once cooked to your liking, remove` from the oven and allow to rest for 8 minutes.

To serve, place the sauce onto a serving platter. Carve the racks of lamb, between each bone and arrange over the sauce. Serve with my Gratin Aloo Boulangère (on page 179).

ASLAM'S BUTTER FISH

SERVES 6

6 thick steaks or
   darnes of halibut
150g (5½oz/scant ⅔ cup)
   unsalted butter
1 tbsp chaat masala

Marinade:
150g (5½oz/scant ⅔ cup)
   Greek yoghurt
1 tbsp vegetable or
   sunflower oil
2 tsp Kashmiri chilli
   powder
1 tsp garam masala
¾ tsp salt
Juice of 1 lemon
3 garlic cloves, finely grated
2cm (¾in) piece of ginger,
   finely grated
2 tsp dried fenugreek
   leaves (kasoori methi)

Yoghurt cream sauce:
125g (4½oz/½ cup)
   natural full-fat yoghurt
50g (1¾oz/3½ tbsp)
   double (heavy) cream
Zest of 1 lemon
½ tsp ground white pepper

To serve (optional):
Boiled new potatoes
Asparagus
Courgettes (zucchini)
A squeeze of lemon juice

This dish is perfect for a summer barbecue and works brilliantly with thick-cut steaks of meaty fish with the bone in. Turbot or halibut work well, as does monkfish tail. Whole Dover or lemon sole, with the skin removed can also be used – just ask your fishmonger to remove the skin. If you don't fancy making this recipe with fish, you can even use chicken thighs and drumsticks or a whole spatchcocked chicken. Just make sure that after barbecuing the chicken you put it through a hot oven for 10 minutes or so, to ensure that it is thoroughly cooked through.

Combine all the marinade ingredients in a shallow dish wide enough to hold the fish. Add the fish and coat thoroughly in the marinade. Cover and place in the fridge for 1 hour.

For the sauce, mix together the yoghurt, cream, lemon zest and white pepper. Keep in a bowl at room temperature.

Light your barbecue – a charcoal one always gives the best flavour. When it has come up to temperature, making sure it's not too hot, you can start to grill the fish. I like to put the fish inside grill cages, which protects the fish when turning and reduces the risk of it breaking. Place the fish onto the coals and cook on each side for around 4 minutes, until nicely charred.

You can also use the grill (broiler) function of your oven preheated to its highest setting. Place the fish onto a cooking rack suspended over the grill pan and grill for 4–5 minutes on each side, until nicely charred.

Place the butter in a pan and melt, until hot.

When the fish is ready, transfer it to a warm serving dish, season generously with chaat masala, then cover with the yoghurt cream sauce. Season with yet more chaat masala – be really generous – then finish by drizzling over all the butter, hot and melted straight from the pan.

Serve with boiled new potatoes, which you can char on the barbecue, along with some asparagus or courgettes, finished with lemon juice.

PUDUCHERRY BOUILLABAISSE

SERVES 4

4 tbsp olive oil
2 bay leaves
10 black peppercorns
1 star anise
1 tsp fennel seeds
1 tsp cumin seeds
4 green cardamom
pods, crushed
1 tsp red chilli flakes
1 piece of orange peel
4 shallots, finely sliced
1 fennel bulb,
finely chopped
6 garlic cloves, crushed
3cm (1¼in) piece of
ginger, grated
A bunch of coriander
(cilantro) stalks,
finely chopped
2 green finger chillies,
halved
4 large whole tiger prawns
(shrimp), heads removed
but reserved
4 fresh tomatoes,
finely chopped
1 tbsp tomato purée (paste)
2 tsp Kashmiri chilli
powder
1 tsp ground turmeric
150ml (5fl oz/scant ⅔ cup)
white wine
750ml (26fl oz/3¼ cups)
good-quality fish stock
(see page 233)
A pinch of saffron
4 white fish fillets
(eg. halibut, cod, turbot,
sea bass, sea bream, red
mullet), skin removed,
each weighing around
100g (3½oz)
300g (10½oz) mussels
or clams
4 thin slices sourdough
bread or 8 slices
baguette, toasted,
to serve

The French colonised Pondicherry, now Puducherry, on the east coast of India – a rule which lasted for 280 years. Pondicherry was known as the 'Riviera of the East' – rich in fish and seafood. The French brought their classic dishes with them to Pondicherry and used whatever ingredients they could find in India. Even today you'll see bouillabaisse on the menu of many restaurants in this city, but with a spicy Indian twist. It's such a fascinating history! You can use whatever seafood and fish you like for this recipe and I think that it's nice to have two types of fish – red mullet or brill work very well – with some langoustines and a handful of mussels or clams, but the choice is yours!

Warm your largest heavy-based saucepan over a medium heat. When hot, add the olive oil, bay leaves, peppercorns, star anise, fennel and cumin seeds, cardamom pods, chilli flakes and orange peel. Allow the spices to sizzle in the hot oil for 30 seconds, to release their aroma.

Add the shallots, fennel, garlic, ginger, coriander stalks, green chillies and the reserved prawn heads and fry for 10–15 minutes, until lightly golden. Add the fresh tomatoes, tomato purée, chilli powder and turmeric and cook for a further 3–4 minutes. When the mixture is starting to look a little dry, add the white wine, fish stock and saffron. Bring to a boil, then reduce the heat so the soup is at a gentle simmer. Simmer for 30–45 minutes – this really intensifies the flavour.

While the soup is simmering, make the rouille. To the bowl of a mini food processor, add the egg yolk, garlic, bread, lemon juice, saffron, chilli powder and salt. Blend to a smooth paste. You can also do this by pounding all of the ingredients together in a mortar and pestle. With the machine running, slowly drizzle in the olive and rapeseed oils to make a thick mayonnaise-like rouille. If using the mortar and pestle, slowly drizzle in the oil whilst mixing with the pestle to emulsify. Avoid adding the oil too quickly, as this will cause the rouille to split. Keep aside in a small dish.

To make the fennel pickle, very finely shred the fennel using a mandoline or sharp knife. Mix together the other ingredients and pour over the fennel. Allow to macerate until ready to serve.

Recipe continued overleaf

Rouille:
1 egg yolk
2 garlic cloves, peeled
½ slice sourdough
Juice of ½ lemon
A pinch of saffron
1 tsp Kashmiri
    chilli powder
A pinch of salt
75ml (2½fl oz/5 tbsp)
    olive oil
75ml (2½fl oz/5 tbsp)
    rapeseed (canola) oil

Fennel pickle:
1 fennel bulb
Juice of ½ orange
1 tsp chilli flakes
1 tsp fennel seeds
50ml (1¾fl oz/3½ tbsp)
    Pernod
50ml (1¾fl oz/3½ tbsp)
    white wine vinegar
1½ tbsp olive oil
½ tsp salt
1 tsp sugar

After the soup has simmered, remove as many whole spices as you can find. Blend until smooth – you may have to do this in batches. Pour the blended soup through a sieve, pushing through as much liquid as you can with the back of a spoon. Discard whatever pulp is left behind in the sieve and pour the strained soup into a wide pan. Bring the soup to a gentle simmer for around 25 minutes. After this time, the soup should be a lovely rusty brown colour.

Add the prawns, fish fillets and mussels or clams to the soup and poach gently for about 8 minutes, making sure that the mussels and clams have opened; discard any shellfish that haven't opened.

To serve, drain the fennel and place a spoonful into the centre of four wide bowls. Fill each bowl with soup, dividing the fish, prawns and mussels or clams evenly between the bowls. Spread the toasted bread with a generous amount of rouille and serve.

DUCK & FENNEL CASSOULET

SERVES 4

4 duck legs
4 tbsp duck fat or
    vegetable oil
3 green cardamom pods,
    lightly crushed
1 black cardamom pod,
    lightly crushed
10 black peppercorns
4 cloves
1 bay leaf
2 tsp cumin seeds
1 medium onion, diced
1 small fennel bulb,
    core removed and
    thinly sliced
100g (3½oz) smoked
    bacon or pancetta
2cm (¾in) piece of
    ginger, finely grated
3 garlic cloves, finely grated
2 x 400g (14oz) tins beans
    (flageolet, cannellini
    or haricot beans –
    whichever you prefer),
    drained and rinsed
1 tsp dried thyme
1 tsp ground coriander
2 green finger chillies,
    slit in half
1 tsp garam masala
Zest of 1 lemon
500ml (17fl oz/2 cups)
    chicken stock
Salt and pepper

Cassoulet is one of the most famous dishes of south-west France. It is a delicious rustic bean stew which is simmered for hours in an earthenware pot, with a gutsy helping of the region's famous duck fat to help it along. Toulouse sausage, smoked bacon and confit duck are some of the ingredients which complete this venerable ensemble! There is a great history of preserving for the less bountiful winter months and you'll find jars and tins filled with an assortment of duck products all over this part of France, from tongues, to hearts, gizzards, duck legs and foie gras – you name it, they sell it!

    I'm not going down the traditional route with this recipe – I've added fennel and some aromatic spices, which I think really complement the duck legs and the beans.

Preheat the oven to 160°C fan/350°F/Gas 4. Place the duck legs in a roasting tin, prick the skin all over with a fork and season with salt. Roast in the oven for 1 hour.

While the duck legs are roasting, warm a large, deep pan over a medium–high heat. Add the duck fat and the whole spices. Allow the spices to sizzle in the hot oil for a minute to release their aroma. Add the onion, fennel and bacon to the pot. Fry for around 15 minutes, until golden. Add the ginger and garlic and cook for another 2 minutes. Add a splash of water if it begins to catch.

Stir in all the remaining ingredients and season with salt and pepper. Transfer to a ceramic baking dish and place into the centre of the oven for 1 hour.

Remove the duck legs from the oven, pour the rendered duck fat into a bowl (this can be used again for cooking) and allow the legs to rest for 15 minutes, by which time, your beans should be ready.

To serve, spoon some beans into a bowl and top with a duck leg.

GRANDMA TANDOORI PIZZA

**MAKES 2 LARGE
PIZZAS, SERVES 4**

Dough:
5g (⅛oz) instant dried yeast
540ml (18¾fl oz/2⅓ cups)
  lukewarm water
1 tbsp olive oil, plus extra
  for greasing
8g (¼oz/2 tsp) sugar
830g (1lb 13oz/6¼ cups)
  '00' flour, or strong
  white bread flour
22g (¾oz/4 tsp) salt

Chicken or paneer tikka:
150g (5½oz/scant ⅔ cup)
  Greek yoghurt
1 tbsp oil
½ tsp ground turmeric
2 tsp dried fenugreek leaves
  (kasoori methi)
1 tsp garam masala
2 heaped tsp Kashmiri
  chilli powder
1 tsp salt
Juice of ½ lemon
400g (14oz) chicken thigh
  fillets or paneer, cut into
  2cm (¾in) cubes

Makhani tomato sauce:
30g (1oz/2 tbsp) unsalted
  butter
3 green cardamom pods,
  crushed
3 cloves
2cm (¾in) cinnamon stick
4 garlic cloves, finely grated
2cm (¾in) piece of ginger,
  finely grated
3 green chillies, halved
2 x 400g (14oz) tins good-
  quality plum tomatoes
  (San Marzano are best)
1 tbsp Kashmiri chilli powder
1 tsp garam masala
1 tsp sugar
1 tsp salt

'Grandma' is a style of pizza that you'll find all over New York. It's different to that quintessential thin and round New York slice you might think of – the Grandma Pie is a large rectangular pizza, baked in a metal tray, which gives the crust a nice crisp base. It was invented by Italian-American grandmas, who would make this style of pizza at home and therefore it has the benefit of being very easy for the home cook to replicate, needing of a powerful pizza oven. Another unique trait of this pizza is that the cheese is spread onto the dough, before the tomato sauce – I love how the cheese soaks into the dough! I'm topping my Grandma Pie with some classic Desi pizza toppings: Makhani tomato sauce, peppers, onions and chicken or paneer tikka.

The recipe makes two large pizzas which are baked in large trays. Make the dough at least 24 hours in advance – 48 is actually better. The dough proves slowly in the fridge, which gives a great complexity of flavour and texture and makes it easier to handle. You can use '00' flour from the supermarket or strong white bread flour. For best results, look online for a good-quality high-protein pizza flour.

To make the dough, mix together the yeast, water, olive oil and sugar and leave for 5 minutes. Add the flour and salt to the bowl of a stand mixer fitted with the dough hook. Pour the yeast water into the bowl and knead for 10 minutes on a medium speed. You can also knead this by hand. It will start off quite sticky, but don't be tempted to add more flour – it will become less sticky when it has been kneaded properly. Divide the dough into two pieces. Tightly shape each piece into a ball and place in a wide shallow pasta bowl which has been lightly greased with olive oil. Grease the tops of the dough with a bit more oil and cover tightly with cling film (plastic wrap). Place into the fridge to prove slowly for 24–72 hours.

To make the chicken or paneer tikka, mix together the ingredients for the marinade, then add the chicken or paneer. Marinate for 1–24 hours. The chicken or paneer can be cooked a day in advance. Preheat the grill (broiler) function of your oven to 250°C (480°F). If using paneer, thread the paneer cubes onto skewers, leaving a gap between each cube. Line the bottom of a grill tray with kitchen foil and place the chicken thighs or paneer skewers on a rack suspended over the tray. Space everything out nicely and place

Toppings:
600g (1lb 5oz) mozzarella
    (Galbani Cucina is best),
    cut into 3mm (⅛in) slices
1 red onion, sliced
½ green pepper, seeds
    removed and cut into
    1cm (½in) slices
½ red (bell) pepper, seeds
    removed and cut into
    1cm (½in) slices
Chilli flakes, for sprinkling

Garnish:
2 tbsp fresh coriander
    (cilantro), finely chopped
70g (2½oz) pecorino
    cheese, grated
1 recipe quantity Mint
    and Coriander Chutney
    (page 232)
75g (2½oz/5 tbsp)
    mayonnaise

under the hot grill. Grill for 4–6 minutes on each side, until lightly charred and sizzling. Allow to cool, before cutting the chicken into bite-sized chunks. Cover and refrigerate.

To make the Makhani sauce, melt the butter in a large pan over a medium heat. Add the whole spices and allow them to sizzle in the butter for 30 seconds, to release their aroma. Add the garlic, ginger and green chillies. Fry for 2–3 minutes until lightly golden, then add the remaining sauce ingredients and cook over a medium heat, uncovered for 30 minutes. Purée with a stick blender. Allow to cool and refrigerate.

When you're ready to bake the pizza, preheat your oven to 220°C fan/475°F/Gas 9 and grease a 30 x 40cm (12 x 16in) baking tray with 3 tablespoons of olive oil.

Remove one of the dough balls from the fridge and gently transfer it from the bowl into the tray. With your hands, gently push the dough outwards and stretch it to cover the base of the tray. You won't be able to do this in one go. Cover with cling film and leave to rest for 30 minutes. After resting, you should be able to stretch the dough right into the corners. If the dough still doesn't stretch completely, cover with cling film again, and leave for 20 minutes.

Completely cover the dough with a layer of cheese slices (using roughly half the cheese), leaving a 5mm (¼in) border around the edge. Spread the Makhani sauce across the pizza in diagonal lines. Scatter with half the chicken or paneer pieces and slices of red onion and peppers then sprinkle with some chilli flakes.

Bake for 10 minutes, then turn the tray around and bake for a further 10–15 minutes. Check underneath the pizza after this time – it should be golden and slightly caramelised and the top nicely golden. Place onto a large wooden board, garnish with fresh coriander and a handful of grated pecorino. Cut into eight slices.

Allow the tray to cool before making the next pizza.

Combine the chutney with the mayonnaise and serve this on the side of the pizzas.

BIRYANI

If there's one dish in the world that I love, it's biryani. After my first taste of the real, authentic Hyderabadi biryani in India, I knew immediately that I had never tasted anything so complex or exquisite. I was blown away by the intense waft of saffron perfume and the deep nutty aroma of fried onions rising from the pot. Digging to the depths of the biryani, through the seemingly endless layers of moist saffron-stained rice, to find succulent chunks of lamb, falling apart and perfectly glazed with aromatic sticky masala, I could have gorged for days. Imagine what a life it must have been for the Mughals, who would have extravagantly feasted on exquisitely-made dishes like this every day. It was the most spectacular meal I can remember. The aromatic blend of spices was so subtle, yet at the same time it had such an addictive punch. I have never experienced food like it – food cooked with such evident know-how. Forget the pomp of Michelin; this is where food is really at! The ancient royal Hyderabadi, Awadhi and Mughlai cuisines are famed for their biryanis and melt-in-the-mouth kebabs. The pride of these cuisines is built on the fine balancing act of blending complex aromatic spices with luxurious ingredients such as ghee, fried onions, nut pastes and perfumed essences – all of which create an extraordinary myriad of flavours and textures. The processes and ancient techniques that were employed by these royal chefs were as sophisticated as those used by any Michelin-starred restaurant to this day. The ancient art of dum pukht *or slow cooking was commonly used. It translates to 'breath cooking'. A dish would be cooked in a dough-sealed pot very slowly over a gentle fire. The sealing of the pot means that no flavour escapes and the food cooks deliciously in its own steam. Discovering the captivating magic of these ancient royal techniques made me want to learn how to master this art form and recreate my biryani moment!*

EDDIE'S HYDERABADI LAMB BIRYANI

**SERVES 4
GENEROUSLY**

500g (1lb 2oz) diced lamb,
   or lamb chops, cut into
   3 pieces
1 tsp salt
4 green cardamom pods,
   gently crushed
2cm (¾in) cinnamon
   stick, crushed
1 tsp caraway seeds
6 cloves
1 tbsp Kashmiri chilli
   powder
1 heaped tsp garam masala
½ tsp green cardamom
   powder, made from
   grinding the seeds of
   4 green cardamom pods
½ tsp ground turmeric
2cm (¾in) piece of
   ginger, peeled
3 garlic cloves
4 green finger chillies
Juice of ½ lime
160g (5¾oz/⅔ cup)
   full-fat natural yoghurt
15g (½oz) mint leaves,
   finely chopped
15g (½oz) coriander
   (cilantro), finely chopped
100g (3½oz/7 tbsp) ghee
60g (2oz) crispy fried
   onions
A large pinch of saffron
2 tsp rosewater
90ml (3fl oz/6 tbsp)
   warm milk

Raita:
6 garlic cloves, peeled
A splash of oil
400g (14oz/1¾ cups)
   natural full-fat yoghurt
½ tsp salt
½ tsp Kashmiri chilli
   powder
½ tsp ground cumin

Here is an easy-to replicate version of my famous Hyderabadi lamb biryani! Many people often tell me how time-consuming a biryani can be to make. But the Hyderabadi version really isn't. Once you've done your prep and mixed together all the ingredients, there's actually very little cooking to be done. You can get ahead of the game by marinating the lamb in the fridge the day before and all that will be left to do is boil some rice and cook the biryani! But, equally you'll still have a delicious biryani if you make it on the same day. The crispy onions can be bought from a supermarket – they come in little plastic tubs and are very handy. You can make your own: finely slice a medium red onion and deep-fry in vegetable oil over a medium heat until golden and crisp. Allow them to cool on kitchen paper and sprinkle them into the marinade. I'm serving the biryani with a Hyderabadi Burani raita, which is the traditional accompaniment. This raita is flavoured with red chilli powder, cumin and garlic, rather than the usual cucumber people might be more accustomed to.

Preheat your oven to 180°C fan/400°F/Gas 6. Place a heavy baking sheet, pizza stone or steel inside the oven to heat up.

In a large bowl, season the lamb with the salt and add the rest of the dried spices. Stir well to coat.

Using a food processor, blend the ginger, garlic, green chillies and lime juice to a smooth paste.

Add the paste to the lamb, with the yoghurt, chopped mint and coriander, half the ghee and all the crispy onions. Mix well. This is the point at which you can put the meat into the fridge to marinate for up to a day. If you're making the biryani straightaway, leave the meat out at room temperature for 45 minutes–1 hour.

To make the raita, wrap the garlic cloves in a piece of foil adding a splash of oil and a pinch of salt. Bake in a hot oven for 45 minutes. Crush the soft roasted garlic with the back of a knife to make a smooth purée. Add the garlic to the yoghurt with the salt, chilli powder and cumin. Whisk well and leave in the fridge.

For the rice, bring a large pot of salted water to the boil – it should taste like the sea! The quantity of salt in the water

Rice:
Plenty of salt
2 bay leaves
6 cloves
4 green cardamom pods
2cm (¾in) cinnamon
  stick, crushed
1 tsp caraway seeds
425g (15oz/2½ cups)
  basmati rice (aged
  basmati rice is best)

is important, as it's the only opportunity to season the rice. Add the bay leaves and spices to the pan and allow them to infuse the water for 20 minutes.

Transfer the lamb to a large cast-iron casserole with a lid, approximately 24–30cm (9½–12in) wide. Spread the lamb mixture on the bottom of the pan in an even layer. Ladle out 100ml (3½fl oz/scant ½ cup) of the boiling salted water for the rice and add it to the lamb. Stir to mix.

Add the rice to the boiling water and cook for around 4–5 minutes, over a rolling boil. Remove a grain of rice after 4 minutes to check; it should be almost cooked, with a slight al dente bite to it. Using a spider strainer or sieve, scoop out half of the rice from the boiling water, draining most of the water. Sprinkle the rice over the lamb, making sure that you have an even layer of rice. Cook the remaining rice for another minute. Drain in a colander and add the last of the rice to the pot.

Stir the saffron and rosewater into the warm milk. Spoon the remaining ghee over the rice, followed by the milk. Cover and place the pan onto the hob over a medium heat for 10 minutes. Transfer to the preheated baking sheet and cook in the oven for 25 minutes. Allow the biryani to rest for 10 minutes with the lid on before serving with the raita.

CHICKEN, MUSHROOM & TARRAGON BIRYANI

SERVES 4

3 tbsp ghee or vegetable oil
6 chicken thighs, on the
  bone, skin on
1 bay leaf
1 star anise
½ tsp fennel seeds
½ tsp cumin seeds
2 black cardamom pods
1 medium onion,
  finely diced
2cm (¾in) piece of
  ginger, finely grated
3 garlic cloves, finely grated
125ml (4fl oz/scant ½ cup)
  white wine
2 tsp Dijon mustard
200ml (7fl oz/generous
  ¾ cup) good-quality
  chicken stock
200g (7oz/generous
  ¾ cup) crème fraîche
A small bunch of tarragon,
  picked from the stalks
  and finely chopped
20g (⅔oz) fresh mint,
  finely chopped
60g (2oz) shop-bought
  crispy fried onions
25g (1oz) dried porcini
  mushrooms, soaked in
  80ml (2½fl oz/⅓ cup)
  of boiling water for
  10 minutes
1 tsp ground black pepper
1 tsp nutmeg, finely grated
½ tsp ground turmeric
1 tsp Kashmiri chilli
  powder
1 tsp garam masala
2 green finger chillies,
  halved
Salt

To finish:
500g (1lb 2oz) basmati rice
A large pinch of saffron
60ml (2fl oz/4 tbsp)
  warm milk
40g (1½oz/2½ tbsp
  butter, melted

Someone once asked me how I could create a French-inspired biryani to tie in with my love of fusion cooking. The challenge was set! A fricassée of chicken, mushroom and tarragon, with white wine and mustard, is a truly classic dish. Sometimes, the French will even serve these types of dishes with a steamed pilaf, so the idea of a French biryani seems quite sensible.

Preheat your oven to 180°C fan/400°F/Gas 6, and place a heavy baking sheet in the centre of the oven to heat up.

Warm the ghee or oil in a large heavy-based pan with a lid over a medium–high heat. When hot, season the chicken thighs with salt and cook, skin side down, for 6 minutes until golden and crispy. Turn over and brown on the underside for 3–4 minutes, until golden. You may have to do this in batches. Set the chicken aside on a plate.

Turn the heat down to medium and add the bay leaf, star anise, fennel, cumin and black cardamom pods to the oil. Allow them to sizzle for 30 seconds to release their aroma. Add the onion and fry for 10 minutes until lightly golden. Add the ginger and garlic and cook for 2 more minutes, until lightly golden. Add the white wine and give the pan a good stir to deglaze. Allow the wine to reduce by half, then add the mustard and chicken stock. Add the chicken and any juices back to the pan with the remaining ingredients and give it all a good stir. Allow to simmer gently while you cook the rice.

Bring a large pot of salted water to the boil – it should taste like the sea! When the water is boiling, add the rice and cook for 4–5 minutes over a rolling boil. Test a grain of rice after 4 minutes – the outside should be cooked, with a slight al dente bite in the centre. Using a strainer or sieve, scoop out half of the rice from the boiling water, draining most of the water. Sprinkle the rice over the chicken, making sure that you have an even layer of rice. Cook the remaining rice for another minute, then drain in a colander and add the drained rice to the chicken pot.

Stir the saffron into the warm milk. Top the rice with the melted butter and saffron milk and cover. Place the pan onto the hob over a medium heat for 10 minutes, then transfer to the baking sheet in the oven and cook for 20 minutes. Allow the biryani to rest for 5 minutes with the lid on before serving.

GRATIN ALOO BOULANGÈRE

SERVES 4

50g (1¾oz/3½ tbsp)
  unsalted butter
1 tsp black mustard seeds
1 tsp cumin seeds
½ tsp chilli flakes
3 medium onions,
  finely sliced
2 green finger
  chillies, halved
2cm (¾in) piece of
  ginger, finely grated
2 garlic cloves, finely grated
2 sprigs fresh curry leaves
  (optional)
1 tsp garam masala
1 tsp ground coriander
700g (1lb 9oz) small waxy
  potatoes (Charlotte
  or Ratte work well)
500ml (17fl oz/2 cups)
  good-quality chicken
  or lamb stock
50g (1¾oz/3½ tbsp)
  salted butter, to finish
Salt and pepper

This potato gratin is delicately spiced, which adds a new dimension to the classic French pommes Boulangère. The unctuous potatoes soak up all the flavours of the stock and butter, making this a very indulgent and elegant side dish. It makes a fine accompaniment to a Sunday roast leg of lamb, or indeed many of the recipes from this chapter including Lamb Rogan Chops (Pictured on page 162), Murgh Mussallam, Manipurchetta or Salmon Coulibiac.

Set a large cast-iron pot with a lid over a medium heat. When hot, melt the unsalted butter and add the mustard seeds, cumin seeds and chilli flakes. Allow the spices to sizzle in the butter for 30 seconds to release their aroma. Add the sliced onions, green chillies, ginger, garlic and curry leaves (if using). Cook for 15 minutes with the lid on. Don't worry if the onions stick a little – the caramelised bits equate to more flavour. After 15 minutes, remove the lid and cook for a further 20 minutes. Give the onions a stir every 5–10 minutes. You really want the onions to be beautifully caramelised and concentrated. Remove from the heat and stir through the garam masala and ground coriander.

Preheat your oven to 180°C fan/400°F/ Gas 6.

Slice the potatoes into 2mm (¹⁄₁₆in) thick rounds using a mandoline or a sharp knife.

Spread the caramelised onions over the base of a 20cm (8in) ovenproof pan or a 23cm (9in) gratin dish. Arrange the slices of potatoes into stacks, then arrange the stacks in the pan, curling them round in a circular pattern, so that all the potato slices are standing on edge (see photograph) .

Season the potatoes with salt and pepper, then pour the stock over, so that the potatoes are just covered. Place dots of the salted butter over the top, then place into the centre of the oven. Bake for 1 hour 20 minutes, until most of the stock has been absorbed and the potatoes are golden. Allow to rest for 20 minutes before serving.

NIHARI CHIMICHANGAS

SERVES 4

20g chickpea (gram) flour
    (or plain flour if you
    can't find gram flour)
800g–1kg (1¾lb–2¼lb)
    beef brisket
60ml (2oz/4 tbsp) ghee
    or vegetable oil
6 garlic cloves, finely grated
1 tbsp ground ginger
1 tbsp Kashmiri chilli
    powder
400ml (14fl oz/1¾ cups)
    beef stock
1 bay leaf
4cm (1½in) cinnamon
    stick
80g (2¾oz) shop-bought
    crispy fried onions
2 tsp ground turmeric
8 large flour tortillas
1 egg yolk, mixed with 1 tbsp
    of milk for brushing
Vegetable or sunflower oil,
    for frying (optional)

Masala spice blend:
6 cloves
6 green cardamom pods
2 black cardamom pods
½ star anise
1 tbsp coriander seeds
1 tsp black peppercorns
½ tsp cumin seeds
½ tsp fennel seeds
½ tsp caraway seeds
½ piece mace
¼ nutmeg

To serve:
A large handful of fresh
    coriander (cilantro)
2–3 green finger chillies,
    finely chopped
3cm (1¼in) piece of ginger,
    sliced into matchsticks
2 limes, cut into wedges
300g (10½oz/1¼ cups)
    sour cream

My dad was a bit of an experimental cook when I was growing up. His recipe for chimichangas was in an old and very unfashionable Tex-Mex book; they were like a burrito – but deep-fried – filled with the most delicious slow-cooked brisket, in a dark and smoky sauce laden with hot jalapeños. They took him all day and night to make, but the chimichangas were unstoppable and quickly became a regular on the menu at home.

The Mughlai cuisines of India specialise in slowly braised meat stews that are cooked for hours and hours, bubbling away in huge pots over charcoal fires. The nihari is the epitome of such dishes; a rich, fragrantly-spiced stew. Nihar means 'morning' in Urdu, and this dish would have been eaten as a hearty breakfast across Muslim India and Pakistan, to set you up for the long day ahead. It is this slow-cooked, rich curry that I'm using to fill my chimichangas, for the ultimate in Tex-Mex-Mughlai fusion. Traditionally, nihari is garnished with lime juice, fresh juliennes of ginger, green chillies and coriander to add a bit of zip. I'm also serving these with some sour cream, in true Tex-Mex fashion.

Brisket is the ideal cut of beef for this richly satisfying dish, but you can also use braising steak, skirt, beef shin, feather blade or beef cheeks – anything that benefits from a long and slow cook! If using smaller cuts, however, reduce the cooking time to 2–3 hours and check for tenderness.

To make the masala, grind all the whole spices in a coffee or spice grinder until you have a fine powder. Set aside in a bowl.

Toast the chickpea flour in a frying pan over a gentle heat for 7–8 minutes, until lightly toasted. Set aside.

Preheat your oven to 140°C fan/325°F/Gas 3. Pat the brisket dry with kitchen paper and season well with plenty of salt.

Heat the ghee or oil in a large cast-iron pot with a lid over a medium–high heat. When the oil is hot, sear the brisket for 3–4 minutes on each side, until browned all over. Remove from the pan and add the garlic to the pan. Fry for 2–3 minutes, until golden. If it starts to stick, add a splash of water. Add the ground ginger and chilli powder and stir for a minute before adding the stock, bay leaf, cinnamon stick and 500ml (17fl oz/2 cups) water. Stir in the toasted flour and masala powder mix and bring to a simmer, stirring to make sure that there are no lumps. Return the brisket to the pot, as well as any juices, and add the crispy fried onions. Cover and place in the preheated oven for 3 hours.

After 3 hours, stir in the turmeric and cook for a further 1 hour. The meat should be really tender by this point, and you should be able to pull it apart. You can test it with a fork to check. If it isn't tender enough, return the pot to the oven for 45 minutes or so.

When the meat is cooked, remove it from the pot and shred with two forks. Dress the meat with 300–400ml (10½–14fl oz/1¼–1¾ cups) of sauce, so that it is nice and moist. Reserve the remaining sauce in the cooking pot for serving. Allow to cool.

When cooled, spoon a generous amount of brisket into the centre of each tortilla – the chimichangas should be quite generously filled. Fold the sides into the centre, like you would fold a burrito and brush with egg, which acts like glue. Tightly fold the tortilla up, along the length – again, brushing with egg so that the tortilla is sealed shut. Repeat, until all of the tortillas have been folded or the filling has been used up.

Preheat the oven to 180°C fan/400°F/Gas 6. Brush the tortillas with a generous amount of oil and place onto two baking sheets, so that they are well-spaced out. Bake for 20 minutes, until they are golden and crisp. Turn the chimichangas halfway through the cooking. They can also be shallow-fried – the results are a little better, but it's not as straightforward as baking them in the oven. Fill a large non-stick frying pan with oil to a depth of 2cm (¾in) and place over a medium heat. When hot, fry the chimichangas in batches, making sure not to overcrowd the pan. They should take around 3 minutes to cook on each side to a golden brown. When they are golden, place on a baking sheet and give them 5 minutes in the oven to make sure they are piping hot inside.

To serve, reheat the sauce and pour into a serving bowl. Place a chimichanga on a plate with some of the coriander, chillies and ginger, a wedge of lime and some sour cream. Serve the sauce on the side to dip the chimichanga into, or pour the sauce all over!

COUSCOUS ROYALE

SERVES 6

5 tbsp vegetable or
   sunflower oil, plus a
   splash for the sausages
6 chicken thighs, skin on
300g (10½oz) diced lamb
   leg or shoulder
1 large onion, diced
3cm (1¼in) cinnamon
   stick
6 garlic cloves,
   finely chopped
2 tbsp tomato purée (paste)
2 tbsp harissa paste
   (Harissa du Cap Bon
   is very good)
1 tbsp ras el hanout
1 tsp ground cumin
1 tsp ground ginger
2 tsp Kashmiri chilli
   powder
1 litre (35fl oz/4¼ cups)
   good chicken stock
3 baby turnips, peeled
   and quartered
3 medium carrots,
   peeled and cut into
   chunky batons
2 courgettes (zucchini),
   each cut into 4 pieces
2 x 400g (14oz) tins
   chickpeas, drained
   and rinsed
6 Merguez sausages, or
   any other spicy sausage
600g (1lb 5oz) couscous
50g (1¾oz/3½oz)
   butter, melted
Salt

Couscous was brought to France by immigrants from the French colonies of North Africa. North African food is to France as chicken tikka masala is to Britain, and wherever you are, you'll be sure to find this hearty spicy stew on the menu. It starts with a huge pile of fluffy couscous piled into the centre of the plate, followed by chunks of slow-cooked lamb, chicken and of course, the spicy merguez sausage. Next, the vegetables: chickpeas, courgette, turnip and carrot. The whole plate is then doused in a ladle or two of the spicy broth that everything was gently simmered in. You could see why they call it 'royale', it is a real blow-out! This dish makes for an impressive meal, brilliant for a weekend centrepiece!

In a large, ovenproof casserole, heat 3 tablespoons of the oil over a medium–high heat. When hot, add the chicken thighs to the pan and fry on the skin side for 4–5 minutes, until golden. Turn the thighs over and brown for a further 3 minutes. Remove and set aside on a plate. Add the diced lamb and cook until browned all over and set aside.

Turn the heat down to medium, add another 2 tablespoons of oil to the same pan and fry the onion with the cinnamon stick for around 15 minutes until golden. Add the garlic and fry for a further 2 minutes. Add the tomato purée, harissa paste and spice powders and cook for a further minute before adding the stock. Loosen any caramelised bits which have stuck to the bottom of the pan. Add the chicken, lamb, vegetables and chickpeas to the pot and bring to a gentle simmer. Season with plenty of salt, cover with a lid and cook for 1 hour, until everything is deliciously tender.

Heat a splash of oil in a large frying pan over a medium–high heat and colour the sausages to a golden brown. Add to the pot and simmer for a further 15 minutes.

Meanwhile, cook the couscous according to the instructions on the packet, then stir through the melted butter.

To serve, make a mound of the couscous in the centre of a large serving platter, making sure that you leave a 6cm (2½in) border around the edge. Arrange the meat and vegetables on top of the couscous, alternating between the different ingredients. Finally, spoon over the broth.

MUMBAI PAV BHAJI

SERVES 6

Masala:
1 tbsp coriander seeds
¾ tbsp cumin seeds
½ tbsp fennel seeds
1 bay leaf
4 cloves
2cm (¾in) cinnamon stick
1 star anise
1 black cardamom pod
5 dried red Kashmiri chillies
1 tsp dried fenugreek leaves
  (kasoori methi)
½ tsp ground turmeric
½ tsp ground ginger
½ tsp dried mango powder
  (amchoor)
½ tsp black salt (kala namak)

Spice Paste:
8 garlic cloves
2cm (¾in) piece of ginger
4 dried red Kashmiri chillies
1 medium fresh tomato
2 green finger chillies

Bhaji:
4 medium potatoes, peeled
  and diced into 2cm
  (¾in) cubes
¼ cauliflower, stalks
  removed, cut into
  2cm (¾in) pieces
1 large carrot, peeled and
  diced into 1cm (½in) cubes
75g (2½oz/¾ cup)
  frozen peas
100g (3½oz/7 tbsp)
  unsalted butter
50ml (1¾fl oz/3½ tbsp)
  vegetable oil
1 tsp cumin seeds
2 red onions, finely diced
3 medium fresh
  tomatoes, diced
1 green (bell) pepper,
  deseeded and
  finely chopped
A handful of fresh coriander
  (cilantro), finely chopped

A visit to Mumbai isn't complete without a trip to eat the ultimate pav bhaji. This dish of mashed vegetables cooked in spices and obscene amounts of butter may sound simple, but it is the most famous and delicious dish of Mumbai. There really is no better place to eat the perfect pav bhaji than Sardar. This little restaurant, open to the street, is so popular that there has been a constant queue to get in for the past 57 years. Every Mumbaikar – from Bollywood royalty to cricketing legends – comes here for the best bhaji. You watch the chef cooking the thick brown paste of vegetables on a giant iron hotplate over a smoky wood fire, slicing massive bricks of butter which are laid on top of the bhaji. When you get in, you're blinded by the intense clinical lighting, which they have obviously turned up to max so you don't get too comfortable and the next set of punters can come in quick. Seconds after you order, the pav bhaji arrives. The waiter carries a tray piled high with at least 12 plates stacked on top of each other. I'm sure he's never dropped a single one. You break the pav – little soft white rolls – which, like everything here have been toasted in copious amounts of butter. Take a dip into the fantastically rich, spicy and tangy vegetables and now you're in Mumbai proper.

....

To make the masala, add all of the ingredients to a spice or coffee grinder and blend until you have a fine powder. Set aside in a sealed jar. This will last for up to 3 months.

For the spice paste: add all of the ingredients to a blender with 200ml (7fl oz/generous ¾ cup) water and blitz to a smooth paste. Set aside.

For the bhaji, put the potatoes, cauliflower and carrot in a large pan. Top up with water until just covered and season with a generous pinch of salt. Bring to a simmer, cover with a lid and cook for 20 minutes. Add the frozen peas and continue to cook for a further 5 minutes. By this time, the vegetables should be extremely tender. Drain the water and set the vegetables aside.

For this next step, to get the best flavour, it is best to use a wide cast-iron pan, about 30cm (12in) diameter (a large frying pan will do the job if you don't have one). Place the pan over a medium heat. When the pan is hot, add half the butter and the oil. Add the cumin seeds and diced red onions and fry over a medium heat for 10–15 minutes until golden. Add the tomatoes and green pepper and fry for another 8–10 minutes, until softened.

¼ tsp ground turmeric
1 tsp Kashmiri chilli
    powder
1 tsp ground coriander
Salt

Pav:
6 brioche burger buns
50g (1¾oz/3½ tbsp)
    unsalted, softened butter

To serve:
75g (2½oz/5 tbsp)
    unsalted butter
A small handful of fresh
    coriander (cilantro),
    finely chopped
1 medium red onion,
    finely diced
1 lime, cut into wedges

Add the reserved spice paste to the pan, along with the cooked vegetables, fresh coriander, turmeric, chilli powder and ground coriander. Stir the mixture to combine well and cook for a further 5 minutes, stirring every minute.

Add 1½ tablespoons of the masala powder to the pan, along with 400ml (14fl oz/1¾ cups) water. Turn the heat down to medium-low and, with a potato masher, mash everything in the pan together until you are left with quite a smooth saucy purée. The bhaji shouldn't be too dry; it should have a nice saucy consistency, so add a splash of water, if required. Add 1 teaspoon of salt and taste, adding a bit more salt if you need to. Allow the bhaji to cook for a further 20 minutes over a medium-low heat. By this time, it should have a rich and dark colour. Add the remaining butter and stir through to melt.

For the pav: place a large non-stick frying pan over a medium–high heat. Slice the buns in half and spread the inside and outside of each bun with butter. Place in the pan and allow to toast nicely for a couple of minutes on each side.

To serve, fill six small bowls with the bhaji. Add a healthy dollop of butter to each one. Garnish with a sprinkling of fresh coriander and red onion and a spritz of lime juice. Enjoy with the toasted pav.

PUDDING

For the uncompromising glutton, a meal isn't complete without a sweet ending. The word 'dessert' brings to mind the overly fussy offering you might find in a restaurant – an over-thought quenelle of empty mousse, the plate painted with an array of textures: gels, fake snows, granitas, edible flowers. It disappears in a single mouthful and we feel we have to say, 'Oh WOW, I've never had anything like it...' Dissatisfied, on your way home, you feel compelled to burst into the nearest supermarket bakery section, sprinting away with a six-pack of jammy doughnuts in your hand. After reading this book, you've probably realised that this isn't really my style. What I'm after is a good old-fashioned PUDDING. The word itself is just so much more inviting, with connotations of generosity, indulgence, conviviality – a wholesome family delight. The feeling of complete satisfaction, sitting on the sofa, thinking about how you'll never fit into those jeans you bought last year. These are the sorts of hearty, rustic and homely desserts I grew up loving. We're talking about proper puddings.

I have delicious teenage memories of travelling to France on Brittany Ferries, which has a well-deserved reputation for its excellent, buffet restaurants. The immaculate art-deco restaurant could easily be confused for a really up-market place in Paris. Waiters dressed in black waistcoats wore bowties; the grand piano playing standards in the background. We could never afford a restaurant at home in the UK, but this was a special trip for just me and my dad (I must highlight the huge secrecy of these meals, as my mum certainly would never have approved of this sort of extravagance). I used to walk into the dining room with so much excitement, combining my two loves: ships and food! I guess the clientele was mainly the classic British type of holiday maker-cum-professional gourmand – driving south to their château in the Dordogne, red wine complexion from enjoying the benefits of competitively-priced claret and Camembert for perhaps a few too many years. I'm getting off-topic here slightly, but I want to really paint the scene – to convey the competitive nature of the buffet. As soon as you ordered with the waiter, you'd be off like a shot, as if at the start of the 100-metre sprint. Gannets feasting on infinite shoals of sardines springs to mind. The course which caused the most frantic commotion would always be pudding. I remember eating my main course with *anxiety* in case my favourite dessert would be all gone. To avoid this, I set off prematurely towards the mountain of puddings – a huge selection of all the French classics:

pear frangipane tarts, chocolate mousse, crème brûlée, croustillant au chocolat. Proper puds. But there was only one thing that I was looking for – the legendary meringue! It used to be the best-kept secret of the buffet, but of course, word got out and now everyone wanted a big slice of the action. We didn't know the name, so we coined it 'The Meringue': towering layers of meringue, sandwiched between thick, unctuous layers of crème mousseline (custard and cream). The balance of lightness and decadence was perfect: sweet perfection. I'd usually cut myself a slice, the size of which was calculated by whatever I thought I could comfortably eat and then doubled. On one occasion, returning from the buffet with a massive slice of meringue enrobed in raspberry coulis, a woman at a neigbouring table gasped 'No!' I would always add a couple of customisations: more crème anglaise, because you can never have too much of a good thing, *and* raspberry coulis to cut through the sweetness of the meringue and cream.

I inherited my love of sugar from my grandfather, who regularly treated me and my brother to a box of warm *jalebi* from the Indian sweetshop: crisp swirls of warm, deep-fried batter were soaked in a thick sugary cardamom syrup. We understood the need for secrecy so that my mum would never find out. Between the three of us, we could polish off a box of these sticky heavenly treats in one go. My grandmother, Nani, would make classics like carrot halwa and creamy kheer (a rice pudding studded with sultanas and raisins). Her apple crumble, made from her garden windfalls, was legendary. There were always fantastic puddings around while I was growing up, but I've always felt that Indian sweets have been overlooked in the UK. In a British-Indian restaurant, you might end the meal with bought-in ice cream or kulfi, sometimes garnished with a squirt of cream. It's a non-event. Whereas actually in India, you'll find many delightful, freshly-made sweet treats and puddings; something delicious and often unfamiliar to really get excited about! Milk is invariably at the heart of these puddings: from airy clouds of whipped milk – *makhan malai* – to deliciously thick and creamy *phirni*, a variation of rice pudding, or *shahi tukda* bread pudding; there's a wonderful diversity and tradition of puddings in India, which need to be revealed. In this section of the book, I'm going to share with you the kind of puddings that I want to eat. New and exciting flavour combinations and Indian twists on much-loved classics. I hope you're in the mood for some no messing, drop-dead gorgeous puddings – you're in for a treat!

SHRIKHAND PANNA COTTA WITH MANGO COMPOTE

SERVES 4

100ml (3½fl oz/scant
½ cup) whole milk
200ml (7fl oz/generous
¾ cup) double (heavy)
cream
120g (4¼oz/½ cup
plus 1½ tbsp) caster
(superfine) sugar
Seeds of 10 green
cardamom pods, crushed
in a mortar and pestle,
or 1 tsp green ground
cardamom
2½ leaves platinum
leaf gelatine
400g (14oz/1¾ cups)
full-fat natural yoghurt
2 ripe mangoes
4 shortbread biscuits,
to serve

This ultra-creamy, tart panna cotta reminds me of a classic Indian shrikhand: strained yoghurt, sweetened with a hint of sugar and green cardamom. The tang of the yoghurt brings a lightness, making it the perfect way to end a meal. So, I've combined two puddings, which I love and which I think both share a similar DNA. It's the kind of thing I have to have double helpings of.

For the panna cotta, put the milk, cream, sugar and cardamom in a saucepan over a low heat. Allow to come to a very gentle simmer, then leave to infuse for 15 minutes over a very low heat.

Soften the gelatine leaves in a bowl of cold water for 5 minutes. Squeeze the leaves with your hand to remove the excess water, then add to the hot milk and whisk in until dissolved.

Put the yoghurt in a bowl and pour over the milk. Stir to combine, then divide the mixture between four dessert glasses or ramekins and place in the fridge to set for 8 hours, or overnight.

Slice the cheeks off the mangoes, cutting around the stones. With a spoon, scoop out the flesh, leaving behind the skin. Dice one of the mangoes into 5mm (¼in) dice and put in a small bowl. Add the other mango to a blender and purée until smooth. Add the purée to the diced mango and set aside until ready to serve.

Either serve the panna cotta as it is – simply spoon a generous amount of mango over the top – or, if you are using ramekins, demould them onto a plate. To do this run a knife around the edge of the panna cottas. Fill a bowl with boiling water and place the ramekin inside the water so that it comes three-quarters of the way up the sides. Hold in the water for 15 seconds, then remove the ramekin and carefully place it upside-down on a bowl or plate. Gently shake the ramekin to tease the panna cotta out. Spoon the mango around the panna cotta and serve with a buttery shortbread biscuit.

NEW DELHI BAKED CHEESECAKE

SERVES 8–10

Base:
400g (14oz) ginger
  nut biscuits
½ tsp salt
150g (5½oz/scant ⅔ cup)
  unsalted butter, melted

Filling:
800g (1lb 12oz)
  Philadelphia Original
  cream cheese, at
  room temperature
250g (9oz/1¼ cups) caster
  (superfine) sugar
2 tbsp cornflour
  (cornstarch)
50g (1¾oz/⅔ cup)
  skimmed milk powder
2 tsp green cardamom
  powder
1 tsp rosewater
2 medium eggs, at room
  temperature, beaten
1 x 170g (6oz) tin
  evaporated milk

The cheesecake at Juniors in New York is the real deal. The recipe hasn't changed since it opened in 1950 and it's the best you'll get anywhere! Don't be tempted by the strawberry or chocolate versions; it's the classic plain cheesecake you want. My New Delhi Cheesecake, just like its American relative, doesn't need accompaniments, its unrefined natural beauty does not need any distractions. Evaporated milk, cardamom and rose replaces vanilla, creating a classic Indian flavour.

Preheat your oven to 180 °C fan/350°F/Gas 6.

Put the biscuits and salt in the bowl of a food processor and blend to a very fine crumb. If you don't have a food processor, simply put everything in a freezer bag and smash with a rolling pin. Put the crumbs into a bowl, add the melted butter and mix together. Tip the mixture into a 23cm (9in) springform cake tin and press down firmly and evenly, so that the biscuit lines both the base and sides of the tin – you can use a flat-bottomed glass as a tamper to achieve this. Bake for 10 minutes. Remove from the oven and allow to cool.

For the filling, put the cream cheese and sugar into the bowl of a stand mixer fitted with a paddle attachment (or use a mixing bowl and wooden spoon) and mix together slowly until nicely blended and smooth. Add the cornflour, milk powder, cardamom and rosewater and mix again. Add the beaten eggs and mix slowly until combined. Add the evaporated milk and give it a final mix.

Pour the cheesecake filling into the cooled tin and tap the tin on the worktop a few times to knock any air out of the filling. Place in the centre of the oven and immediately turn the oven down to 160°C fan/350°F/Gas 4. Bake the cheesecake for 1 hour. After an hour, check the cheesecake – it should be set but still have a wobble in the centre. Turn the oven off and leave the cheesecake to cool in the oven for 45 minutes. Remove the cheesecake from the oven after this time and allow it to cool down to room temperature. When cool, place into the fridge for 8 hours. Baked cheesecakes take a long time to set, so don't be tempted to try and remove it from the tin until it's had enough time to chill. After 8 hours, remove the mould and place the cheesecake on a large serving plate. To slice, heat a large kitchen knife in a deep glass of hot water – this will ensure that you get a clean slice. Cut the cheesecake, cleaning the blade in hot water with kitchen paper after each cut. Enjoy.

MAKHAN MALAI AWADHI MESS

SERVES 4–6

Makhan Malai:
200g (7fl oz/generous
    ¾ cup) gold-top milk
200g (7oz/generous
    ¾ cup) clotted cream
50g (1¾oz/generous
    ¾ cup) icing
    (confectioners') sugar
1 generous pinch of saffron
1 tsp rosewater

Strawberry compote:
1½ tbsp caster
    (superfine) sugar
1 tsp pink peppercorns
500g (1lb 2oz)
    strawberries, hulled
    and halved

For the meringues:
3 medium egg whites
160g (5½oz/¾ cup
    plus 1 tbsp) caster
    (superfine)sugar
or
1 packet shop-bought
    meringue nests

I dream of going back to Lucknow to taste the makhan malai: soft, pillowy, airy clouds of saffron- and rose-scented whipped milk. Not overly sweet, the intense creaminess of the milk allows you to appreciate the beauty of India's milk products. The milk is richer and more delicious. This light milk foam is similar to the texture of whipped cream. As soon as you taste a spoonful, it dissolves on the tongue giving you a delicious creamy hit. It's simple yet addictive and gone in seconds; you're left wanting more...and more. I'm adding meringue and strawberries for a Lucknowi twist on Eton mess.

In a large bowl add the milk, clotted cream, icing sugar, saffron and rosewater. Mix and leave in the fridge for an hour to infuse.

To make the compote, grind the sugar and peppercorns to a fine powder using a mortar or spice grinder. Put the strawberries in a bowl with the sugar, stir to mix, then cover and leave for 1–2 hours at room temperature. Add half of the strawberries to a blender jug and blitz to a fine purée. Mix the purée back through the reserved strawberries. Set aside until ready to serve.

If making the meringues, preheat your oven to 120°C fan/275°F/ Gas 1, and line a baking sheet with baking parchment. Whisk the egg whites in a very clean bowl until soft peaks are formed. At this stage, add the sugar to the meringues, 1 tablespoon at a time, giving a good whisk after each addition of sugar. You will be left with a lovely glossy and thick meringue. Spoon little uniform mounds of meringue onto the baking sheet, then place into the centre of the oven. Bake for 2 hours, turn the oven off and leave the meringues to cool inside the oven.

Remove the milk and cream from the fridge and with the help of an electric whisk, whip until very soft peaks are formed. This may take around 10 minutes – so be patient – but rest assured, you'll be left with the most heavenly whipped makhan malai.

To serve, spoon some of the cream into the bottom of a dessert bowl or glass. Add a couple of spoons of the strawberry compote, followed by crushed meringue (avoiding any uniformity). Repeat and enjoy.

LE MERINGUE FROM BRITTANY FERRIES

SERVES 4

6 medium egg whites
300g (10½oz/1½ cups)
    caster (superfine) sugar
30g (1oz) pistachios,
    chopped

Cream:
200ml (7fl oz/generous
    ¾ cup) whole milk
3 egg yolks
70g (2½oz/⅓ cup) caster
    (superfine) sugar
1 heaped tbsp plain
    (all-purpose) flour
1½ tbsp cornflour
    (cornstarch)
1 tsp vanilla bean paste
    or vanilla extract
125g (4½oz/½ cup)
    mascarpone cheese
200ml (7fl oz/generous
    ¾ cup) double (heavy)
    cream

Raspberry coulis:
350g (12oz) frozen
    raspberries
1 star anise
4 cloves
1 black cardamom pod
2 tbsp icing
    (confectioners') sugar

This great dish is a flagship pudding of my repertoire. But for those of you who didn't read the introduction, I'll briefly describe one of my all-time favourite puddings. It may look like a pavlova, but a pavlova this is not. The meringue is filled with a rich but at the same time, fluffy crème diplomate filling – don't worry about the posh-sounding name; I'm here to break it down for you. It is better served with an aromatic raspberry coulis, for ultimate pleasure. You might say that it sounds very similar to my Awadhi mess; yes – it is indeed another meringue and cream; totally different, equally good.

Preheat your oven to 120°C fan/275°F/Gas 1, and line a large baking tray with baking parchment.

First make the meringue. In a large very clean bowl, either with an electric hand-held whisk or stand mixer, whisk the egg whites to soft peaks. Add the sugar, one spoon at a time, whisking well after each addition until all the sugar has been incorporated. You should be left with a stiff glossy meringue. Spoon four equally sized dollops of meringue, nicely spread out, onto the tray. Dip a spoon in hot water and use it to make a dip in the centre of each meringue, which will hold the cream. Bake for 2 hours, then turn the oven off and leave them to cool in the oven.

To make the cream, warm the milk in a saucepan over a medium heat. Beat together the egg yolks, sugar, both flours and vanilla. When simmering, add the milk to the egg yolks and whisk together. Pour the mixture back into the pan and cook for 5 minutes, by which time you will have a very thick crème pâtissière. Transfer to a bowl, cover the surface with cling film (plastic wrap) and allow to cool.

When the crème pâtissière has cooled, beat in the mascarpone, using a whisk. In a second bowl, whisk the double cream to form stiff peaks. Fold the two creams together and keep in the fridge.

For the raspberry coulis, add all of the ingredients to a pan with 1½ tablespoons water, cover with a lid and simmer for 5 minutes over a medium heat. Remove the star anise and blend the warm coulis with a stick blender then push through a sieve to remove the pips to give a smooth raspberry sauce. Allow to cool.

Top each meringue with an overly generous dollop of cream and a sprinkling of pistachios. Serve with plenty of coulis on the side.

FENNEL & CARDAMOM APPLE CRUMBLE CAKE

SERVES 6

Apple filling:
25g (1oz/1²/₃ tbsp)
    unsalted butter
6 green cardamom pods,
    lightly crushed
2cm (¾in) cinnamon stick
4 cloves
1 star anise
6 eating apples, cored
    and diced into 1cm
    (½in) chunks
100g (3½oz/½ cup)
    caster (superfine) sugar
1 tbsp fennel seeds,
    ground to a powder

Crumble topping:
75g (2½oz/½ cup
    plus 1 tbsp) plain
    (all-purpose) flour
75g (2½oz/¾ cup)
    ground almonds
75g (2½oz/6 tbsp) caster
    (superfine) sugar
½ tsp salt
1 tsp mixed spice
75g (2½oz/5 tbsp)
    unsalted butter, cold
1 tbsp milk

Sponge:
100g (3½oz/7 tbsp)
    unsalted butter,
    softened, plus extra
    for greasing
2cm (¾in) cinnamon stick
4 green cardamom pods
1 tsp fennel seeds
4 cloves
100g (3½oz/¾ cup)
    self-raising flour
100g (3½oz/½ cup) caster
    (superfine) sugar
1 tsp almond extract
2 eggs

Spices like fennel, cardamom and cinnamon really enhance the natural apple flavour, raising the humble crumble a notch. I try to avoid using Bramley apples as they disintegrate when cooked and are devoid of any texture. Any good eating apples such as Cox, Gala or Braeburn will work brilliantly.

For the filling, heat a wide, deep pan over a medium heat. Melt the butter with the cardamom, cinnamon stick, cloves and star anise, allow to sizzle for 1 minute before adding the apples, sugar and fennel. Stew for 25–30 minutes, stirring every 5 minutes, until the apples are soft, then remove from the heat and allow to cool.

For the crumble, in a large bowl, mix together the dry ingredients. Add the chilled butter and rub it in with your hands, so that all the large pieces are incorporated and you're left with a sandy texture. Add the milk and run a fork through briefly, so that you have a range of rubbly textures, some large, some small. Set aside.

Preheat the oven to 180°C fan/400°F/Gas 6, and grease a 23cm (9in) loose-based cake tin with some soft butter.

For the sponge, add the whole spices to a spice grinder and blitz to a fine powder. Add the spices to the flour.

In a mixing bowl, beat together the butter, sugar and almond extract until smooth and creamy. Beat in the eggs and mix well, before adding the flour and spices. Fold together until just combined – don't over-mix as the cake will become tough.

Tip the batter into the cake tin and smooth level. Next, spread the stewed apple over the batter, and finally scatter over the crumble. Bake in the centre of the oven for 45 minutes, until golden. Serve warm with plenty of custard.

SPICED CHAI CHOCOLATE MOUSSE WITH POACHED PRUNES

SERVES 4

2cm (¾in) cinnamon stick
3 cloves
½ nutmeg
Seeds from 4 green
   cardamom pods
½ tsp black peppercorns
1 black teabag (Assam or
   English Breakfast)
10g piece of ginger, crushed
225ml (8fl oz/scant 1 cup)
   whole milk
4 egg yolks
½ tsp cornflour
   (cornstarch)
50g (1¾oz/¼ cup) caster
   (superfine) sugar
175g (6oz) dark chocolate
   (70% cocoa solids),
   chopped
½ tsp salt
200ml (7fl oz/generous
   ¾ cup) whipping cream

Poached prunes:
16 pitted prunes
   (Agen are best)
2cm (¾in) cinnamon stick
3 cloves
1 star anise
2 lemon slices
1 teabag (Assam or
   English Breakfast)
Peel of ½ orange,
   (pared with a peeler)
75g (2½oz/6 tbsp) sugar
75ml (2½fl oz/5 tbsp)
   brandy or Armagnac

To serve (all optional):
Gold leaf to garnish
Clotted cream
Cardamom biscuits
   (see page 16)

The idea of infusing chocolate with spices has been around for the last 4,000 years, originating from where we now call Mexico, so it's not a new idea by any stretch of the imagination. I'm infusing my chocolate mousse with a few aromatic Indian spices which add a sparkle of magic and depth to a dark and rich chocolate mousse.

For the prunes, put all of the ingredients except the brandy in a small saucepan. Cover with water and bring to the boil, then turn the heat down and simmer gently for 20 minutes. Transfer the prunes to a jar along with 100ml (3½fl oz/scant ½ cup) of the poaching syrup and the brandy or Armagnac. This will keep in the fridge for up to 2 weeks.

Grind the whole spices for the mousse to a fine powder in a spice grinder, or pestle and mortar. Add the spices, teabag and ginger to the milk and warm gently. Once simmering, remove from the heat and leave to infuse for 20 minutes.

Whisk together the egg yolks, cornflour and sugar until pale and fluffy. Return the milk to the boil and strain it through a fine sieve into the egg-yolk mixture. Whisk together, before returning the mixture to the pan and cooking for 2–3 minutes over a medium heat, stirring well until slightly thickened. Put the chopped chocolate in a heatproof bowl and pour the hot liquid over it. Stir until the chocolate has melted. Add the salt and set aside.

Whip the cream to soft peaks and fold into the chocolate mixture. Divide the mousse between four pudding glasses or ramekins and place in the fridge for 3 hours to set.

To serve, add two prunes to each serving and garnish with some gold leaf for a royal finish, if you wish. Serve with clotted cream and cardamom biscuits.

CHILLI MARMALADE OR ROSE & RASPBERRY BAKEWELL TART

SERVES 8

150g (5½oz/1 cup plus 2 tbsp) plain (all-purpose) flour, plus extra for dusting
50g (1¾oz/3½ tbsp) cold unsalted butter, chilled
50g (1¾oz/generous ⅓ cup) icing (confectioners') sugar
A pinch of salt
1 egg
Extra-thick cream or clotted cream, to serve

Frangipane filling:
150g (5½oz/scant ⅔ cup) unsalted butter, softened, plus extra for greasing
150g (5½oz/¾ cup) caster (superfine) sugar
1 tsp almond extract
3 medium eggs, at room temperature
150g (5½oz/1½ cups) ground almonds
2 tsp mixed spice

Chilli marmalade:
200g (7oz/generous ¾ cup) + 70g (2½oz) good-quality bitter marmalade
2 scant tsp Kashmiri chilli powder
2 scant tsp chilli flakes
2 tbsp Cointreau (optional)
Or
Rose and raspberry:
200g (7oz/generous ¾ cup) + 70g (2½oz) gulkand (rose jam)
125g (4½oz) raspberries
2 tbsp Cointreau (optional)
30g (1oz) toasted flaked almonds
Icing (confectioners') sugar, for dusting

As a child, I was always interested in the places things came from. I would spend hours looking at the beautifully made old bone-handled knives we used to eat with at home, with 'SHEFFIELD' embossed on every single one of them. I'd spend all day thinking about all of the banging and clanging of hot iron, smelting, forging, clouds of steam and 'Rocket Ronnie' furiously potting snooker balls. All of this was exciting stuff that must have been going on in Sheffield. Another place that took my interest was Bakewell, coincidentally, not that far from Sheffield. For me, Bakewell was the capital of my world – Britain's most significant town – the home of the Bakewell tart and the original, lesser-known Bakewell pudding! I dreamt of a shop packed to the rafters with almond tarts, the heady perfume of almond extract and buttery pastries. Tarts flying out of the oven with cups of tea and clotted cream. My mum always made the best Bakewell tart. It was in fact one of my happiest memories of baking at home in the kitchen and I've carried my love of fruit-filled frangipane through life with me, cherishing it as my signature. If anyone comes round to my house for dinner, pudding will almost certainly be a frangipane tart of some sort. As with most things in life, our palate becomes more complex and we want something with more of a kick; so here's a recipe for two very much more grown-up Bakewell tarts. You could use shop-bought ready rolled shortcrust pastry to save time, but I love to make my own! You'll be able to order gulkand or rose jam online and from specialist shops.

For the pastry (if making), add the flour, butter, icing sugar, and salt to the bowl of a food processor. Process for around 30 seconds, or until the mixture resembles fine breadcrumbs. Add the egg to the food processor and pulse until the dough comes together. Don't be temped to pulse this for too long, as it will make the pastry tough. Wrap the pastry in cling film (plastic wrap) and flatten it out to a rough circle, about 1cm (½in) thick. Chill for 1 hour.

Meanwhile make the frangipane. In a large bowl, using an electric beater (or hand whisk if you fancy a workout), cream together the butter, sugar and almond extract until pale and creamy (it's so much easier if the butter is really soft). Next, add the eggs, one by one, making sure to beat the mixture thoroughly between adding each egg. Add the ground almonds and mixed spice and gently mix until all the ingredients have been combined thoroughly. Set aside.

Remove the pastry from the fridge 15 minutes before you want to roll it out, to allow it to soften. Grease a 23cm (9in) loose-based tart tin with a small amount of soft butter. Remove the pastry from the cling film. On a lightly flour-dusted surface, gently dust the surface of the pastry and roll it out to a circle slightly larger than the tin, around 3–4mm (1/8in) thick. Keep dusting under and onto the pastry with flour if it is slightly tacky, to help with the rolling. When rolled to the correct size, fold the pastry over the rolling pin and lift it into the greased tin. Make sure that the pastry is pushed into all of the corners of the tin, then trim the excess from the edge of the tin.

Preheat the oven to 180°C fan/400°F/Gas 6, and place a baking tray (large enough to hold the tart tin) in the centre of the oven to heat up.

If making the chilli marmalade tart, combine the marmalade with the chilli powder and chilli flakes. Spread the marmalade over the bottom of the pastry case in an even layer. Dollop the frangipane over the jam and, with a small palate knife, spread evenly to cover the jam.

If making the rose and raspberry tart, spread the rose jam over the bottom of the pastry case in an even layer. Dollop the frangipane over the jam and spread out evenly with a small palette knife, then push the fresh raspberries into the frangipane.

Place the tart in the oven, onto the preheated baking tray, and bake for 20 minutes. Reduce the temperature of the oven to 150°C fan/337°F/Gas 3, and bake for a further 50 minutes until golden brown on top and firm to the touch.

Remove the tart from the oven and allow to cool in the tin while you make the glaze. In a small saucepan, combine the 70g (2½oz) of marmalade (for the chilli marmalade tart) or jam (for the rose and raspberry tart) with either the Cointreau, if using, or 2 tablespoons water. Bring to a boil, giving it a good stir, then brush over the surface of the warm tart.

When cool, remove the tart from the tin. If you have made the rose and raspberry tart, scatter the top with the almonds and dust with icing sugar. Slice the tart into portions and serve with lots of extra thick or clotted cream.

QUBANI TRIFLE

SERVES 6

1 shop-bought Madeira
   loaf cake
125ml (4½fl oz/½ cup)
   brandy
600ml (21fl oz/2½ cups)
   double (heavy) cream
1 tsp vanilla bean paste
   or vanilla extract
2 tbsp icing
   (confectioners') sugar
30g (1oz) flaked almonds,
   toasted in the oven for
   7–8 minutes until golden
A handful of crunchy
   amaretti biscuits,
   crushed

*Rosemary cardamom
   custard:*
500ml (17fl oz/2 cups)
   whole milk
3 sprigs rosemary
8 green cardamom pods,
   lightly crushed
4 egg yolks
70g (2½oz/⅓ cup) caster
   (superfine) sugar
20g (⅔oz/3 tbsp)
   cornflour (cornstarch)

Apricot compote:
200g (7oz) dried apricots,
   halved and soaked in
   hot water for 2 hours
400g (14oz) fresh apricots,
   halved and de-stoned
200g (7oz/1 cup) caster
   (superfine) sugar

A beautiful summer pudding – trifle! In Hyderabad there is a dessert called qubani ka meetha, *which is Urdu for 'sweet apricots'. It's a very simple dish of dried apricots, soaked and slowly stewed in sugar until they are a lovely jammy consistency. No spice is added; it's all about the flavour of the dried apricots. It's served with cream, and sometimes almonds. The first time I tasted this dish I wanted to make a trifle with it and after some research, my version of the qubani ka meetha trifle was devised!*

Start with the custard. In a saucepan over a medium heat, warm the milk with the rosemary and cardamom pods. Bring to a simmer, then turn off the heat and allow the milk to infuse for 30 minutes, while you make the compote.

To make the apricot compote, in a saucepan over a medium heat, combine the dried and fresh apricots with the sugar and 350ml (12fl oz/1½ cups) water. Bring to the boil, then turn the heat down and simmer gently for 45 minutes. Briefly pulse the apricots with a stick blender to make a nice chunky compote, then leave to cool.

To finish the custard, bring the milk back up to a simmer. Add the egg yolks, sugar and cornflour to a large bowl. Give it a brief whisk to combine. Strain the hot milk into the egg mixture through a sieve, discarding the rosemary and cardamom pods. Give it a mix, then pour the custard back into the saucepan. Cook over a medium heat for 5–6 minutes, whisking all the time so that the custard doesn't go lumpy, after which time, the custard should be nice and thick. Pour the custard into a bowl and leave to cool.

When everything is cool, it's time to build the trifle. Slice the cake into 1cm- (½in-) thick slices and soak with the brandy. Cover the base of a trifle bowl with the cake, then top with the apricot compote. Next, pour over the custard. Gently whip the double cream with the vanilla and icing sugar to soft peaks, then spoon this over the top. Finish with a sprinkling of toasted almonds and crushed amaretti biscuits and serve.

KERALAN BANANA SPLIT

Sunflower oil, for frying
2 bananas
1 tbsp caster (superfine)
   sugar mixed with
   1 tbsp ground cumin
12–16 fresh curry leaves
2 scooops chocolate
   ice cream
2 scoops coconut ice cream
2 scoops vanilla ice cream
2 scoops mango sorbet
   or ice cream
Hundreds and thousands,
   (sugar strands),
   to sprinkle
A few glacé cherries

Batter:
60g (2oz/generous ½ cup)
   cornflour (cornstarch)
60g (2oz/scant ½ cup)
   plain (all-purpose) flour
35g (11/4oz/3 tbsp) caster
   (superfine) sugar
150ml (5fl oz/scant ⅔ cup)
   cold sparkling water

Lime cream:
250ml (9fl oz/1 cup)
   double (heavy) cream
Zest of 1 lime
1 tbsp icing
   (confectioners') sugar
2 tbsp rum
1 tsp vanilla bean paste
   or vanilla extract

White chocolate sauce:
75g (21/2oz) white
   chocolate
50ml (1¾fl oz/3½ tbsp)
   double (heavy) cream

Every summer holiday growing up, we would go back to a beautiful campsite in the village of Saint-André-des-Eaux. Situated between the famous resort of La Baule and the industrial port city of Saint-Nazaire, it wasn't the obvious choice for a family holiday, but over the years it became like a second home to us. On sunny days we would go to the beach and my brother and I would spend the entire day in the sea bodyboarding. Sometimes we would visit the port town of St Nazaire, on the Loire estuary; always fascinated by ships, I would force the family to go on a tour of France's largest shipyard – Les Chantiers de l'Atlantique – to see what ships were being built. My long weeks in France were hugely influential for me – but I've not told you about the best part of these holidays yet…

Our favourite place to eat was 'L'Opaline': a caféteria, located in an old E.Leclerc supermarket. The supermarket must have been built in the 1970s and was definitely showing its age but it had charm and we loved it. Walking in, you were greeted by a huge hand-painted abstract mural of the fantastic suspension bridge spanning the Loire at Saint-Nazaire – ahhhh, we're back in good old Opaline! There were two dishes that stick with me vividly. Firstly, the pizzas were legendary, and the one to have was the 'Pizza Bismarck'. It got its name from an egg cracked into the middle of it, which resembled a torpedo piercing the German battleship. Dish number two: banana split! I used to love watching it being made: banana halves; perfect scoops of vanilla, strawberry and chocolate (the holy trinity of ice creams!); chocolate sauce; squirty cream from a can; followed by colourful sprinkles; and the pièce de résistance – the glacé cherry on top! I have to honour L'Opaline by reconnecting spiritually with the banana split – but with a Keralan twist. The bananas have become large fritters – because banana fritters are an essential dish in Kerala. I have added tropical ice cream flavours and a little hint of spice – taking this simple dessert to dizzy new heights.

This is an easy dessert to throw together as the ice cream is all shop-bought and all you have to do is fry the bananas, whip the cream and build the split! If you don't fancy frying the bananas, you can make an old-fashioned raw banana split, although I highly recommend that you opt for my deep-fried ones!

....

Recipe continued overleaf

To make the batter, whisk together the cornflour, plain flour and sugar with the sparkling water, which will make a batter roughly the same consistency as single (light) cream. Set aside to rest in the fridge.

For the lime cream, whip the cream with the lime zest, sugar, rum and vanilla until you have soft peaks. Transfer to a piping bag with a star nozzle fitted if you have one (I like the retro piped effect). If not, you can simply spoon the cream onto the pudding.

To make the white chocolate sauce, melt the chocolate and cream together in a heatproof bowl set over a pan of gently simmering water. As soon as the chocolate has melted, give it a stir and remove from the heat.

Fill a deep pan (or a deep-fat fryer) to 5cm (2in) depth with sunflower oil and heat it to 180°C (350°F) over a medium–high heat. Be very careful whilst doing this. I recommend that you use a chef's probe thermometer to monitor the temperature of the oil. Slice the bananas in half lengthway and dip each half into the batter, then slowly lower into the hot oil. Make sure that the fritters don't stick to the bottom of the pan. I would do this in batches, cooking two halves at a time. Fry for 4 minutes, until golden brown, then remove the fritters from the oil and allow to drain on kitchen paper. Dust in the cumin sugar whilst still hot.

After frying the banana fritters, add the curry leaves to the hot oil and fry for 3 minutes until they are translucent. Drain the curry leaves on kitchen paper.

To serve, use two small oval serving dishes and line the sides of each with two banana fritters. Scoop a ball of each flavour of ice cream between the fritters. Drizzle over a couple of spoonfuls of white chocolate sauce. Generously top both dishes with whipped cream, then decorate with the fried curry leaves, hundreds and thousands and glacé cherries.

PEANUT KULFI SEMIFREDDO WITH SESAME BRITTLE

SERVES 6–8

1 litre (35fl oz/4¼ cups)
    whole milk
120g (4¼oz/½ cup)
    condensed milk
50g (1¾oz/⅔ cup)
    skimmed milk powder
200g (7oz/generous
    ¾ cup) best-quality
    crunchy peanut butter
½ tsp green cardamom
    powder, made from
    grinding the seeds of
    5 green cardamom pods
300ml (10½fl oz/1¼ cups)
    double (heavy) cream
50g (1¾oz) milk chocolate

Sesame peanut brittle:
50g (1¾oz) chopped
    peanuts
70g (2½oz/⅓ cup)
    caster (superfine) sugar
2 tbsp maple syrup
35g (1¼oz) white
    sesame seeds
1½ tbsp black
    sesame seeds
½ tsp salt

I love the combination of peanut and sesame. In the winter in India you'll find street stalls selling chikki *– a crunchy sesame brittle, both sweet and nutty in taste. The deep nutty flavour is really enhanced by the natural sweetness of milk. Sugar is added to this recipe in the form of condensed milk, to bolster the milky taste of the kulfi. The brilliant thing about kulfi is that it doesn't require churning in an ice-cream machine, so it's a doddle to make at home!*

In a wide non-stick pan, warm the milk over a medium heat and bring to the boil. Once boiling, reduce the heat slightly and simmer until the milk has reduced by approximately two-thirds, stirring every few minutes to prevent the milk sticking to the bottom of the pan. This process will take approximately 45 minutes–1 hour and can be done well in advance. When reduced, the milk will be nice and thick. Stir in the condensed milk, milk powder, peanut butter and green cardamom and allow to cool.

Meanwhile, line a loaf tin, measuring approximately 25 x 11cm (10 x 4¼in), with a double layer of cling film (plastic wrap).

When the milk mixture is cool, whip the cream to stiff peaks. Whisk the kulfi base into the cream, then pour the mixture into the loaf tin. Place in the freezer for 6 hours, or until frozen.

Preheat your oven to 180°C fan/400°F/Gas 6. Put the peanuts on a small baking tray and bake for 8–10 minutes until toasted, turning the nuts halfway through cooking. Allow to cool.

To make the brittle, put the sugar and maple syrup in a non-stick frying pan. Cook over a medium heat until the sugar has dissolved, then add the toasted nuts, sesame seeds and salt. Coat everything in the caramel using a wooden spoon and cook for a further 3–4 minutes. Carefully turn the brittle out onto a baking sheet lined with baking parchment and spread into a thin, even layer. Allow to cool, then break into shards. The brittle will keep for around 4–5 days in an airtight container.

Remove the kulfi from the freezer 20 minutes before serving.

Melt the chocolate in a heatproof bowl set over a pan of gently simmering water. Unmould the kulfi and place it on a serving platter. Drizzle with the melted chocolate and with some chopped peanut sesame brittle.

GULAB JAMUN PEACH MELBA SUNDAE

MAKES 4 SUNDAES

300g (10½oz/1½ cups)
    caster (superfine) sugar
4 ripe yellow peaches,
    halved 150ml (5fl oz/
    scant ⅔ cup) double
    (heavy) cream
1 tbsp icing
    (confectioners') sugar
½ tsp vanilla extract
6 gulab jamun (Royal is the
    usual brand you'll find)
8 scoops good-quality
    vanilla ice cream
30g (1oz) flaked (sliced)
    almonds, toasted in the
    oven for 7–8 minutes
    until golden

Raspberry coulis:
150g (5½oz) raspberries,
    fresh or frozen
1 tbsp lemon juice
2 tbsp icing
    (confectioners') sugar

The illustrious 'Peach Melba' was invented by the great Auguste Escoffier and is one of my go-to French caféteria pudding staples. I think adding a spongy texture to this classic is a brilliant idea and I'm going with shop-bought gulab jamun. *If you've not tried these Indian sweets before, please do, because they are out of this world.*

If peaches aren't in season, I can see no reason not to use the tinned variety – which will only enhance the retro vibes, meaning that you can enjoy this pudding all year round. The melba is best served in tall sundae glasses that have been chilled or frozen, but a bowl will work too.

To poach the peaches, put the 300g (10½oz) sugar in a saucepan with 500ml (17fl oz/2 cups) water and bring to the boil, then turn the heat down and add the peaches. Simmer gently for 5 minutes, until tender, turning halfway through cooking if they are not completely submerged in the syrup. Remove from the heat and allow to cool. When cool, remove the stones and peel the skin off – it should come off very easily. Cut each peach half in two.

To make the raspberry coulis, add all the ingredients to a food processor and blitz until smooth. Push through a fine sieve into a bowl to remove the seeds. Set aside.

Whip the cream with the icing sugar and vanilla to soft peaks. If you like, you can put this into a piping bag with a star nozzle fitted.

Warm the gulab jamun in their syrup, either in a pan for 7 minutes or in the microwave for 2 minutes.

To build the sundae, cut all the gulab jamun in half. Place two halves in the bottom of each sundae glass and drizzle with a spoonful of their syrup. Top with a ball of ice cream, followed by three pieces of peach. Add another half of gulab jamun, followed by more ice cream. Finish by topping with raspberry coulis, another piece of peach, and some whipped cream and sprinkle with flaked almonds.

GREEN CHILLI KEY LIME PIE

SERVES 8

Crust:
200g (7oz) malted
   milk biscuits
60g (2oz/4 tbsp) unsalted
   butter, melted, plus
   extra for greasing

Filling:
1 x 400g (14oz) tin
   condensed milk
3 egg yolks
Finely grated zest
   and juice of 5 limes
5 green finger chillies,
   finely chopped
1 tsp black salt
6 dried kaffir (Makrut) lime
   leaves, ground to a fine
   powder in a spice grinder
   or mortar and pestle

*Candied lime slices
(optional):*
2 limes
200g (7oz/1 cup) sugar

Cream topping:
150ml (5fl oz/scant 2/3 cup)
   double (heavy) cream
1 tbsp icing
   (confectioners') sugar
50g (1¾oz/3½ tbsp)
   full-fat Greek yoghurt

Kaffir limes are so integral to the cuisine of Bengal. They give a sickly sweet flavour, almost toned down in acidity compared to our supermarket ones. This is my version of a familiar pudding – Key Lime Pie – which I've spiced up! Black salt really is worth finding and gives this dessert an edge of personality – it is complex, sulphurous and pungent. You'll find it in South-Asian supermarkets or online and is called 'kala namak'.

Preheat your oven to 160°C fan/350°F/Gas 4, and lightly grease a 20cm (8in) loose-based tart tin with butter.

In a food processor, blitz the biscuits to a fine crumb. You can also do this by putting the biscuits in a freezer bag and smashing them with a rolling pin. Stir in the melted butter, mix together, then tip into the bottom of the tin and press down well (the flat base of a glass is useful for this). Bake for 10 minutes until golden, then allow to cool.

To make the filling, whisk together the condensed milk and egg yolks for around 2 minutes, until creamy. Add three-quarters of the lime zest, all the lime juice, the green chillies, black salt and kaffir lime powder. Whisk again for a minute, then pour into the biscuit-lined tin. Bake in the centre of the oven for 15–20 minutes until set. Remove the pie from the oven and allow to cool, before placing in the fridge to set for 2 hours.

To make the candied limes, slice the limes into 5mm- (¼in-) thick slices – a mandoline is useful for this. Bring a pan of water to the boil and cook the slices of lime for a minute. Remove the limes and plunge into a bowl of ice-cold water. Leave to cool. Repeat this process once more, using fresh water to boil the limes in. Bring the sugar and 200ml (7fl oz/generous ¾ cup) water to a boil in a pan and gently simmer the slices for 20–30 minutes, until glassy and almost transparent. Remove the slices from the syrup and place on a rack to cool.

When ready to serve, remove the chilled pie from the tin and place on a large serving plate. Whip the cream and sugar to soft peaks. Add the yoghurt and whisk again until stiff. Cover the pie with cream in an even, pillowy layer, then decorate with the remaining lime zest and some of the candied lime slices, if making.

SHAHI TUKDA BREAD & BUTTER PUDDING

SERVES 6

80g (2¾oz/⅓ cup)
    softened salted butter,
    plus extra for creaming
8 slices brioche loaf or
    8 slices day-old bread
Icing (confectioners')
    sugar, for dusting
Extra-thick double (heavy)
    cream or clotted cream,
    to serve

Custard:
200ml (7fl oz/generous
    ¾ cup) whole milk
200ml (7fl oz/generous
    ¾ cup) double
    (heavy) cream
200ml (7fl oz/generous
    ¾ cup) condensed milk
A pinch of saffron
Seeds from 5 cardamom,
    pods crushed in a mortar
    and pestle (or ½ tsp
    ground cardamom)
Zest of 1 orange
1 tsp vanilla bean paste
    or vanilla extract
4 egg yolks

Shahi tukda is a Mughlai classic, a bread pudding, with its origins firmly rooted in Old Delhi. Bread is fried in ghee, then soaked in a saffron and cardamom syrup before being topped with luxurious sweetened cream and milk. Shahi translates to 'royal' and this dish would definitely have adorned the royal tables of the Mughal Emperors – decorated with saffron, nuts, and silver-leaf bling! The first time I tasted shahi tukda, I couldn't help thinking how similar it is to a very traditional British bread and butter pudding.

Grease a medium gratin dish with butter. Butter the slices of brioche generously on both sides and cut into squares, then throw them into the gratin dish in a higgledy-piggledy fashion – a very random arrangement gives a nice range of textures when baked.

For the custard, add the milk, cream, condensed milk, saffron, cardamom, orange zest and vanilla to a saucepan. Over a medium heat, slowly bring the liquid to a simmer. Meanwhile, put the egg yolks in a bowl. Once simmering, pour the hot liquid over the egg yolks and whisk immediately until combined. Pour the custard over the bread so that it is completely covered and leave to soak for at least 30 minutes, making sure that the bread is submerged. While the bread is soaking, preheat the oven to 160°C fan/350°F/Gas 4.

To make a water bath, place the gratin dish into a larger, deep roasting tin and pour boiling water around the edge so that it comes around halfway up the gratin dish. Place in the centre of the preheated oven and bake for 25–30 minutes. To check if done, the custard on the surface should have started to set, but the centre of the pudding should still have some wobble. Remove the pudding from the water bath, sift over an even layer of icing sugar, and blowtorch the top to give a nice caramelised crust. If you don't have a blowtorch, place under a hot grill (broiler) for a minute or two to caramelise the sugar and give the pudding some colour. Serve with lashings of extra-thick cream, without delay.

PEAR & GINGER SPONGE PUDDING WITH WHISKY CARAMEL SAUCE

SERVES 6

120g (4¼oz/½ cup)
    unsalted butter, melted,
    plus extra for greasing
80g (2¾oz/⅓ cup)
    buttermilk
50g (1¾oz/3 tbsp)
    black treacle
4 medium eggs, beaten
150g (5½oz/¾ cup)
    dark muscovado sugar
200g (7oz/3½ cups)
    self-raising flour
2 tsp garam masala
1 tsp bicarbonate of soda
    (baking soda)
2 tsp ground ginger
A pinch of salt
120g (4¼oz) stem ginger,
    finely chopped
Clotted cream, vanilla
    ice cream or custard,
    to serve

Poached pears:
2 conference pears, peeled,
    halved and cored
200ml water
150g (5½oz/¾ cup)
    caster (superfine) sugar
2cm (¾in) cinnamon stick
4 cloves
1 bay leaf
1 star anise
2 slices of lemon

Caramel sauce:
100g (3½oz/7 tbsp)
    salted butter
100g (3½oz/½ cup)
    dark muscovado sugar
125ml (4½fl oz/½ cup)
    double (heavy) cream
100ml (3½fl oz/scant
    ½ cup) whisky

Top of my list, king of sponge puddings, has to be ginger. Fiery warmth with a hint of spice, magically enveloped with sticky-sweet sauce. I'm adding a hit of whiskey to the sauce because the combination of pear, ginger, warming spice and whiskey is a heavenly combination. The pears can be poached ahead of time and kept in a jar in their syrup for a couple of weeks.

Preheat your oven to 180°C fan/400°F/Gas 6. Line the bottom of a 20cm (8in) cake tin with baking parchment and grease the sides with softened butter.

To poach the pears, put the pear halves in a saucepan with all the other ingredients and set over a medium heat. When simmering, turn the heat down and allow the pears to poach gently for 20 minutes. Turn the heat off and allow them to cool in the syrup.

For the sponge, combine all the wet ingredients, except the stem ginger and cream, in one bowl and all the dry ingredients in another. Pour the wet ingredients over the dry and mix until you have a smooth batter. Don't be tempted to mix for too long as you will have a tough cake.

Drain the pear halves and arrange them in the bottom of the cake tin. Sprinkle the chopped ginger into the gaps between the pears to make an attractive pattern.

Pour the batter into the cake tin and bake for 40 minutes. You can check that the cake is ready by inserting a skewer into the centre of the cake – if it comes out clean it is ready, if not check after a further 5 minutes. Remove the cake from the oven and allow it to cool for 10 minutes before turning it out of the tin.

For the sauce, melt the butter and sugar in a non-stick frying pan over a medium heat, stirring so they combine. Add the cream and whisky and bring to the boil. Simmer for one minute, stirring all the time. Remove from the heat and pour into a sauce jug.

To serve, cut a slice of the warm cake, pour over a generous serving of sauce and top with some clotted cream, vanilla ice cream or custard. Or why not all three?

COCONUT TIRAMISU

SERVES 6

Mascarpone cream:
80g (2¾oz) desiccated (dried shredded) coconut
125g (4½oz/½ cup) mascarpone
160g (5¾oz/⅔ cup) coconut cream
25g (1oz/2 tbsp) caster (superfine) sugar
Zest of 2 limes
75ml (2½fl oz/5 tbsp) double (heavy) cream
150ml (5fl oz/scant ⅔ cup) coconut rum
100ml (3½fl oz/scant ½ cup) cold strong coffee, or 2 tsp good-quality instant coffee powder mixed with 100ml (3½fl oz/scant ½ cup) water
3 green cardamom pods, seeds removed and ground to a fine powder
1 packet (about 24) sponge fingers (Savoiardi)
30g (1oz) grated frozen milk chocolate to garnish

The palm trees in Kerala stretch into the distance as far as the eye can see. Almost every dish will contain coconut in one form or another: everything is fried in coconut oil, curries are finished with varying grades of coconut milk; fresh coconut is grated into dishes; desserts are sweet with coconut! The famous Malabar biryani is even cooked using burning coconut shells. As part of our honeymoon, my wife and I stayed on the most amazing plantation in the tea hills of Munnar, in Kerala – a working coffee and cardamom plantation. Every day heaped coffee beans dried in the afternoon sun. What a treat it was to visit the thatched-roofed open-air café to enjoy a cup of locally-grown coffee with biscuits, while listening to mountain birdsong. In South India it is very common for people to drink coffee, rather than tea. Perhaps a reaction to the imposition of tea-drinking from the British colonists. Here's my Keralan-inspired tiramisu.

In a non-stick frying pan over a medium-low heat, toast the desiccated coconut until light gold. Remove from the pan and leave to cool.

For the mascarpone cream, in a large bowl whisk the mascarpone, coconut cream, sugar, lime zest and half of the toasted desiccated coconut with an electric hand mixer until soft. Add the double cream and 3½ tablespoons of the coconut rum and whisk again. Keep mixing until the cream reaches soft peaks – this may take up to 5 minutes. Keep in the fridge until needed.

Find yourself a deep ceramic dish, measuring around 30 x 20cm (12 x 8in) to build the tiramisu in.

Mix together the coffee, ground cardamom and remaining coconut rum and pour it into a separate shallow dish. Soak the biscuits in the coffee mixture (around six at a time) for 10 seconds on each side, then place them in a single layer in the serving dish, using about half of them to cover the base. Just break them up to fill in any gaps. Pour over half the coconut mascarpone cream, followed by half the remaining desiccated coconut. Repeat with another layer of soaked sponge finger biscuits, followed by the remaining cream. With a small spatula or palate knife, smooth the top, then sprinkle with the remaining desiccated coconut and the grated milk chocolate. Chill for 2 hours before serving.

GINGER MISHTI DOI CRÈME BRÛLÉE WITH RHUBARB COMPOTE

SERVES 4

Mishti doi:
300ml (10½fl oz/1¼ cups)
   evaporated milk
100ml (3½fl oz/scant
   ½ cup) double (heavy)
   cream
50g (1¾oz) stem ginger in
   syrup, roughly chopped
125g (4½oz/scant ⅔ cup)
   caster (superfine) sugar
300g (10½fl oz/1¼ cups)
   full-fat Greek yoghurt
Demerara (turbinado)
   sugar, for finishing
   the crème brûlée

Rhubarb:
400g (14½oz) rhubarb, cut
   into 5cm (2in) batons
125g (4½oz/scant ⅔ cup)
   caster (superfine) sugar

Mishti doi is a most famous Bengali sweet – yoghurt and milk, gently sweetened with caramelised sugar to produce the smoothest, silken, custard-like cream. It is so similar in texture to the perfect crème brûlée, which is why this recipe makes complete sense!

For the mishti doi, heat the evaporated milk, cream and stem ginger in a saucepan. When simmering, remove from the heat and allow to infuse for at least 20 minutes. Meanwhile, preheat your oven to 160°C fan/350°F/Gas 4.

Place a large wide non-stick pan over a medium heat. Add the sugar and cook for around 10 minutes until you are left with a rich, amber-coloured caramel. It is important to let the sugar caramelise as it adds a complex hint of bitterness, but don't let it burn. When the caramel is ready, remove from the heat. Strain the warm ginger cream through a sieve into the caramel. Be careful, it will splutter. Return the pan to a medium heat, making sure that the caramel fully dissolves into the liquid – you can use a whisk to make this easier. After about 3 minutes, when dissolved, remove from the heat. Place the yoghurt into a large bowl and pour the caramel cream over. Whisk to combine.

Transfer the cream mixture to a ceramic baking dish, roughly 20 x 10cm (8 x 4in), then place the dish into a large deep roasting tin. Pour boiling water from your kettle into the roasting tin, so that it comes halfway up the side of the dish. Carefully place in the centre of your preheated oven and bake for 15 minutes. Allow to cool, still inside the water bath. When cool, place in the fridge and allow to chill for at least 8 hours, or overnight.

For the rhubarb, turn the oven up to 180°C fan/400°F/Gas 6. Place the rhubarb into a large roasting tin and cover with the sugar. Roast in the top of the oven for 10–15 minutes, until tender. Place into a serving dish and allow to cool.

Remove the crème brûlée from the fridge just before you want to serve and dust with a thin, even layer of demerara sugar. With a blowtorch, caramelise the sugar, so that it is evenly melted with a slight burnt tinge. This can also be done under a hot grill (broiler). Serve with the rhubarb compote.

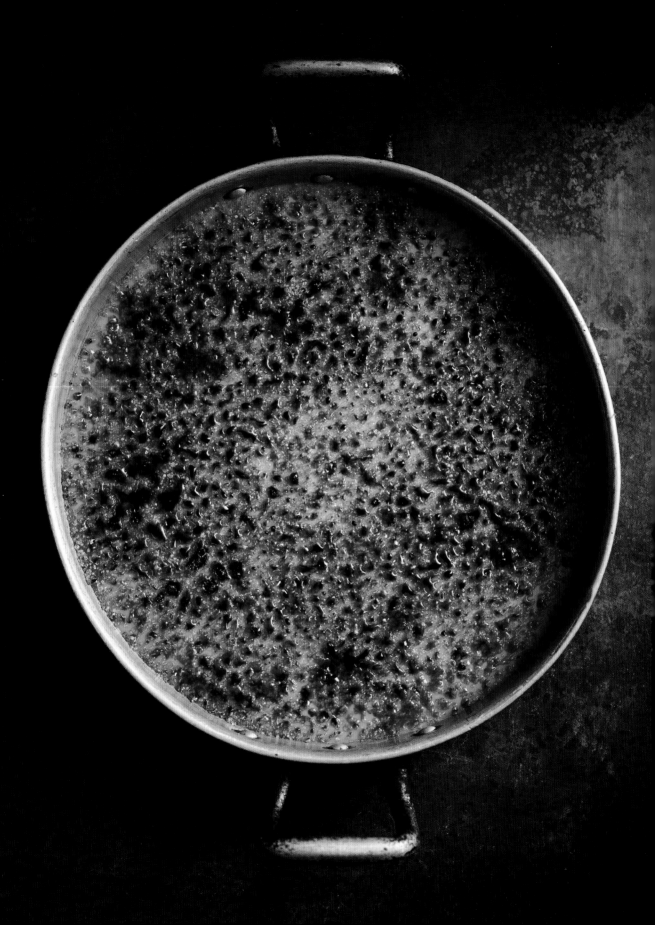

TEURGOULE

SERVES 4

Seeds from 8 green
   cardamom pods
1.2 litres (40fl oz/5 cups)
   whole milk
1 x 410g (14½oz) tin
   evaporated milk
125g (4½oz/scant ⅔ cup)
   caster (superfine) sugar
70g (2½oz/scant ⅓ cup)
   short-grain rice (pudding
   rice, paella rice or risotto
   rice all work fine)
A generous pinch of saffron
1 tsp vanilla bean paste
   or vanilla extract
1 tsp rosewater
½ tsp salt

India and Normandy share a love of rice pudding. Across India you'll find many variations, often packed full of different dried fruits and spices – some of them even taste very similar to cousin Teurgoule. For those of you who are a bit put off by the idea of rice pudding, please, please, give this one a go – it's so good that it will convert any sceptic!

....

Preheat your oven to 140°C fan/325°F/Gas 3.

Using a spice grinder or mortar and pestle, grind the cardamom seeds to make a fine powder. Add it to a large saucepan along with all the remaining ingredients and set over a medium heat. Bring to a gentle simmer, stirring often so that the milk doesn't catch on the bottom of the pan.

Once simmering, transfer the mixture to a ceramic baking dish. Bake for 2 hours, after which time, the pudding will be covered by a glorious dark skin. Allow to cool to room temperature and serve. Nothing else is required; the rice pudding is perfect just by itself.

GÂTEAU BASQUE

SERVES 6

200g (7oz/generous ¾ cup plus 2 tbsp) unsalted butter, at room temperature
200g (7oz/1 cup) caster (superfine) sugar
3 medium eggs, at room temperature
300g (10½fl oz/2¼ cups) plain (all-purpose) flour
1½ tsp baking powder
A pinch of salt
150g (5½oz/½ cup) cherry jam (Bonne Maman is very good)
1 egg yolk mixed with 1 tbsp whole milk, to make an egg wash

Crème pâtissière:
300ml (10½fl oz/1¼ cups) whole milk
4 egg yolks
70g (2½oz/⅓ cup) caster (superfine) sugar
30g (1oz/¼ cup) cornflour (cornstarch)
1 tsp vanilla extract
½ tsp ground cloves
1 tsp ground cinnamon
A pinch of saffron
Zest of 1 orange, finely grated

I have chosen this pudding as the finale to my book. It is is one that I fell in love with as soon as I tasted it on a family holiday to the French Basque country. You may have heard of the very fashionable Basque cheesecake, which is so over-rated that I prefer to avoid it. This traditional pudding is in fact a cousin to the famous cheesecake, and I think far superior. It consists of the richest, most buttery sponge – it is almost like a pastry; the edges have a wonderful crispness, but the centre is soft. It is filled with cherry jam and a thick custard, which I'm injecting with saffron, orange, clove and cinnamon – a combination which works marvellously with the cherries. Cut yourself a hearty wedge and *Basque* in the glory (if you'll pardon the pun).

....

To make the crème pâtissière, bring the milk to a simmer in a saucepan over a medium heat.

In a large bowl, whisk together the remaining crème ingredients for 1–2 minutes until well combined. Pour the hot milk over the egg yolk mixture and whisk immediately to combine. Pour this custard back into the pan and continue to cook, whisking all the time, over a medium heat until you are left with a thick crème pâtissière – this will take around 4–5 minutes. When thick, transfer to a deep baking tray or shallow bowl and cover the surface of the custard with cling film (plastic wrap) to stop a skin forming. When cool, place in the fridge.

Grease a 23cm (9in) loose-based tart tin with butter.

To make the cake, cream together the butter and sugar until light and fluffy. Add the eggs, one by one, whisking well after each addition. Mix together the flour, baking powder and salt, then fold this into the butter mixture until combined – don't overwork the batter, as this will make the cake tough.

Put a piece of baking parchment on to your work surface and put two-thirds of the cake mixture on top. Cover with another piece of parchment then roll it into a circle large enough to line the base and sides of a tin.

Roll the remaining one-third of the mixture again, between two sheets of baking parchment, into a 23cm (9in) circle. This will be for the top of the gâteau.

Recipe continued overleaf

Place both sheets of rolled cake mixture, still between the sheets of baking parchment, into the freezer for 30 minutes.

After 30 minutes in the freezer, the dough should be almost frozen and the baking parchment should peel off nicely without leaving much dough behind. If not, return to the freezer for another 15 minutes.

Line the base of the tart tin with the larger circle, pushing it well into the sides and corners of the tin. Don't trim the sides yet. Spread the cherry jam over the bottom of the cake in an even layer.

Remove the crème pâtissière from the fridge, transfer to a bowl and whisk until smooth. Dollop this over the jam and spread out in an even layer. Top with the remaining circle of dough, sealing well around the edges with a palette knife. With a small sharp knife, trim any excess pastry from the edge then place the tin in the fridge for 20 minutes.

Meanwhile, preheat your oven to 170°C fan/375°F/Gas 5, and place a metal baking sheet in the centre of the oven to heat up.

Remove the gâteau from the fridge and brush with the egg wash. Using the back of a fork, score a tartan-style pattern over the cake (see photograph). Place on the preheated baking sheet in the oven and bake for 1 hour, until golden brown. Remove from the oven and allow to cool before removing from the tin. Serve at room temperature.

PANTRY

SPICES

At the heart of Indian cooking lies an alchemy of spicing. The blending of many different varieties of aromatic spices is unique to the cooking of the Indian subcontinent. The mastery of this style of cooking depends on blending spices which create dishes of harmonious balance and unique flavour. Different regions use contrasting blends of spices to create their distinctive aromatic qualities. Kerala is known as the spice garden of India and is responsible for growing the majority of the country's spices. On a recent trip, I stayed on a green cardamom plantation in the lush tea hills of Kerala. We trekked into the plantation, amongst the leafy cardamom plants, picking fresh pods straight off the tree. They had an unbelievable freshness and were packed full of rich essential oils. For a chef who cooks with spice, it really was inspirational to see where one of the most important ingredients that I use comes from and how it is processed. Across India, you'll visit any spice market and be blown away by the quality, freshness and variety of spices. Everything has more aroma and flavour – and the piles of colourful whole spices and powders are a wonder to experience. You'll find extraordinary ingredients that you'll only have seen in encyclopaedias – yellow chilli powder, tailed cubeb pepper or long pepper. Spice is the ingredient which defines this part of the world.

Most people will have a cupboard of basic spices, some of which may sit, unused for years – perhaps because they were bought for a particular recipe then left. This book relies on having your storecupboard stocked with an arsenal of spices. It may seem like a lot of different ingredients to buy but, once you've got them, you'll be able to recreate every dish with ease and you'll realise that once you've added the spices, there really aren't that many more ingredients to go and find. So once you have your spices, you'll be set to start exploring this wonderful world of exciting flavours! Freshness of spice is paramount. Store them in sealed jars and keep in a cool dark place. Use them regularly, because they will degrade and lose their flavour over time – especially ground spices. I recommend buying a quantity that you'll comfortably use within a six-month period. I would replace any ground spice powders which have been opened for more than six months – I doubt they will have much flavour left. Whole spices will last longer, up to one year.

Here is a list of spices which you will find in this book and where to find them. Many of the spices in this book are available in major supermarkets, although, for some, it may pay to look a little further. You'll also realise that if you go to your local Asian supermarket you'll get much better value for money. I hope that this section will help you create spice blends which will enhance your creations.

Green Cardamom (Choti Elaichi)

For me, green cardamom is the king of spice. Bright and floral, with a delicious herbal aroma, you'll find these aromatic pods being used all over India. Green cardamom is liberally used in Indian desserts, just as you might use vanilla. It is used in two forms: the whole pod, or by crushing the seeds within the pod to a fine powder. The cardamom seeds actually contain all of the flavour. You can buy ready-ground powder, although this is more perishable, so it's better to grind pods at home in a heavy mortar and pestle as you go, unless you are planning to use it in large quantities. You can also buy packets of the seeds, which are great. When buying, look for pods with a vibrant green colour. The best green cardamoms come from Kerala and may be branded as 'Malabar'. They are sold in varying grades, '8mm', 'extra-bold' or 'bold' being the best. You can find cardamom in most supermarkets, although for the best-quality look either online or in your local Indian supermarket. Fudco brand produce excellent Malabar green cardamom, which is available in larger supermarkets which often have a good Asian section.

Black Cardamom (Moti Elaichi)

Black cardamom may share some of its name with the green variety, but that's about as far as any similarities go. These pods have a dark, smoky, menthol flavour. They will either be used whole, or ground into fresh powdered masalas. Black cardamom is mainly used in north India; it is an integral spice of the famous rich meat stews of the northern regions. Look for pods which have a rich dark colour, and avoid black cardamoms which are very grey as they will be quite dry and lack aroma. Black cardamom is hard to find in supermarkets; head to my list of online suppliers or to your local Indian supermarket.

Clove (Laung)

Cloves are a very strong, aromatic, warming spice. They are used in northern Indian and Mughlai cooking extensively and are widely available in most supermarkets. The longer the clove, the better.

Mace (Javiertri) and Nutmeg (Jaiful)

These two spices are related. Mace is the outer shell of the nutmeg. They both have a sweet and peppery flavour, mace being the stronger and more powerful of the two. Nutmeg is used in many British desserts, and you'll often find mace in sausages and pork pies. In Indian cooking, the combination of both spices is used in many Mughlai spice blends to add warmth and aroma. Nutmeg is available in most supermarkets, whereas mace is harder to find. I would advise buying both in whole spice form, as they will deteriorate quicker as a powder. Nutmeg can be grated using a fine grater and both spices can be ground in a spice grinder.

Star Anise (Chakra Phool)

Star anise has a very strong liquorice-aniseed flavour. It is used in many biryani masalas as well as in my grandmother's garam masala recipe. It is widely available in supermarkets.

Cinnamon (Dalchini)

There are two main types of cinnamon: cassia and Sri Lankan, also known as Ceylon. You'll find the Ceylon variety in most supermarkets, rolled into soft cigar-like quills. Buying cinnamon from the supermarket is expensive and the quality tends to be mediocre. Cassia cinnamon, on the other hand, may also be found rolled into quills, but they are much thicker and sturdier and will snap rather than crumble. They have a more intense, darker flavour, and are much better for Indian cookery. I recommend buying cassia cinnamon quills for use in the recipes in this book. You can snap them into whatever length the recipe calls for. They are available from all Indian supermarkets and online.

Caraway Seeds (Shahi Zeera or Kala Zeera)

Caraway seeds are similar in appearance to cumin, but are darker in appearance. They have a powerful citrus, herbal and menthol flavour. Caraway is used in the famous Hyderabadi biryani and is a popular spice in other Mughlai cuisines. They are available in most supermarkets.

Fennel Seeds (Saunf)

Fennel seeds are bright green and, again, quite similar in appearance to cumin. They have a mild aniseed aroma and are frequently served after a meal in Indian restaurants, as they have a refreshing liquorice flavour. The fennel seeds you'll find in the spice aisle of supermarkets are OK, but the best fennel seeds are known as Lucknow fennel seeds – they have a brighter, more powerful flavour and aroma.

Black pepper (Kali Mirch)

You will all have black pepper kicking around your kitchen, I'm sure. In Indian cooking it is used either whole, or ground into powdered masalas. The best black pepper is from Tellicherry in Kerala and you'll find this in good supermarkets. I've even seen it being sold in Tesco. Only buy whole pepper; don't buy ready ground – it will lose its potency very quickly. I would advise that you invest in a good-quality pepper mill, so you can grind your pepper fresh. Peugeot make the best ones, which allow you to adjust the coarseness of the grind. Ausha and Banyan Tree Foods (see page 230) sell Tellicherry black pepper on their websites.

White Pepper (Safed Mirch)

White pepper is simply black pepper with the husk removed. It is softer and more delicate in flavour and is used mainly in the Awadhi cuisine of Lucknow. It is best to buy whole white pepper and grind when needed.

Saffron (Kesar)

Saffron is my favourite spice, and it's also more expensive than gold. Saffron is originally from Persia and is an integral ingredient in the royal Mughlai cuisines of India. It has a luxurious floral aroma and gives a wonderful colour to both sweet and savoury dishes, such as makhan malai and Hyderabadi biryani. You can find saffron in supermarkets, but I would advise against it. The price is extremely high and it is usually very dry. Look for a reputable online retailer of Iranian saffron – this is the best and the strands should be plump and long. I buy my saffron from Sara Saffron. It will keep in an air-tight jar, in a dark cupboard for up to a year. The best way to use saffron is to infuse it in warm milk or water for a few hours. I buy mine from sarasaffron.com.

Cumin (Jeera)

Cumin is a spice which you will be very familiar with, appearing in many cuisines of the world. It has a warming and earthy flavour. It is used in whole seed or powdered form. This spice is one of the most widely used in India. It is available in most supermarkets.

Coriander (Dhaniya)

Coriander, along with cumin, is probably the most widely used spice in India. The round seeds have a bright, zesty and lemony flavour. Coriander is available in most supermarkets. Darker, smaller seeds have the best flavour.

I would advise you to have both ground and whole cumin and coriander, as they are used in relatively large quantities.

Turmeric (Haldi)

Turmeric is used in powdered form, mainly as a colouring. It has brilliant health benefits and is used in the ancient Indian practice of Ayurveda. It has a dusty, earthy and musky flavour. It is very powerful – a little goes a long way and if used excessively, will overpower your food. Many recipes in this book call for the use of turmeric as it is widely used in India, although you may be interested to hear that the Mughlai cuisines of northern India seldom use turmeric in any of their cooking. It's available in supermarkets.

Dried Fenugreek Leaves (Kasoori Methi)

Dried fenugreek leaves are used mainly in Punjab and north India to add depth and nuttiness to tandoori marinades and spinach curries. They round out the flavour of dishes and they are an essential ingredient in Old Delhi butter chicken. They keep well and are ground in a mortar and pestle before sprinkling into dishes. Dried fenugreek leaves are not commonly found in supermarkets. You may see fenugreek powder in supermarkets, but this is not a suitable substitute. Fenugreek leaves are available online and from Indian supermarkets.

Chilli Powder (Kashmiri Mirch, Deggi Mirch and Lal Mirch)

Chilli powder is used to add both warmth and colour to dishes. The chilli powder which I use throughout this book is Kashmiri chilli powder. This powder, made from mild Kashmiri chillies, adds a lovely red hue to dishes. It is not excessively hot and a great all-round chilli powder, which you should have lots of. It is not widely available in supermarkets and is worth seeking out either online or in Indian supermarkets.

Deggi mirch is a blend of chilli powder with red pepper powder and it is similar to Kashmiri chilli powder and can be used in a similar way.

Chilli powder (*lal mirch*) can also be used for the recipes in this book. It is, however, much hotter than Kashmiri or deggi chilli powders and doesn't give as vibrant a colour. If using, reduce the quantity in the recipe.

I tend to avoid buying supermarket own-brand chilli powders, as they lack flavour and often have other ingredients added, such as garlic, cumin and oregano. Buy chilli powder which only contains chilli.

Dried Red Chillies

Dried red chillies are used in a variety of ways to add flavour to Indian dishes. They may be fried in hot oil or ground into a paste with water. There are two main types used in Indian cooking: Kashmiri or red whole dried chillies. The Kashmiri variety are much milder and add a more vibrant colour. It is best to source dried Kashmiri chillies or dried red chillies online or from Indian supermarkets – they tend not to be available from most supermarkets.

Chilli flakes, which can be found in supermarkets, can be substituted for recipes which require dried red chillies, but not the softer Kashmiri variety.

Avoid buying dried bird's eye chillies – they are not suitable for use in this book.

Green Chillies

Green chillies are a vital ingredient in Indian cooking. The type of chilli which you must use in this book are green finger chillies. They are small, thin and have moderate heat. More importantly, they have the correct flavour profile for Indian cooking. These are not to be confused with bird's eye chillies, which are much smaller and hotter. The larger, fatter green chillies you may find are not suitable for use in these recipes. Green finger chillies are widely available in most major supermarkets.

Black Mustard Seeds (Rai)

Black mustard seeds are used extensively in south-Indian and Bengali cuisines. They add a lot of flavour with a slightly bitter pungency and warm depth. In south India, almost every dish will call for their use, frying them in oil to release their flavour. In Bengal, mustard seeds are ground with chillies and water to make a thick mustard paste. Black mustard seeds are available in some supermarkets. They cannot be interchanged with more commonly available white mustard seeds. Available in all Indian Supermarkets.

Curry Leaves

It is difficult to describe the smell and taste of curry leaves – all I can tell you is that when they are cooking in a pan, they have the most heavenly scent, which is probably my favourite smell in the kitchen. These green leaves are a staple in south Indian cookery. You can pick them up fresh in some major supermarkets, and in your local Indian supermarket. Dried curry leaves can also be found in supermarkets, but I wouldn't bother – they are nothing in comparison to the fresh variety. Buy a large quantity of fresh ones and put them in the freezer in a plastic bag – this will ensure that you always have them on hand.

Asafoetida (Hing)

This pungent, sulphurous and funky-smelling powder is derived from the resin of the Ferula plant (giant fennel). It is added very sparingly to daals and many south-Indian vegetable dishes. The powder is added to hot oil, which brings out its flavour. You don't need a large quantity of this spice and it is available in most supermarkets.

Fenugreek Seeds (Methi Seeds)

Fenugreek seeds have a bitter, nutty flavour and are mainly used in south-Indian sambhar and vegetable curries in combination with asafoetida, black mustard seeds, cumin seeds and curry leaves. You can buy these from good supermarkets and in Indian supermarkets. It is possible to substitute the fenugreek powder for the seeds – the powder is more widely available in supermarkets.

Carom Seeds (Ajwain)

These tiny seeds have a very strong savoury flavour, similar to that of dried thyme, but more intense. They are used in north Indian samosas and paratha flatbreads, as well as in the famous Amritsari fish. You'll find these in some big supermarkets but it may be better to buy from your local Indian supermarket.

Indian Bay Leaves (Tej Patta)

The Indian bay leaf is different to the variety which grows in Europe. These have a smoky aromatic flavour, similar to that of cinnamon and clove. They are used in the cuisines of north India, by infusing them first in hot oil. If you can't find them, simply leave them out of the recipe. You'll be able to find a bag of these in your local Indian supermarket and they will last you a very long time – up to two years.

Chaat Masala

Chaat masala is a sharp, tangy seasoning which is sprinkled over kebabs and various types of chaats. It contains spices such as cumin, coriander, dried mango, black salt, dried mint, ginger, asafoetida and chilli powder. You can buy it in larger supermarkets quite easily. An excellent brand to look for is MDH, which you'll find in Indian shops and online.

Black Salt (Kala Namak)

Black salt has a very unique flavour profile. This salt is mined in the Himalayan region and is very high in minerals. It is kiln-dried at high temperature, which brings out a sulphurous complexity. As soon as you open a jar, it'll knock your socks off. It is found in chaat masala and can be used in lassi (buttermilk yoghurt drinks), desserts and Indian lemonade (*nimbu pani*). I have used it in my Key Lime Pie recipe. Your local Indian supermarket will definitely have it, as well as Spice Mountain (see suppliers, opposite).

Dried Mango Powder (Amchoor)

This sharp, acidic powder is made from green unripe mangoes. It is used as an ingredient in chaat masala and I have used it in my Amritsari fish. You'll often find Punjabi dishes calling for amchoor to act as a souring agent. It is also sprinkled onto tandoori chicken to add a tangy note. It can be found in large supermarkets and Indian supermarkets. MDH also do a good one.

Jaggery

Jaggery is an unrefined sugar made from pure sugar cane juice. It is slowly cooked and has a wonderful complex, almost acidic flavour profile. It can be substituted with demerara sugar. You will find this easily online and in Indian supermarkets.

Rosewater and Kewra Water

Kewra water is a very fragrant water that is distilled from the pandan leaf. It has a glorious perfumed aroma, similar to that of rosewater. These fragrances are used in Mughlai cooking, which is famed for its luxurious use of natural essences and highly aromatic spices. Rosewater and kewra water can be used interchangeably if you can only find one or the other. Rosewater is available in most supermarkets – Nielsen-Massey brand makes a good rosewater. You'll also be able to find these in Indian supermarkets and in some larger supermarkets.

Stock

You can buy excellent stocks from good supermarkets or online from True Foods (this company makes stock for probably most Michelin-starred restaurants in the UK). You can keep True Foods stock in the freezer to extend its life. You can also use Knorr stock pots, which are very convenient.

Spice suppliers:

ausha.co.uk
banyantreefoods.co.uk
fudcoshop.com
indiangrocerystore.co.uk
renspantry.com
spicemountain.co.uk

Vist your local Indian supermarket – they are great one-stop shops for picking up all of your spices. Good Sainsbury's stores with large Asian aisles stock a particularly comprehensive range of Fudco spices, which I recommend.

Grinding Spices

Many of the recipes in this book will call for a fresh masala to be made from whole spices. Freshly grinding whole spices is much better than having lots of ready ground spices in your cupboard because they will take longer to perish and will therefore have a far superior flavour.

Do not use heat before grinding spices – you may have read that spices should be dry roasted in a pan before grinding. This technique actually cooks off the aroma. Simply measure out the spices and add them to an electric or hand grinder. Below are the spice grinders which I recommend you buy for the job.

Peugeot Roellinger: this is my most prized piece of kitchen equipment and I love it so much! I use it every day and it does a perfect job of grinding cumin seeds, fennel seeds, coriander seeds and black and white pepper.

Moulinex spice/coffee mill or Krups coffee mill: I have used these two grinders my entire life. The Moulinex belongs to me and the Krups to my parents. Both designs have stood the test of time. Simply throw your whole spices in and blend until they have transformed into a fine powder.

Peugeot pepper mills: I use two Peugeot pepper mills for daily pepper grinding. The first is the classic Paris design and the second – the Maestro. Both grinders have an adjustment setting, so you can decide how coarse you would like your pepper to come out, which is a game-changing function. The Maestro has the added capability of being able to swap pepper varieties – different peppers are kept in small jars which screw into the base of the grinder. This is a brilliant function.

A heavy stone mortar and pestle: this will last you a lifetime and will help you to crush or grind any spice, although it may take you a little longer and require a touch more elbow grease.

How to make a masala

This is a good basic guide to the method of starting many Indian dishes.

Whole spices are very often added as the first step of Indian cooking. Oil is heated in a hot pan and the whole spices are added. The spices are fried gently in the oil for a minute, which brings out their aromas, infusing them into the oil.

Onions are added and fried until golden – for a good 10–15 minutes. This adds depth to dishes.

When the onions are golden, it's time to add ginger and garlic and other ingredients such as green chillies or curry leaves, which will cook more quickly. The ginger and garlic is fried for 2–3 minutes, until lightly golden. Always have a little water on hand to splash into the pan if it starts to catch on the bottom. At this stage, the powdered spices are added with liquid. If they are added dry, they will burn and go bitter very quickly.

A sprinkling of garam masala is usually added at the end of cooking, to finish the dish

BASIC RECIPES

Garam Masala
This is my grandmother's recipe for a very fragrant Punjabi garam masala, which you can use throughout this book whenever a recipe calls for garam masala. This fresh garam masala is so much better and more fragrant than a shop-bought variety and is very simple to make. It will keep in an airtight jar for 6 months.

Makes about 90g (3oz)

15g (1/2oz) cumin seeds
15g (1/2oz) black pepper corns
15g (1/2oz) black cardamom pods
15g (1/2oz) cinnamon stick
8g (1/4oz) star anise
8g (1/4oz) cloves
8g (1/4oz) mace

Add all the spices to a spice or coffee grinder and grind until you have a fine powder. Sieve the garam masala into a bowl to catch any tough fibres. Place the sieved powder into a clean airtight jar until ready to use.

Ginger-Garlic Paste
Ginger and garlic paste forms the fundamental base of most Indian recipes. It can either be made fresh to-order, on a recipe-by-recipe basis, or in advance – in larger quantities. You can buy ready-made jars of ginger garlic paste or purée in the supermarkets. I wouldn't recommend these products as vinegar is usually added to preserve them. I use a Cuisinart mini food processor which makes an excellent ginger garlic paste.

Makes 200g (7oz)

100g (3½oz) ginger, peeled and roughly chopped
100g (3½oz) garlic cloves, peeled
2 tbsp vegetable oil
½ tsp salt

Add all the ingredients to a mini food processor with 2 tablespoons water and blend until you have a very smooth paste.
    The ginger-garlic paste can be kept in the fridge in a sterilised jar for up to a week. Alternatively, it can be portioned into large ice-cube trays and frozen for up to 3 months.

If a recipe calls for 2–3 garlic cloves and 2cm (¾in) of ginger, this roughly equates to 30g (1oz) of ginger-garlic paste.

Tamarind Purée

Tamarind purée is an ingredient which is used quite frequently in this book. It is used in recipes to add sharpness and sourness. You can buy it ready-made from the supermarket (it usually comes in small 100g/3½oz jars). The shop-bought version is a decent product, which I am more than happy to endorse. You can, alternatively, make your own and freeze it in large ice-cube trays. The usual way to buy tamarind, other than as a purée, is in a compressed block from Asian supermarkets.

Makes about 1.5 cups

200g (7oz) block of tamarind, broken into pieces
300ml (10½fl oz/1¼ cups) boiling water

Pour the boiling water over the tamarind block and allow to steep in the water for 45 minutes.

After 45 minutes, pour the mixture through a sieve. Using a metal spoon, push as much purée as you can through the sieve, leaving behind the stones. Pour the purée into a medium-sized pan and cook over a medium heat for 15 minutes. You should be left with a thick paste. Allow to cool and keep in the fridge for up to a week or in the freezer for 3 months.

Ghee and Cooking Oils

I recommend using a variety of oils and cooking fats in this book, from duck fat to ghee and everything in-between.

For deep-frying I recommend using sunflower or vegetable oil. Some recipes will call for beef dripping – this is entirely optional, as I understand that it will not be to everyone's taste.

For salads and dressings I recommend using cold-pressed rapeseed (canola) oil or extra virgin olive oil.

For general cooking and frying, I recommend using vegetable oil or sunflower oil. In some recipes I will also specify ghee, as this is a traditional cooking medium in India and has an excellent flavour.

Ghee is simply clarified butter – the butter is cooked slowly in a pan to separate the milk solids

from the butter fat. It is this process which separates the proteins and impurities from the butter and transforms it into ghee. The ghee is cooked slowly to build up a complex, nutty flavour and a golden-brown colour. Traditionally, ghee is cooked from butter made from natural set yoghurt using a laborious process of churning called the 'Bilona method'. In Europe, however, butter is usually made from churning cream. Bilona-method ghee is made from indigenous breeds of Indian Desi cows and is the most pure and flavourful ghee you can buy. These ghees, however, are not easily available in the UK. I recommend that you buy artisanal ghee, preferably made from grass-fed Jersey or Guernsey cattle. There should be no artificial ingredients or preservatives. I do not recommend the tins of ghee offered in supermarkets.

You can also make your own ghee, from top-quality unsalted butter:

Makes about 190g (6¾oz)

250g (9oz/generous 1 cup) butter

Melt the butter in a saucepan over a medium-low heat. Cook slowly for 15–25 minutes, until the ghee is golden in colour and smells wonderfully nutty. Remove from the heat and strain through a very fine tea strainer or muslin cloth (cheesecloth).

The resulting ghee can be kept in a sealed and sterilised jar in the fridge for 1 year.

Mint and Coriander Chutney

A fresh, vibrant mint and coriander chutney is one of the most popular condiments in India and is always served with a variety of starters and chaat dishes.

Makes about 1.5 cups

25g (1oz) fresh mint leaves
30g (1oz) fresh coriander (cilantro)
3 green finger chillies
1 tsp sugar
Juice of ½ a lime
2 tbsp vegetable oil
1 tbsp natural yoghurt
A pinch of salt
Ice cubes

Place all the ingredients into the jug of a nutri-blender with a couple of ice cubes and blitz for

2–3 minutes until you are left with a vibrant green chutney. Cover closely with cling film (plastic wrap) and use within 2 days.

To make mint and coriander mayonnaise, simply mix 2 tablespoons of the chutney with 75g (2½oz) of good-quality mayonnaise.

Tomato and Ginger Chutney

This can be used in a variety of ways. I like to spread it on buttered crumpets or toast. It can also be mixed with boiled rice and ghee to make a simple but delicious meal. The secret is to mix a couple of teaspoons with the rice, so that it coats every grain. Drizzle over some ghee and have yourself a perfect dinner, which is a great favourite of mine.

Makes about 1.5 cups

80ml (2½fl oz/^{1}/₃ cup) vegetable oil
1 tsp black mustard seeds
1 tsp cumin seeds
1 tsp fenugreek seeds
1 tbsp chilli flakes
1 tbsp chana dal or yellow split peas
¼ tsp asafoetida
4 garlic cloves, finely chopped
70g (2½oz) fresh ginger, finely chopped
200g (7oz) tomatoes, roughly chopped
1 tbsp tamarind purée
1 tbsp brown sugar
1 tsp salt
2 tsp Kashmiri chilli powder

Place a large deep pan over a medium heat. When hot, add the oil with the whole spices, chilli flakes, chana dal and asafoetida. Fry for 1 minute to allow the spices to release their aroma. As soon as the mustard seeds start to splutter, add the garlic and ginger and cook for 3–4 minutes, or until light brown. Add the tomatoes, tamarind purée, sugar, salt and chilli powder. Cook uncovered, still over a medium heat, for 25–30 minutes, stirring every 5 minutes or so. By this time the moisture will have cooked out and you will be left with a thick purée with the oil pooling on the surface.

Remove from the heat and transfer to the bowl of a food processor. Pulse the chutney for 30 seconds or so to combine, then refrigerate in a sterilised jar. It will keep for up to 1 month.

Green Chutney

20g (²/₃oz) fresh mint leaves
30g (1oz) fresh coriander (cilantro) leaves
3 green finger chillies
1 tsp sugar
Juice of ½ lime
1 garlic clove
2 tbsp vegetable oil
1 tbsp natural yoghurt
A pinch of salt
2 ice cubes

Place all the ingredients into the jug of a blender and blitz to a vibrant green chutney. Decant into a serving bowl.

Fish Stock

To make your own fish stock, ask a fishmonger to give you some bones: they shouldn't cost you anything, and will make something far more fragrant than any stock that you can buy.

Makes about 750ml (26fl oz/3¼ cups)

700g (1lb 9oz) fish bones
1 onion, chopped
2 garlic cloves
½ leek, sliced
1 stick of celery, sliced
1 glass white wine
½ tsp black peppercorns
1 bay leaf
Herbs of your choice
2 slices of lemon

In a large saucepan or stock pot, lightly sweat the onion, garlic, leek and celery. Add the fish bones, wine, peppercorns, bay leaf, herbs and lemon. Reduce by half, without stirring, then top up with a litre (35fl oz) of water. Slowly simmer for an hour, skimming away any scum which appears on the surface. After straining, you can keep this in the fridge for a couple of days or freeze it for up to three months.

USEFUL EQUIPMENT

Nutri-Blender
A nutri blender is a must-buy! They are inexpensive, very powerful and will effortlessly blend sauces and purées in seconds. They are great for jobs which can't be undertaken by a food processor, such as my mint and coriander chutney. These really are great bits of kit – I can't recommend them enough.

Mini food processor
A mini food processor is brilliant for chopping green chillies, making ginger-garlic paste and even making pastry. They are inexpensive and don't take up much kitchen space. I recommend the Cuisinart mini food processor – it's something I use everyday.

Japanese Mandoline
Benriner is a Japanese brand which makes superb razor-sharp mandolines. Every Michelin-star kitchen will have one of these and they make slicing or julienning everything from onions, to celeriac or cucumbers a breeze. The BN-64 model also has a brilliant thickness adjustment tool which is so intuitive to use. I am never without my Benriner.

These are available from Amazon, Borough Kitchen and Knives from Japan, to name a few.

Microplane
These graters are brilliant for finely grating ginger and garlic and they are also the best tools in the business to zest citrus fruit. I always have three in my kitchen drawer. The fine microplane is great for zesting, whereas the medium one is great for grating ginger and garlic.

Spider Strainer
Spiders are very simple but useful pieces of equipment for removing things quickly and effectively from hot oil or boiling water. I use them for straining rice when making biryani.

Cast-Iron Pot
A large cast-iron pot is the workhorse of my kitchen. It is the perfect vessel for cooking anything from curries to soups, biryanis or slow cooking in the oven for hours. They may require a fair outlay, but they will last you a lifetime. The heavy cast-iron material heats very evenly and provides the perfect cooking surface for Indian food.

Heavy Flat Iron Pan
When making paranthe breads, khameeri roti or naan, the best pan to use is a heavy flat iron pan – they can withstand high heat far better than non-stick pans (the non-stick coating of some pans can degrade when exposed to very high temperatures) and these heavy pans will cook the breads much more evenly. You should also definitely have a good non-stick frying pan for general cooking – it will make your life so much easier.

Digital Thermometer Probe
These are invaluable pieces of equipment, especially useful when deep frying to monitor the temperature of the oil safely. I have a Thermapen and it measures the temperatures quicker than any other temperature probe that I've used. (Thermapen.co.uk)

Digital Scales
A good pair of digital scales will cost you between £10–15, but they will make measuring and weighing ingredients so much easier – and if you look after them, they will last you at least 10 years.

Knives
People are always asking me about which fancy Japanese knives to buy ... *but*, if you don't know how to sharpen them or don't have the sharpening equipment, they will dull faster than any other blade (the blades of Japanese knives are generally cut at a shallower angle when compared to European knives, meaning that they need more sharpening maintenance). I recommend buying a 16–20cm (6¼–8in) chef's knife or santoku knife, which you'll be able to sharpen easily. Victorinox make great knives which fit this bill. Make sure that you also buy a sharpening steel, so that you can maintain the edge, because having a knife that is sharp in the kitchen is the most important thing! Once you've got some practice in sharpening, go and buy your fabulous, shiny, super-duper Japanese knife – and the three whetstones you'll need to sharpen it!

Other knives that I would recommend are: a small paring knife, a small serrated tomato knife and a large serrated pastry or bread knife.

Metal Sieve
A couple of strong, well-made sieves are extremely useful for passing and straining sauces and will last you a very long time.

INDEX

ACKNOWLEDGEMENTS

Food and cooking is what I live for, but this gift was inherited as part of a long family tradition. A journalist from The Times who interviewed me after I won MasterChef in 2022, summed it up perfectly: 'MasterChef winner Eddie Scott. My family taught me to love food.'

The memory of my Sussex grandmother's damson compote lingers; served with a dollop of thick cream and a buttery shortbread biscuit, her damsons were magic. My dad took a cutting from the cottage garden tree and every year we pick our damsons for jams, jellies and compote. In the Kent-Sussex borders the damson has held a central part in the centuries-old tradition. We are all part of a family who have been brought up with a love of cooking.

I want to thank my parents who unknowingly sparked my enthusiasm for cooking. My fondest memories are baking days with my mum from the age of around 4 years old. Together, we would make jam tarts, biscuits and Bakewell tarts. Since then, I have always cooked. Together, my Mum and I would spend whole weekends recreating Heston Blumenthal's perfect Black Forest gâteau – staying up until well into the night.

My Dad opened my world up to the traditions of French cuisine. We would go on secret trips to our favourite restaurant in Normandy, Auberge du Moulin de la Sée, or 'The Mill', as we would call it. It was here, as a young boy, that I started to experiment with new flavours. We would eat wonderful dishes of gratinated oysters, Andouillette de Vire, Livarot cheese and 'The Mill's' famous trio of crème brûlées – all strictly developed by a devoted chef within the Norman tradition.

I thank my brother, Andrew, for many happy shared culinary memories, adventures and cooking projects from our varied food travels together, which have inspired so many of the recipes in this book.

Nami, my wife, deserves medals for putting up with all of my recipe writing, testing and filming. She has always been so patient and supportive. Her critique has been invaluable in making these recipes the very best they can be. Nami and her parents have also introduced me to the amazing flavours of South-Indian cooking, which has been a revelation to me.

Thank you to my grandmother, Nani, who is still cooking well into her nineties, who has introduced me to the techniques required to cook the very best home-made Punjabi food, from her garam masala to her legendary samosas.

Tribute must be paid to Pa, my grandfather, who is no longer with us. He would tell me and my brother stories of how he could eat a whole bar of butter every day when he first came to the UK from India in the 1960s, using it even for his chapped lips. He loved talking about food and was the real expert cook in the family. He had an instinctive feel for cooking and a knack of making it all look so effortless. His signature was his infamous keema- a dish of lamb mince, slowly braised, until soft and juicy, in a subtle blend of aromatic Punjabi spices. His keema would appear on special occasions, or whenever we grandsons asked for it. You knew he was in the kitchen, because he would appear in an immaculately pressed shirt and trousers and an exquisite smell would pervade the kitchen! He had a way of making it taste melt in the mouth, both subtle and rich in equally fascinating doses. I remember my dad asking him how he made his keema. 'William, you know, it's very easy' is how the lengthy masterclass would start. He would reel off the list of ingredients and talk with clear authority on each and every subtle detail, including the cuts of meat which should be used in the mince. But the truth was and still is, that only Pa had the magic Keema touch.

Quarto

First published in 2024 by Carnival
an imprint of The Quarto Group.
One Triptych Place, London, SE1 9SH
United Kingdom
T (0)20 7700 6700
www.Quarto.com

Art Direction and Design: Smith & Gilmour
Cover illustrator: nancy@nancyeckels.com
Editor: Charlotte Frost
Food Stylist: Rob Morris
Photographer: Jamie Orlando Smith
Project Editor: Rebecca Woods
Prop Stylist: Hannah Wilkinson
Publisher: Eleanor Maxfield
Senior Production Controller: Eliza Walsh

A catalogue record for this book is available from the British Library.

ISBN 978-0-7112-9248-2
EBOOK ISBN 978-0-7112-9249-9

10 9 8 7 6 5 4 3 2 1

Printed in China

FSC
www.fsc.org

MIX
Paper | Supporting
responsible forestry
FSC® C016973